Starter's Guide to Verilog™ 2001

Starter's Guide to Verilog™ 2001

Michael D. Ciletti
Department of Electrical and Computer Engineering
University of Colorado at Colorado Springs

PEARSON
Prentice
Hall

Upper Saddle River, NJ 07458

Library of Congress Cataloging-in-Publication Data.

Ciletti, Michael D.
  Starter's guide to Verilog / Michael D. Ciletti.
    p. cm.
  ISBN 0-13-141556-5
   1. Verilog (Computer hardware description language) 2. Electronic digital
computers—Design and construction. I. Title.

TK7885.7.C57 2003
621.39'2—dc22

                                    2003059652

Vice President and Editorial Director, ECS: *Marcia J. Horton*
Acquisitions Editor: *Laura Fischer*
Vice President and Director of Production and Manufacturing, ESM: *David W. Riccardi*
Executive Managing Editor: *Vince O'Brien*
Managing Editor: *David A. George*
Production Editor: *Daniel Sandin*
Director of Creative Services: *Paul Belfanti*
Creative Director: *Carol Anson*
Art and Cover Director: *Jayne Conte*
Art Editor: *Greg Dulles*
Manufacturing Manager: *Trudy Pisciotti*
Manufacturing Buyer: *Lisa McDowell*
Marketing Manager: *Holly Stark*

©2004 Pearson Education, Inc.
Pearson Prentice Hall
Pearson Education, Inc.
Upper Saddle River, NJ 07458

Printed in the United States of America

ISBN 0-13-141556-5

Pearson Education Ltd., *London*
Pearson Education Australia Pty. Ltd., *Sydney*
Pearson Education Singapore, Pte. Ltd.
Pearson Education North Asia Ltd., *Hong Kong*
Pearson Education Canada, Inc., *Toronto*
Pearson Educación de Mexico, S.A. de C.V.
Pearson Education—Japan, *Tokyo*
Pearson Education Malaysia, Pte. Ltd.
Pearson Education, Inc., *Upper Saddle River, New Jersey*

Contents

Preface

Hardware description languages (HDLs) are widely used in design flows for modern integrated circuits, yet many engineers lack this background. Furthermore, many electrical and/or computer engineering students and computer science students are not exposed to HDLs in their studies, particularly at the undergraduate level. This book is intended to help bridge that gap by introducing the Verilog™ HDL in a brief format that is suitable for self-study by an engineer, and which serves as a companion text for an undergraduate course in logic circuits.

The Verilog HDL underwent its first revision in 2000, and emerged as IEEE Standard 1364-2001, known as *Verilog 2001*, with significant changes aimed at improving the utility and clarity of the language. The Verilog Standards Committee clarified ambiguous syntax and semantics in IEEE Standard 1364-1995[1] and removed errors in the LRM. The language was strengthened by the addition of enhancements supporting higher-level modeling and abstract modeling, while maintaining backward compatibility with IEEE Standard 1364-1995. We will present a selected set of those changes so that the reader can develop models that exploit the features of Verilog 2001. An appendix includes the complete formal syntax of IEEE Standard 1364-2001, which also encompasses IEEE Standard 1464-1995.

This volume will address the main features of Verilog that support the design of combinational and sequential logic. It will emphasize synthesizable models, with a limited discussion of the theoretical framework for synthesis. Features of the language that have marginal or specialized utility will not be addressed.

Intended Audience

Our intended audience includes designers and students who are taking or who have taken a first course in logic circuits, including the design of synchronous sequential circuits. Students in electrical engineering, computer engineering, and computer science can use this book to gain background in the main features of Verilog. Designers who have no background in HDLs can use the book to acquire a foundation for additional study. Designers who are familiar with Verilog 1995 can use the book to learn about the new features introduced by Verilog 2001.

---

[1] Referred to as Verilog 1995.

Chapter Descriptions

Chapter 1 briefly discusses the role of hardware description languages in design flows for cell-based ASICs (Application-Specific Integrated Circuits) and FPGAs (Field Programmable Gate Arrays). Chapter 2 introduces primitives, data types and operators to establish a foundation for the remaining chapters. Chapters 3 covers Verilog constructs for structural modeling, including user-defined primitives and top-down design methodology. Chapter 4 covers event-driven simulation, which is used to verify the models in chapters 5 and 6. Chapter 5 presents constructs for modeling combinational and sequential logic, and includes new constructs introduced in Verilog 2001. Chapter 6 uses Verilog to model finite-state machines and to design a controller for a datapath.

Special Features

- Focuses on modern digital design methodology
- Covers the design of finite-state machines to control datapaths
- Highlights modeling tips with a special icon
- Highlights features of Verilog 2001 with a special icon
- Illustrates and promotes a synthesis-ready style of modeling with Verilog
- Demonstrates the utility of ASM and ASMD charts for behavioral modeling
- Thoroughly covers behavioral modeling
- Includes numerous graphical illustrations
- Provides problems after each chapter
- Contains 100 verified examples
- Includes an indexed list of all models developed in the examples
- Contains an appendix with full formal syntax of IEEE Std 1364-2001
- Supported by a regularly updated website containing source files of all models developed in the examples

Web Site

All models developed in the book will be available at a companion website. (See www.prenhall.com.)

Acknowledgments and Dedication

I am grateful to my editor, Tom Robbins, and his production team for supporting and skillfully managing the development and production of this book. I dedicate it to Jerilynn, who is the gift and blessing of my life.

Starter's Guide
to Verilog™ 2001

CHAPTER 1   Introduction to Digital Design Methodology

Classic design methods relied on schematics and manual methods to design a circuit, but today's methods use computer-based hardware description languages (HDLs) to describe designs of enormous size and complexity. There are several reasons for this shift in practice. No team of engineers can correctly design and manage, by manual methods, the details of state-of-the-art integrated circuits (ICs) containing several million gates, but designers using HDLs easily manage the complexity of large designs. Even small designs rely on language-based descriptions, because designers have to quickly produce correct designs targeted for an ever-shrinking window of opportunity in the marketplace.

Language-based designs are portable and independent of technology, allowing design teams to modify and reuse designs to keep pace with improvements in technology. As devices shrink, denser circuits with better performance can be synthesized from an original HDL-based model.

HDLs are a convenient medium for integrating a proprietary design with intellectual property (IP) from a variety of sources. By relying on a common design language, models can be integrated for testing, and synthesized, separately or together, with a net reduction in the design cycle. Some simulators also support mixed descriptions based on multiple languages.

The most significant gain from the use of an HDL is that a working circuit can be synthesized automatically from a language-based description, bypassing the laborious steps that characterize manual design methods (e.g., logic minimization with Karnaugh maps).

HDL-based synthesis is now the dominant design paradigm used by industry. Today, designers build a software prototype of the design, verify its functionality, and then use a synthesis tool to automatically optimize the circuit and create a netlist in a physical technology.

HDLs and synthesis tools focus an engineer's attention on functionality, rather than on individual transistors or gates. They synthesize a circuit that will realize the desired functionality and satisfy area and/or performance constraints. Moreover, alternative architectures can be generated from a single HDL model and evaluated quickly to perform design tradeoffs. Functional models are also referred to as behavioral models.

HDLs serve as a platform for several tools: design entry, design verification, test generation, fault analysis and simulation, timing analysis and/or verification, synthesis, and automatic generation of schematics. This breadth of usage improves the efficiency of the design flow by eliminating translations of design descriptions as the design moves through the tool chain.

Two languages enjoy widespread industry support: Verilog™ [1, 2] and VHDL [3]. Both languages are IEEE standards and are supported by synthesis tools for ASICs (application-specific integrated circuits) and FPGAs (field programmable gate arrays). Languages for analog circuit design, such as Spice [4], play an important role in verifying critical timing paths of a circuit. However, these languages impose a prohibitive computational burden on large designs, cannot support abstract styles of design, and become impractical when used on a large scale. Hybrid languages (e.g., Verilog-A) [5] are used in designing mixed-signal circuits, which have both digital and analog circuitry. System-level design languages, such as System Verilog™ [6] and SystemC [7], are now emerging to support a higher level of design abstraction than can be supported by Verilog or VHDL.

1.1   Design Methodology—An Introduction

ASICs and FPGAs are designed systematically to maximize the likelihood that a design will be correct and fabricated without fatal flaws. Designers follow a design flow like that shown in Figure 1-1, which specifies a sequence of major steps that will be taken to design, verify, synthesize, and test a digital circuit. ASIC design flows involve several activities, from specification and design entry, to place-and-route and timing closure of the circuit in silicon. Timing closure is attained when all signal paths in the design satisfy the timing constraints imposed by the interface circuitry, the circuit's sequential elements, and the system clock. Although the design flow appears to be linear, in practice it is not. Various steps might be revisited as design errors are discovered, requirements are changed, or performance and design constraints are violated. For example, if a circuit fails to meet timing constraints, a new placement and routing step will have to be taken, perhaps including redesign of critical paths.

Design flows for standard-cell-based ASICs are more complex than those for FPGAs because the architecture of an ASIC is not fixed. Consequently, the performance that can be realized from a design depends on the physical placement and routing of the cells on the die, as well as the underlying device properties. Interconnect delays play a significant role in determining performance in submicron designs below 0.18 μm, where prelayout estimates of path delays do not guarantee timing closure of the routed design.

The following sections will clarify the design flow described in Figure 1-1.

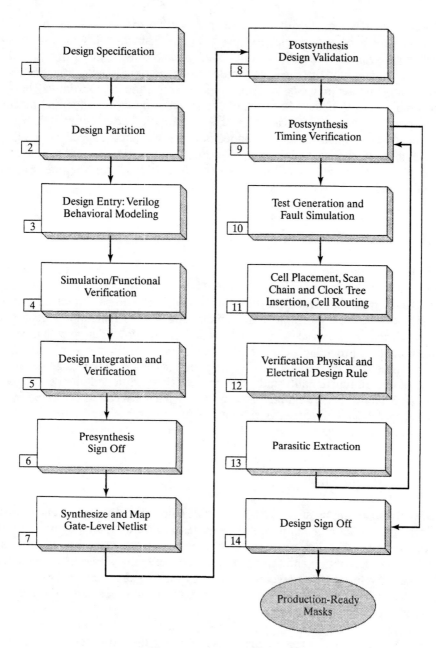

FIGURE 1-1   Design flow for HDL-based ASICs

1.1.1   Design Specification

The design flow begins with writing a specification for the design. The specification document can be a very elaborate statement of functionality, timing, silicon area, power consumption, testability, fault coverage, and other criteria that govern the design. At a minimum, the specification describes the functional characteristics that are to be implemented in a design. Typically, state transition graphs, timing charts, and algorithmic state machine (ASM) charts are used to describe sequential machines, but interpretation of the specification can be problematic, because the HDL-based model might actually implement an unintended interpretation of the specification. The emerging high-level languages, like System Verilog, hold the promise that the language itself provides an executable specification of the design, which can then be translated and synthesized into a circuit.

1.1.2   Design Partition

In today's methodologies for designing ASICs and FPGAs, large circuits are partitioned to form an *architecture*—a configuration of interacting functional units, such that each is described by a behavioral model of its functionality. The process by which a complex design is progressively partitioned into smaller and simpler functional units is called *top-down design* or *hierarchical design*. HDLs support top-down design with mixed levels of abstraction by providing a common framework for partitioning, synthesizing, and verifying large complex systems. Parts of large designs can be linked together for verification of overall functionality and performance. The partitioned architecture consists of functional units that are simpler than the whole, and each can be described by an HDL-based model. The aggregate description is often too large to synthesize directly, but each functional unit of the partition can be synthesized in a reasonable amount of time.

1.1.3   Design Entry

Design entry composes a language-based description of the design and stores it in an electronic format in a computer. Modern designs are described by hardware description languages, like Verilog, because it takes significantly less time to write a Verilog behavioral description and synthesize a gate-level realization of a large circuit than it does to develop the gate-level realization by other means, such as bottom-up manual entry. This saves time that can be put to better use in other parts of the design cycle. The ease of writing, changing, or substituting Verilog descriptions encourages architectural exploration. Moreover, a synthesis tool will find alternative realizations of the same functionality and generate reports describing the attributes of the design.

Synthesis tools create an optimal internal representation of a circuit before mapping the description into the target technology. The internal database at this stage is generic, which allows it to be mapped into a variety of technologies. For example, the technology mapping engine of a synthesis tool will use the internal format to migrate a design from an FPGA technology to an ASIC standard-cell library, without having to reoptimize the generic description.

HDL-based designs are easier to debug than schematics. A behavioral description encapsulating complex functionality hides underlying gate-level detail, so there is less information to cope with in trying to isolate problems in the functionality of the design. Furthermore, if the behavioral description is functionally correct, it is a gold standard for subsequent gate-level realizations.

HDL-based designs incorporate documentation within the design by using descriptive names, by including comments to clarify intent, and by explicitly specifying architectural relationships, thereby reducing the volume of documentation that must be kept in other archives. Simulation of a language-based model explicitly specifies the functionality of the design. Since the language is a standard, documentation of a design can be decoupled from a particular vendor's tools.

Behavioral modeling is the predominant descriptive style used by the industry, enabling the design of massive chips. Behavioral modeling describes the functionality of a design by specifying what the designed circuit will do, not how to build it in hardware. It specifies the input-output model of a logic circuit and suppresses details about physical, gate-level implementation.

Behavioral modeling encourages designers to (1) rapidly create a behavioral prototype of a design (without binding it to hardware details), (2) verify its functionality, and (3) use a synthesis tool to optimize and map the design into a selected physical technology. If the model has been written in a synthesis-ready style, the synthesis tool will remove redundant logic, perform trade-offs between alternative architectures and/or multilevel equivalent circuits, and ultimately, achieve a design that is compatible with area or timing constraints. By focusing the designer's attention on the functionality that is to be implemented, rather than on individual logic gates and their interconnections, behavioral modeling provides freedom to explore alternatives to a design before committing it to production.

Aside from its importance in synthesis, behavioral modeling provides flexibility to a design project by allowing parts of the design to be modeled at different levels of abstraction. The Verilog language accommodates mixed levels of abstraction so that the portions of the design implemented at the gate level (i.e., structurally) can be integrated and simulated concurrently with other parts of the design represented by behavioral descriptions.

1.1.4   Simulation and Functional Verification

The functionality of a design is verified (Step 4 in Figure 1-1) either by simulation or by formal methods [8]. Our discussion will focus on simulation, which is reasonable for the size of circuits we can present here. The design flow in Figure 1-1 iterates back to Step 3 until the functionality of the design has been verified. The verification process is threefold, and includes (1) development of a test plan, (2) development of a testbench, and (3) execution of the test.

Test Plan Development   A carefully documented test plan is developed to specify what functional features are to be tested and how they are to be tested. For example, the test plan might specify that the instruction set of an arithmetic/logic unit (ALU) will be verified by an exhaustive simulation of its behavior, for a specific set of input data. Test plans for sequential machines must be more elaborate to ensure a high level of confidence in the design, because they may have a large number of states. A test plan identifies the stimulus generators, response monitors, and the gold response against which the model will be tested.

Testbench Development   The *testbench* is a Verilog module in which the unit under test (UUT) has been instantiated, together with stimulus pattern generators that are to be applied to the inputs of the model during simulation. Graphical displays and/or response monitors are part of the testbench. The testbench is documented to identify the goals and sequential activity that will be observed during simulation (e.g., "Testing the opcodes"). If a design is formed as an architecture of multiple modules, each must be verified separately, beginning with the lowest level of the design hierarchy, then the integrated design must be tested to verify that the modules interact correctly. In this case, the test plan must describe the functional features of each module and the process by which they will be tested, but the plan must also specify how the aggregate is to be tested.

Test Execution and Model Verification   The testbench is exercised according to the test plan and the response is verified against the original specification for the design (e.g., Does the response match that of the prescribed ALU?). This step is intended to reveal errors in the design, confirm the syntax of the description, verify style conventions, and eliminate barriers to synthesis. Verification of a model requires a systematic, thorough demonstration of its behavior. *There is no point in proceeding further into the design flow until the model has been verified.*

1.1.5   Design Integration and Verification

After each of the functional subunits of a partitioned design have been verified to have correct functionality, the architecture must be integrated and verified to have the correct functionality. This requires development of a separate testbench whose stimulus generators exercise the input/output functionality of the top-level module, monitor port and bus activity across module boundaries, and observe state activity in any embedded state machines. *This step in the design flow is crucial* and must be executed thoroughly to ensure that the design being signed off for synthesis is correct.

1.1.6   Presynthesis Sign-Off

A demonstration of full functionality is to be provided by the testbench, and any discrepancies between the functionality of the Verilog behavioral model and the design specification must be resolved. *Sign-off* occurs after all known functional errors have been eliminated.

1.1.7 Gate-Level Synthesis and Technology Mapping

After all syntax and functional errors have been eliminated from the design and sign-off has occurred, a synthesis tool is used to create an optimal Boolean description and compose it in an available technology. In general, a synthesis tool removes redundant logic and seeks to reduce the area of the logic needed to implement the functionality and satisfy performance (speed) specifications. This step produces a netlist of standard cells or a database that will configure a target FPGA.

1.1.8 Postsynthesis Design Validation

Design validation compares the response of the synthesized gate-level description to the response of the behavioral model. This can be done by a testbench that instantiates both models, and drives them with a common stimulus, as shown in Figure 1-2. The responses can be monitored by software or by visual/graphical means to see whether they have identical functionality. For synchronous designs, the match must hold at the boundaries of the machine's cycle—intermediate activity is of no consequence. If the functionality of the behavioral description and the synthesized realization do not match, painstaking work must be done to understand and resolve the discrepancy.

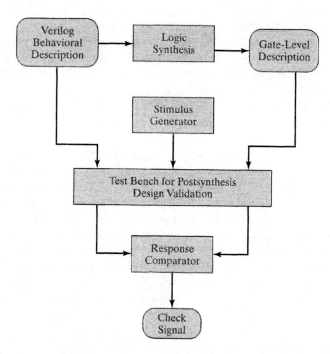

FIGURE 1-2 Postsynthesis design validation

8

Starter's Guide to Verilog 2001

Postsynthesis design validation can reveal software race conditions in the behavioral model that cause events to occur in a different clock cycle than expected.[1] We will discuss how good modeling techniques can prevent this outcome.

1.1.9 Postsynthesis Timing Verification

Although the synthesis process is intended to produce a circuit that meets timing specifications, the circuit's timing margins must be checked to verify that speeds are adequate on critical paths (Step 9). This step is repeated after Step 13, because synthesis tools do not accurately anticipate the effect of the capacitive delays induced by interconnect metalization in the layout. Ultimately, these delays must be extracted from the properties of the materials and the geometric details of the fabrication masks. The extracted delays are used by a static timing analyzer to verify that the longest paths do not violate timing constraints. The circuit might have to be resynthesized, or replaced and rerouted, to meet specifications. Resynthesis might require (1) transistor resizing, (2) architectural modifications or substitutions, and (3) device substitution (more speed at the cost of more area).

1.1.10 Test Generation and Fault Simulation

Integrated circuits must be tested after fabrication to verify that they are free of defects and operate correctly. Contaminants in the clean room can cause defects in the circuit and render it useless. In this step of the design flow, a set of test vectors is applied to the circuit, and the response of the circuit is measured. Testing considers process-induced faults, not design errors. Design errors should be detected before presynthesis sign off. Testing is daunting, for an ASIC chip might have millions of transistors, but only a few hundred package pins that can be used to probe the internal circuits. The designer might have to embed additional, special circuits that will enable a tester to use only a few external pins to test the entire internal circuitry of the ASIC, either alone or on a printed circuit board.

The patterns that are used to verify a behavioral model can be used to test the fabricated part that results from synthesis, but they might not be robust enough to detect a sufficiently high level of manufacturing defects. Combinational logic can be tested for faults exhaustively, but sequential machines present special challenges [9]. Fault simulation questions whether the chips that come off the fabrication line can, in fact, be tested to verify that they operate correctly. Fault simulation is conducted to determine whether a set of test vectors will detect a set of faults. The results of fault simulation guide the use of software tools for generating additional test patterns. To eliminate the possibility that a part could be produced but not tested, test patterns are generated before the device is fabricated, to allow for possible changes in the design, such as a scan path.[2]

---

[1] Postsynthesis validation in an ASIC design flow also includes a step for postlayout timing verification.
[2] Scan paths are formed by replacing ordinary flip-flops with specially designed flip-flops that can be connected together in test mode to form a shift register. Test patterns can be scanned into the design, and applied to the internal circuitry. The response of the circuit can be captured in the scan chain and shifted out for analysis.

1.1.11 Placement and Routing

The placement and routing step of the ASIC design flow arranges the cells on the die and connects their signal paths. In cell-based technology the individual cells are integrated to form a global mask that will be used to pattern the silicon wafer with gates. This step also might involve inserting a customized clock tree into the layout to provide a skew-free distribution of the clock signal to the sequential elements of the design. If a scan path is to be used, it will be inserted in this step too.

1.1.12 Physical and Electrical Design Rule Verification

The physical layout of a design must be checked to verify that constraints on material widths, overlaps, and separations are satisfied. Electrical rules are checked to verify that fanout constraints are met, and that signal integrity is not compromised by electrical crosstalk and power-grid drop. Noise levels are also checked to determine whether electrical transients are problematic. Power dissipation is modeled and analyzed in this step to verify that the heat generated by the chip will not damage the circuitry.

1.1.13 Parasitic Extraction

Parasitic capacitance induced by the layout is extracted by a software tool and then used to produce a more accurate verification of the electrical characteristics and timing performance of the design (Step 13). The results of the extraction step are used to update the loading models that are used in timing calculations. Then the timing constraints are checked again to confirm that the design, as laid out, will function at the specified clock speed.

1.1.14 Design Sign-Off

Final sign-off occurs after all of the design constraints have been satisfied and timing closure has been achieved. The mask set is ready for fabrication. The description consists of the geometric data (usually in GDS-II format) that will determine the photomasking steps of the fabrication process. At this point, significant resources have been expended to ensure that the fabricated chip will meet the specifications for its functionality and performance.

1.2   IC Technology Options

Figure 1-3 shows various options for creating the physical realization of a digital circuit in silicon, ranging from programmable logic devices (PLDs) to full-custom integrated

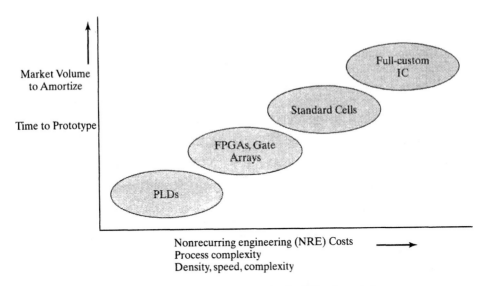

FIGURE 1-3 Alternative technologies for IC implementation

circuits. Fixed-architecture programmable logic devices serve the low end of the market (i.e., low-volume and low-performance requirements). They are relatively cheap commodity parts, targeted for low-volume designs.

The physical database of a design might be implemented as (1) a full-custom layout of high-performance circuitry, (2) a configuration of standard cells, or (3) gate arrays (field or mask programmable), depending on whether the anticipated market for the ASIC offsets the cost of designing it, and provides the required profit. Full-custom ICs occupy the high end of the cost-performance domain, where sufficient volume, or a customer with corporate objectives and sufficient resources, warrants the development time and investment required to produce fully custom designs having minimum area and maximum speed. FPGAs have a fixed, but electrically programmable architecture for implementing modest-sized designs. The tools supporting this technology allow a designer to write and synthesize a Verilog description into a working physical part on a prototype board in a matter of minutes. Consequently, design revisions can be made at a very low cost. Board layout can proceed concurrently with the development of the part because the footprint and pin configuration of an FPGA are known. Low-volume prototyping sets the stage for migration of a design to mask programmable and standard-cell-based parts.

In mask-programmable gate array technology, a wafer is populated with an array of individual transistors that can be interconnected to create logic gates implementing a desired functionality. The wafers are prefabricated and later personalized with metal interconnect for a customer. All but the metalization masks are common to all wafers, so the time and cost required to complete masks is greatly reduced, and the other non-recurring engineering (NRE) costs are amortized over the entire customer base of a silicon foundry.

Standard-cell technology predesigns and characterizes individual logic gates to the mask level and assembles them in a shared library. A place-and-route tool places the cells in channels on the wafer, interconnects them, and integrates their masks to create the functionality for a specific application. The mask set for a customer is specific to the logic being implemented and can cost over $500,000 for large circuits, but the NRE costs associated with designing and characterizing the cell library are amortized over the entire customer base. In high-volume applications, the unit cost of the parts can be relatively cheap compared to the unit cost of PLDs and FPGAs.

1.3   Overview

The following chapters will develop a foundation for the reader's role in a Verilog-based design flow presented in Figure 1-1, but not cell placement and routing, design rule checking, or parasitic extraction. These steps are conducted by separate tools which operate on the physical mask database, rather than on an HDL model of the design, and they presume that a functionally correct design has been synthesized successfully.

In the remaining chapters, we will present the primary features of Verilog that are used in modeling combinational and sequential logic design. Three things matter in learning design with an HDL: examples, examples, and examples. We present several examples.

REFERENCES

[1] *IEEE Standard Hardware Description Language Based on the Verilog Hardware Description Language*, Language Reference Manual (LRM), IEEE Std.1364-1995. Piscataway, New Jersey: Institute of Electrical and Electronic Engineers, 1996.
[2] *IEEE Standard Hardware Description Language Based on the Verilog Hardware Description Language*, Language Reference Manual (LRM), IEEE Std.1364-2001. Piscataway, New Jersey: Institute of Electrical and Electronic Engineers, 2001.
[3] *IEEE Standard VHDL Language Reference Manual* (LRM), IEEE Std, 1076-1987. Piscataway, New Jersey: Institute of Electrical and Electronic Engineers, 1988.
[4] Negel, L.W., *SPICE2: A Computer Program to Simulate Semiconductor Circuits*, Memo ERL-M520, Department of Electrical Engineering and Computer Science, University of California at Berkeley, May 9, 1975.
[5] Fitzpatrick, D., and Miller, I., *Analog Behavioral Modeling with the Verilog-A Language*, Boston: Kluwer, 1998.
[6] System Verilog 3.0, www.Accellera.org.
[7] SystemC Draft Specification, Mountain View, CA: Synopsys, 1999.
[8] Chang, H. et al., *Surviving the SOC Revolution*, Kluwer Academic Publishers, Boston, 1999.
[9] Ciletti, M.D. *Advanced Digital Design with the Verilog HDL.* Upper Saddle River, NJ: Prentice Hall, 2003.

CHAPTER 2

Basic Concepts: Primitives, Data Types, and Operators in Verilog

This chapter will introduce the Verilog HDL, beginning with some language rules, data types, built-in logic functionality, and operators. The concepts presented here provide a foundation for developing models in the remaining chapters.

2.1 Some Language Rules and Lexical Conventions

First, we present a brief summary of some rules governing Verilog models [1, 2]. Verilog has a set of keywords having predefined meanings; they may not be used for any other purpose.[1] All keywords in the text (e.g., *module*) are shown in bold, italicized type; keywords within a model are shown in bold.

2.1.1 Identifiers

An identifier (name) in Verilog is composed of a space-free sequence of upper- and lowercase letters from the alphabet, the digits (*0, 1, ..., 9*), the underscore (_), and

---

[1]See Appendix A for a list of keywords.

the $ symbol.[2] Verilog is a *case sensitive* language, so it matters whether you refer to a signal as *C_out_bar* or *C_OUT_BAR*. Verilog treats these as different names. The name of a variable may not begin with a digit or $, and may be up to 1,024 characters long. The following names are valid: *clock_bar, Clock_, STATE_3*. Identifiers are associated with logic signals and other elements of a model.

2.1.2 White Space

White space may be used freely to format the text of a model, but it may not separate contiguous characters of an identifier or a keyword, or the digits of a number.

2.1.3 Statement Termination

Verilog models consist of a list of statements declaring relationships between a model and its environment, and between signals within a model. The text of a Verilog model is placed between the keywords **module** and **endmodule**. Statements in Verilog are terminated by a semicolon (;). When used in our discussion, the term module will refer to the entire body of code encapsulated within the keywords **module** and **endmodule**. The text within a module consists of declarative statements describing various characteristics of the model, such as the data types of signals, other elements that describe structural details of the model, and executable procedural statements that are used by a simulator to determine the values of signals.

2.1.4 Comments

There are two kinds of comments: single line and multiline. A single-line comment begins with two forward slashes (//) and has the effect of causing the remaining text on that line to be ignored. A multiline comment begins with the pair of characters /* and terminates with the characters */, as in the following code:

```
// This is a single-line comment.
/*This is a multi-line comment.
Do not attempt to nest multiple multi-line comments.
*/
// The following set of nested comments will produce a syntax error:
/* This is a an illegal attempt to nest multiline comments.
/* Remember to use comments correctly */
A nested comment will be rejected.
*/
```

---

[2]The character $ is reserved to denote an identifier of a system task or function; it also identifies a built-in timing check. *Escaped identifiers* may be formed by beginning the identifier with a backslash character (\ ) and ending the identifier with white space. For example, \ *signal###* is an escaped identifier. Any printable ASCII character may be used in an escaped identifier. Escaped identifiers allow Verilog to import names generated in nonstandard formats by other tools.

A comment is not considered to be a statement and does not require a terminating semicolon.

2.1.5 Four-Value Logic System

Verilog has a four-value logic system in which a scalar variable may have the value *0, 1, x*, and *z. x* denotes an unknown value (not a don't care), and *z* denotes a high impedance value, corresponding to a three-state condition.

2.1.6 Number Formats

Numbers in Verilog are stored as binary words in the host machine. There are four base specifiers that determine how a number is interpreted: binary (*b* or *B*), decimal (*d* or *D*), hexadecimal (*h* or *H*), and octal (*o* or *O*). A number without a base specifier will be interpreted as a decimal value.

2.1.7 Sized Numbers

A number representing a logic signal can be sized to a specified word length that determines the length of the word that will hold the value of the number in the memory of the host machine. For example, the sized and formatted number $8'Ha4$ will be stored as *1010_0100* in the machine. The underscore character may be used freely in numbers to separate the characters, but has no other effect. Underscore characters can make the text more readable. For example, the number $16'hACFA$ can be written as *1010_1100_1111_1010*, which is easier to interpret than *1010110011111010*.

The number $16'HACFA$ illustrates the general form of a sized number. The prefix, 16, specifies the size (in bits) of the stored binary word; the base (radix) specifier, *H*, indicates that the characters to its right are to be interpreted as hexadecimal values. Each hexadecimal value has a corresponding 4-bit binary code, so $ACFA_{16}$ can be stored in 16 bits. If a number is sized to more bits than are needed to store its equivalent binary value, the remaining bits are set to 0. If the number of bits required to store a number exceeds the specified size, only the least significant bits are stored – the most significant bits are truncated.

2.1.8 Unsized Numbers

If a number is given without a size (e.g., $'HAA$), it will be stored in a word having a length of at least 32 bits. So $'HAA$ is stored in a machine having a word length of 32 bits as *0000_0000_0000_0000_0000_0000_1010_1010*.

2.1.9 Signed Numbers

Signed numbers (+ or −) are allowed, and real numbers may be represented in scientific notation (*e* or *E*). The characters of a real number are restricted to the digits

(0, 1, ... , 9) and the underscore character. The exponent of a real number must be an integer; the mantissa may contain only numeric values. If the mantissa contains a decimal point there must be at least one number on either side of it. If the most significant bit of a sized number is *x* or *z*, denoting an unknown or high-impedance value, respectively, the representation automatically extends the values *x* or *z* to the length of the word. For example, the sized number 8′*bx*1010 will be stored as *xxxx_1010*. If a number is signed with -, its two's-complement will be stored, for example, −8′*d*6 is stored as *1111_1010*.

Example: Sized, Unsized, and Signed Numbers

Number	#Bits	Base	Dec. Equiv.	Stored
2'b10	2	Binary	2	10
3'o5	3	Octal	5	101
8'ha	8	Hex	10	00001010
3'b5	Not valid!			
8'bx01	8	Binary	-	xxxxxx01
12'hx	12	Hex	-	xxxxxxxxxxxx
-8'd6	8	Decimal		11111010

Example End: Sized, Unsized, and Signed Numbers

2.2   Primitives

Verilog includes a set of 26 predefined functional models of common combinational logic gates called *primitives*. Primitives are the most basic functional objects that can be used to compose a design. Their inputs and outputs are scalar signals. The functionality of each primitive is built into the language by means of internal truth tables defining the relationship between the output of each primitive and its input(s).

Table 2-1 shows an abbreviated list of the predefined primitives and their reserved keywords. Their names suggest their functionality (the **not** primitive corresponds to an inverter). An *n*-input primitive has the same model keyword (e.g., **nand**) regardless of the number of inputs, and automatically accommodates any number of scalar inputs, rather than only a pair of inputs. The *n*-output primitives (e.g., the buffer

TABLE 2-1   Verilog primitives for modeling combinational logic gates

n-Input	n-Output, 3-state
and	buf
nand	not
or	bufif0
nor	bufif1
xor	notif0
xnor	notif0

primitive, *buf*) have a single scalar input but can have multiple scalar outputs (to model a gate that has fanout to more than one location). The primitives *bufif0* and *bufif1* are three-state buffers; *notif0* and *notif1* are three-state inverters.[3]

 The output port(s) of a primitive must be listed first in the list of ports.

Example: Instantiation of a Multiinput Primitive

The nand primitive shown in Figure 2-1 has six inputs and one output. The Verilog statement declaring the use of the primitive is called an instantiation; it lists the keyword, **nand**, encloses the ports in parentheses, and terminates the statement with a semicolon.

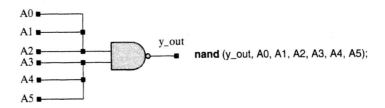

FIGURE 2-1   Instantiation of a *nand* multiinput primitive

Example End: Instantiation of a Multiinput Primitive

 The instance name of a primitive is optional.

In general, a primitive is instantiated within a module by a statement declaring its keyword name, followed by an optional instance name and by a parenthetical list of its terminals.[4] Each primitive has *ports* (terminals) that connect to its environment. If the instance name of the primitive is omitted, the list of ports is placed immediately to the right of the primitive type name as a comma-separated list enclosed by parentheses and terminated by a semicolon (;). The output port(s) of a primitive must be first in the list of ports, followed by the primitive's input port(s).

Only the *bufif0, bufif1, notif0,* and *notif1* primitives may have a *z* output. We'll use these gates to model three-state logic.

---

[3]The complete set of primitives is described in Appendix B.
[4]See Appendix C for a formal description of the language syntax.

Example: Instantiation of a Multioutput Primitive

The **bufif1** primitive in Figure 2-2 has four outputs. Each output may have different electrical loading and timing characteristics associated with the layout of the gate in a physical circuit. When *enable* is asserted, the outputs are determined by *x_in*; when *enable* is deasserted, the outputs have the logic value *z*.

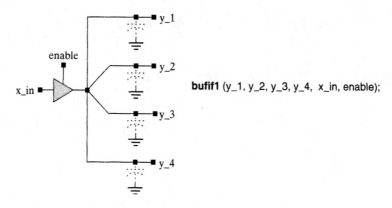

FIGURE 2-2   Instantiation of a *bufif1* three-state primitive

Example End: Instantiation of a Multioutput Primitive

Complex structures can be composed by instantiating and connecting primitives, just as complex logic can be assembled from individual gates. The connections between the gates are made by the named signals in the ports of the primitives.

Example: Instantiated and Connected Primitives

Multiple primitives are instantiated (listed) in Figure 2-3 to form a three-input, three-output combinational logic function. The Verilog description of the structure lists the

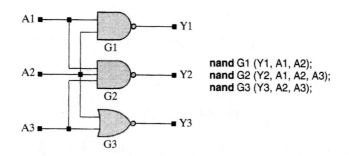

FIGURE 2-3   Formation of logic from multiple primitives

primitives, with their ports establishing the connections apparent in the schematic.[5] The optional primitive instance names, G1, G2, and G3, are each included between the primitive type (e.g., ***nand***) and the list of the primitive's ports. Instance names distinguish instances of primitives from each other. Note that the ***nand*** primitive is used here with two inputs and again with three inputs; the logic of each primitive will be implemented automatically by a simulator.

Example End: Instantiated and Connected Primitives

2.3   Logic Resolution for Primitives

A built-in truth table for each primitive type determines the logic value of its output for given inputs. Figure 2-4 shows how the inputs to the ***and*** primitive, together with its truth table, determine its output, under all possible values of a pair of inputs. Note: if one input of the ***and*** primitive is a 1 and the other input is an x or a z, the output is x.[6]

A simulator uses the built-in truth tables of primitives to form the outputs of primitives during simulation. The values of the inputs attached to a primitive are determined by the circuitry external to the primitive, just as the output of a combinational logic gate is determined by the values of its inputs.

2.4   Data Types for Signals

Computers represent information as constants and variables (e.g., integers and real numbers) that can be retrieved, manipulated, and stored in memory. A variable may represent a number used in computation (such as a loop index governing a repetitive sequence of steps), a value of data (such as a binary word), or a computed value (such

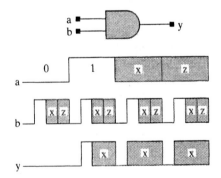

FIGURE 2-4   Signal resolution for the ***and*** primitive

---

[5]The order in which primitives are listed is arbitrary, and has no effect on the meaning of the model or the results of simulation. The order does not establish a precedence of any kind.

[6]Only the output of a three-state primitive can have the value z.

as the sum of two numbers). In Verilog, a variable can also represent a binary-encoded logic signal in a circuit. The value of a signal may be constant or variable.

Logic signals are identified by a name and have a default scalar size (1 bit). Numeric variables are also identified by name, but have a default size dependent upon their type. A vector signal in Verilog is represented by appending square brackets enclosing a contiguous range of bits to an identifier, (e.g., *sum[3:0]* represents a 4-bit value). The individual bits of a vector can be referenced by their index, (e.g., *sum [2]*). The entire vector can be referenced as *sum [3: 0]* or as *sum*. Also, a contiguous range of bits can be referenced as a so-called part-select of the word. The part-select *sum [3: 2]* is a vector of the most significant 2 bits of *sum*.

For the purpose of calculating the decimal equivalent value of a vector, the leftmost index in the bit range is the most significant bit, and the rightmost is the least significant. An expression can be the index of a part-select. If the index of a part-select is out of bounds, the value **x** is returned by a reference to the variable.[7]

There are two kinds of data in Verilog: constants and variables. All variables in Verilog have a predefined type, and there are only two basic families of data types for variables: nets and registers.[8,9] *Net variables* act like wires in a physical circuit and establish connectivity between primitives and other primitives and/or modules. *Register variables* act like variables in ordinary procedural languages—they store logical or numerical information while the program executes. They might synthesize to storage elements (e.g., flip-flops).

2.4.1 Constants

A constant in Verilog is declared with the keyword *parameter* in a statement assigning a name and a value to the constant. The value of a constant is fixed during simulation. Use constants to create symbolic names for state codes and other numerical values to make the description more readable.[10] Constant expressions (with arithmetic) may be used in the declaration of the value of a constant.

Example: Constants

```
parameter HIGH_INDEX = 31;                    // integer
parameter WIDTH = 32, depth = 1024;           // integers
parameter BYTE_SIZE = 8, word_size = 32;      // integer
parameter A_REAL_VALUE = 6.22;                // real
```

---

[7]In Verilog's logic system, the symbol **x** represents an ambiguous (unknown) value, not a don't-care.
[8]All variables in Verilog are static; their memory is allocated before simulation and is not deallocated until the simulation ends.
[9]An abstract data type, called named events, will be introduced in Chapter 5.
[10]Additional types of parameters introduced in Verilog 2001 will be discussed in Chapter 5.

```
parameter AV_DELAY = (MIN_DELAY + MAX_DELAY)/2;    // real
parameter INITIAL_STATE = 8'b1001_0110;            // reg
```

Example End: Constants

2.4.2 Data Type Family: Nets

Nets establish connectivity between design objects within a module, (e.g., a net that connects the output port of a primitive to an input port of another primitive). All structural connections within a module are made with nets. The family of net data types is described in Table 2-2. A primitive is said to *drive* a net if the net is an output port of the primitive. With the exception of the *trireg* net, *the logic value associated with a net is determined by the driver of the net.*[11]

TABLE 2-2   Types of nets in Verilog

	Net Types
wire	Establishes connectivity, with no logical behavior or functionality implied.
tri	Establishes connectivity, with no logical behavior or functionality implied. This type of net has the same functionality as **wire**, but is identified distinctively to indicate that it will be three-stated in hardware.
wand	A net that is connected to the output of multiple primitives. It models the hardware implementation of a wired-AND (e.g., open collector technology).
wor	A net that is connected to the output of multiple primitives. It models the hardware implementation of a wired-OR (e.g., emitter coupled logic).
triand	A net that is connected to the output of multiple primitives. It models the hardware implementation of a wired-AND (e.g., open collector technology). The physical net is to be three-stated.
trior	A net that is connected to the output of multiple primitives. It models the hardware implementation of a wired-OR (e.g., emitter coupled logic). The physical net is to be three-stated.
supply0	A global net representing a connection to the circuit ground.
supply1	A global net representing a connection to the power supply.
tri0	A net that is connected to ground by a resistive pull-down connection.
tri1	A net that is connected to the power supply by a resistive pull-up connection.
trireg	A net that models the charge stored on a physical net.

Example: Driver of a Net

In Figure 2-5, the logic value of *y_out* is determined by the values of *y1* and *y2* and the truth table for the ***nor*** primitive. The logic value of *y1* is determined by the values of *x_in1* and *x_in2* and the truth table for the ***and*** primitive.

---

[11]In Chapter 4, we will consider a behavioral construct that may drive a net.

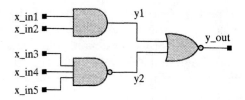

FIGURE 2-5   The drivers of a net determine the logic value of a net.

Example End: Driver of a Net

The **wand** and **wor** net types automatically resolve contention between multiple drivers on a net. The value on a **wand** (wired-AND) net is 0 if any of its drivers is 0; the value on a **wor** net (wired-OR) is 1 if any of its drivers is 0. Use only the type **wire** for structural connections in models intended for synthesis.

A net is declared by a statement associating the keyword of the net type with an identifier. If the net is a vector, the MSB and LSB of its array indices are enclosed in square brackets ([:]) and placed after the type of the net, as shown in the following example (multiple nets of the same type and size may be declared as a comma-separated list):

Example: Declaration of Nets

```
wire [31: 0]    sum, diff;      // 32-bit wires named sum and diff
wire            clock, reset;   // Scalar signals
wire [0: 31]    reverse_sum;    // A 32-bit signal having its MSB as reverse_sum[0]
supply0         ground;         // A net representing a connection to ground
```

Example End: Declaration of Nets

Nets have a default size of one bit (scalar) and a default initial value of x in simulation, retaining that value until it is changed by a driver of the net.

2.4.3   Data Type Family: Registers

Registers store information. Register variables are used in behavioral modeling (beginning in Chapter 4) and are assigned values by procedural statements. A register variable holds its value until an assignment statement changes it. The following are predefined register types: *reg, integer, real, realtime*, and *time*. Logic signals may be a net type, a **reg**, or an **integer**.

Register Variable Type: reg   The data type *reg* is an abstraction of a hardware storage element, but it does not necessarily correspond directly to physical hardware. A *reg* variable has a default scalar size (1 bit) and a default initial value of *x* in simulation The Verilog operators discussed later in this chapter treat a *reg* variable as an unsigned value.

A *reg* variable is declared by the keyword *reg* followed by an optional array range and an identifier.

---

*Example: Declarations of **reg** Variables*

```
reg [31: 0] product;          // A 32-bit register named product
reg clock, reset;             // Scalar register signals
reg [0: 31] reverse_sum;      // A 32-bit register having its MSB as reverse_sum[0]
```

---

*Example End: Declarations of **reg** Variables*

Register Variable Type: integer   The data type *integer* supports numeric computation in procedural statements. *Integers* are represented internally to the word length of the host machine (at least 32 bits). A negative *integer* is stored in two's-complement format. An *integer* variable has a default initial value of 0.

Verilog operates on integers with two's-complement arithmetic, with the MSB indicating the sign of the value. For example, the negative *integer* -4_{10} is stored as 1111_1111_1111_1111_1111_1111_1111_1100. When the size of a nonnegative number assigned to an *integer* is less than the length of the word used by the machine to store an *integer*, the number is padded with 0's to the left. The value assigned to an *integer* must have a decimal equivalent (i.e., *x* and *z* are not allowed). Since integers have fixed word size, their declaration may not have a range specification. Also, it is not advisable to use an *integer* variable where a hardware register is appropriate. A register variable may have significantly fewer bits.

Some examples of valid declarations of integers and arrays of integers follow. An array of integers can be declared by including an array range after the identifier.

Example: Declaration of Integers

```
integer J; K;
integer Array_of_Ints [1:100];
```

Example End: Declaration of Integers

An *integer* will be interpreted as a signed value in two's complement form if it is assigned a value without a base specifier (e.g., A = −24). If the value assigned has a specified base, the *integer* is interpreted as an unsigned value. For example, if A is an *integer*, the result of A = −12/3 is −4; the result of −'d12/3 is 1431655761. Both words evaluate to the same bit pattern, but the former is interpreted as a negative value in two's-complement arithmetic.

Register Variable Type: real Variables having type *real* are stored in double precision, typically a 64-bit value. A *real* variable has a default initial value of 0.0. Real variables can be specified in decimal and exponential notation (e.g., 1.2E12).

Register Variable Type: realtime Variables having type *realtime* are stored in real number format. A *realtime* variable has a default initial value of 0.

Register Variable Type: time A variable of type *time* is stored as a 64-bit unsigned quantity and can be used to hold the value of time as it evolves during simulation.

Undeclared Register Variables Verilog has no mechanism for handling undeclared register variables. An identifier that has not been declared is assumed to reference a net of the default type (e.g., a scalar of type *wire*). A procedural assignment to an undeclared variable will cause a compiler error.

2.4.4 Addressing Nets and Registers

The most significant bit of a part-select of a net or register is always addressed by the leftmost array index; the least significant bit is addressed by the rightmost array index. A constant or variable expression can be the index of a part-select. If the index of a part-select is out of bounds, the value *x* is returned by a reference to the variable. Note that if a vector identifier has an ascending (descending) order from its LSB to its MSB in its declaration, a referenced part-select of that identifier must have the same ascending (descending) order from its LSB to its MSB.

Example : Addressing a Vector

If the 8-bit word *data_bus* is declared with array range *[7: 0]* and has a stored value of decimal 4, then *data_bus[2]* has a value of 1; *data_bus[3:0]* has a value of 4; *data_bus[5:1]* has value 2 (i.e., *data_bus* [7: 0] = 0000_0100_2, and *data_bus* [5: 1] = 0_0010_2). An attempt to address *data_bus[0: 3]* generates a syntax error.

Example End: Addressing a Vector

2.5 Strings

Verilog does not have a data type for strings. Instead, the ASCII code of a string must be stored in a properly sized array with 8 bits allocated for each character of the string.

Example: Strings

A declaration of a **reg**, *string_holder*, that will accommodate a string having *NUM_CHAR* characters is as follows:

```
parameter     NUM_CHAR = 11;
reg           [8 * NUM_CHAR –1: 0] string_code;
…
string_code = "Hello World";
```

Example End: Strings

A string is enclosed within quotes when it is assigned to a register variable. The declaration in the example above implies that 8 bits will encode each of the *NUM_CHAR* characters. If the string "Hello World" is assigned to *string_code*, it is necessary that *NUM_CHAR* be at least 11 to ensure that a minimum of 88 bits are reserved. If an assignment to an array consists of less characters than the array will accommodate, the unused positions are automatically filled with 0's, beginning at the position of the MSB (i.e., the leftmost position).

 Use strings to generate text labels for waveform displays (e.g., the label for a state code).

2.6   Memories

Verilog extends the declaration of a register variable to provide a *memory* (i.e., multiple addressable words of the same size), by adding an array range after the identifier of the register. An example of the syntax for a memory of **reg** variables is shown next.

Example: Declaration of a Memory

With parameters *word_size* = 32 and *memory_size* = 1024, the following code fragment shows how the syntax for declaring a **reg** memory variable simplifies to the form **reg** *word_size array_name memory_size* for an array of 1,024 32-bit words:

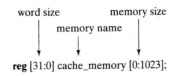

reg [31:0] cache_memory [0:1023];

Example End: Declaration of a Memory

In Verilog 1995 bit-select and part-select are not valid with a memory. Reference may be made to only a *word* of a memory. The MSB of a part-select is the leftmost array index; the LSB is the rightmost. If an index is out of bounds, the result is the logic value *x*. Only a *constant* expression may be used for the LSB and the MSB in a declaration of an array.

2.7 Multidimensional Arrays

Verilog 1995 supports only one-dimensional arrays of type *reg, integer,* and *time*. Verilog 2001 supports multidimensional arrays of nets and all register variables. Arrays can have any number of dimensions in Verilog 2001. The range specifications for the indices of the dimensions of an array follow the declared name of the array.

Example: Arrays in Verilog 2001

---

reg	[15: 0]	data	[0: 127] [0: 127];	// 2-dimensional array of
				// 16-bit words
real		time_array	[0: 15] [0:15] [0:15];	// 3-dimensional array of
				// real values
wire	[31: 0]	d_paths	[15: 0];	// 1-dimensional array of
				// 32-bit words
integer		indices	[7: 0] [63: 0];	// 2-dimensional array of
				// integers

Example End: Arrays in Verilog 2001

A bit or a part-select[12] of contiguous bits of a word in an array cannot be addressed directly in Verilog 1995, but Verilog 2001 allows selection of a bit or a part-select from an array of any number of dimensions. To select a word, reference the array with an index for each dimension. To select a bit or a part, reference the array with an index for each dimension plus a bit or range specification.

Example: Bit-Select and Part-Select in Verilog 2001

---

reg	[15: 0]	data	[0: 127] [0: 127]	// 2-dimensional array of
				// 16-bit words
realtime		time_array	[0: 15] [0: 15] [0: 15];	// 3-dimensional array of
				// realtime values
wire	[31: 0]	d_paths	[15: 0];	// 1-dimensional array of
				// 32-bit words

---

[12]Part-select of a *real* or *realtime* variable is not allowed.

wire	[15: 0]	a_data_word = data [4] [21];	// references a word of // *data*
realtime		a_time_sample = time_array [7] [4] [0];	// references a word of // *time_array*
wire	[7: 0]	a_byte = data [64] [32] [12: 5];	// references a byte of // *data*
wire		a_bit = data [31] [8] [3];	// references a bit of *data*

Example End: Bit-Select and Part-Select in Verilog 2001

2.8   Variable Part-Selects

 Verilog 1995 allows a part-select of contiguous bits from a vector if the range indices of the part-select are constant. Verilog 2001 provides two new part-select operators to support a indexed variable part-select of fixed width, +: and −:, having the syntax [<*start_bit*> +: <*width*>] and [<*start_bit*> −: <*width*>], respectively. The parameter *width* specifies the size of the part select, and *start_bit* specifies the rightmost or leftmost bit in the vector from which the part-select is taken, depending on whether the selection will be made by incrementing (+) or decrementing (−) the index of the bits in the vector.

Example: Variable Part-Select

In Verilog 2001, a reference to $sum[K +: 3]$ forms a 3-bit vector from $sum[K + 2]$, $sum[K + 1]$, and $sum[K]$, depending on the value of K. The syntax for a variable part-select is not supported in Verilog 1995 and would be detected and reported as a syntax error.

Example End: Variable Part-Select

2.9   Operators for Signals

Verilog also has built-in operators for determining the value of a signal from an expression, rather than from a primitive. Operators describe logic symbolically, and can lead to simpler, more compact, and clearer descriptions of functionality than a structural model based on primitives.

2.9.1   Bitwise Operators

Bitwise operators combine a pair of operands on a bitwise basis to form a vector result. Table 2-3 lists the built-in bitwise operators.

TABLE 2-3 Bitwise operators

Bitwise Operators	
Symbol	Operation
~	Negation
&	And
|	Inclusive Or
^	Exclusive Or
~^	Exclusive Nor
^~	Exclusive Nor

Example: Truth Table for the Bitwise Exclusive-Or Operator

Table 2-4 defines the bitwise exclusive-or operator in Verilog's four-value system of logic. If the corresponding bit of either operand is an x or a z, that bit of the result is x. For example, the exclusive-or operation $(1010\_0101) \text{ ^ } (1111\_xx01)$ produces the result (0101_xx00).

TABLE 2-4 Truth table for the Exclusive-Or operator

Exclusive-Or				
^	0	1	x	z
0	0	1	x	x
1	1	0	x	x
x	x	x	x	x
z	x	x	x	x

Example End: Truth Table for the Bitwise Exclusive-Or Operator

The bitwise operators are equivalent to an array of primitives. A single operator may replace several gates.

Example: Equivalent Logic for a Bitwise Operator

The functionality of the bitwise-or operation on the datapaths in Figure 2-6 is equivalent to the functionality of the array of two-input **or** gates:

```
or (y[7], a[7], b[7]);
or (y[6], a[6], b[6]);
or (y[5], a[5], b[5]);
or (y[4], a[4], b[4]);
or (y[3], a[3], b[3]);
or (y[2], a[2], b[2]);
```

```
or (y[1], a[1], b[1]);
or (y[0], a[0], b[0]);
```

The functionality of the array is equivalent to that of the bitwise operation described by $y [7: 0] = a [7: 0] \mid b[7: 0];$

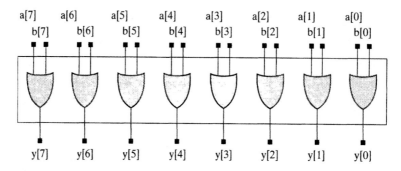

FIGURE 2-6   Array of OR gates.

Example End: Equivalent Logic for a Bitwise Operator

2.9.2   Reduction Operators

The reduction operators shown in Table 2-5 produce a scalar value from a single operand.

2.9.3   Relational Operators

Relational operators (see Table 2-6) compare the value of a pair of words and generate a Boolean result (1 – True) or (0 – False). A word is true (1) only if its decimal equivalent is a positive integer (non-zero value); a word having a value 0 or containing a bit of x or z is treated as false (0). If either operand contains x or z, the result of the comparison is x.

TABLE 2-5   Reduction operators

Reduction Operators			
Symbol	**Operation**	**Operation**	**Result**
&	And	&(010101)	0
~&	Nand	|(010101)	1
|	Or	&(010x10)	0
~|	Nor	|(010x10)	1
^	Exclusive Or	^(010x10)	x
~^	Exclusive Nor	~^(010x10)	x
^~	Exclusive Nor		

TABLE 2-6   Relational operators

Relational Operators	
Symbol	**Operation**
<	Less than
<=	Less than or equal to
>	Greater than
>=	Greater than or equal to

Operation	Result
1101 > 1111	0
1101 < 1111	1
1x11 < 0001	x

2.9.4 Equality Operators

The equality operators in Table 2-7 compare operands bit for bit, with 0s filling in if the operands are of unequal length. The result of a comparison is 1 if the comparison is true, and 0 if false. The comparisons with the operators == and != produce a result of *x* if either operand contains an *x* or *z*. The case equality (===) and inequality (!==) operators compare operands on a bitwise basis for a match in the four-value logic and produce a result of either 0 or 1.

2.9.5 Logical Operators

Expressions combine operands and operators to determine a value. The logical operators **&&** and ‖ in Table 2-8 act as connectives for Boolean expressions to produce a Boolean (true or false) result. The negation operator *!* produces the Boolean complement of the Boolean value of an expression.

Boolean expressions are evaluated from left to right; the evaluation stops as soon as the truth or falsity of the expression is established. In general, use parentheses to clarify the interpretation of a complex expression.

TABLE 2-7   Equality operators

Expression	Interpretation	
A===B	A is identical to B, including *x* and *z*	"case equality"
A!==B	A is not identical to B, including *x* and *z*	"case inequality"
A==B	A is identical to B, not including *x* and *z*	
A!=B	A is not identical to B, not including *x* and *z*	

Equality Operators	
Symbol	**Operator**
===	Case equality
!==	Case inequality
==	Logical equality
!=	Logical inequality

TABLE 2-8   Logical operators

Logical Operators	
Symbol	**Operator**
! && ‖	Logical negation Logical and Logical or

Example: Expression Evaluation with Logical Operators

Of the following two expressions, the intent of the second is clear:

    A < size −1 && B != C && Index != Lastone
    (A < size −1) && (B != C) && (Index != Lastone)

Example End: Expression Evaluation with Logical Operators

Use logical operators only as logical connectives in Boolean expressions; use bitwise operators only to perform bitwise operations on signals. Logical operators might produce the correct result when used with scalar signals, but it is strongly recommended that these operators not be used in place of bitwise operators. A syntax checker will not detect an error caused by misuse of the logical operators.

Example: Misuse of Logical Operators

Suppose that A = 3'b001 and B = 3'b11x. The results of the logical-and (&&) and the bitwise-and operator (&) on these words are as follows:

Operation	Result	Boolean Value
A && B	1'b1	True
A & B	3'b00x	False

Example End: Misuse of Logical Operators

Syntax errors result from using white space improperly with multisymbol operators.

Example: Syntax Errors

Expression	Syntax
A && B	Valid
A| |B	Invalid

A ||B	Invalid
A & (&B)	Valid

Example End: Syntax Errors

2.9.6   Shift Operators

Verilog was originally implemented with only the logical shift operators; Verilog 2001 includes the arithmetic shift operators.

Logical Shift   The logical shift operators in Table 2-9 shift the bits of a word to the left or right and fill the vacated position with 0. The operator does not rotate the operand.

TABLE 2-9   Logical shift operators

Symbol	Operator
<<	Logical Shift Left
>>	Logical Shift Right

Example: Logical Shift Operator

Suppose A is an 8-bit word having the value $8'b1010\_0001$. Some results of shifting A are as follows:

Expression	Before	After
A > 1	1010_0001	0101_0000
A << 2	1010_0001	1000_0100
A >> A	1010_0001	0000_0000

Example End: Logical Shift Operator

Arithmetic Shift

The arithmetic shift operators in Table 2-10 fill the vacated cell with the MSB if the shift is to the right, and a 0 if the shift is to the left. The right-shift arithmetic operation preserves the sign bit of a two's-complement number. The left-shift arithmetic operator is equivalent to the left-shift logical operator (i.e., <<< and << have the same effect).

TABLE 2-10   Arithmetic shift operators

Symbol	Operator
<<<	Arithmetic Shift Left
>>>	Arithmetic Shift Right

Example: Arithmetic Shift

Suppose A is an 8-bit word having the value $8'b1010\_0001$. Following are some results of shifting A with the arithmetic shift operators:

Expression	Before	After
A >>> 1	1010_0001	1101_0000
A <<< 2	1010_0001	1000_0100
A >>> A	1010_0001	1111_1111

Example: Arithmetic Shift

2.9.7   Arithmetic Operators

The arithmetic operators in Table 2-11 treat regs as unsigned words, and implement signed arithmetic on integers.

2.9.8   Conditional Operator

The conditional operator (? :) uses the Boolean value of an expression to select one expression from a pair of expressions. In the syntax shown below, *true_expr* is returned if *Boole_expr* evaluates true; *false_expr* is returned if *Boole_expr* evaluates false. The conditional operator acts like a switch controlled by *Boole_expr*, with syntax:
Boole_expr ? true_expr : false_expr

TABLE 2-11   Arithmetic operators

Symbol	Operation
+	Addition
−	Subtraction
*	Multiplication
/	Division
%	Modulus

Example: Conditional Operator

Expression	A	B	Result
(A > B) ? 1 : 0	4	2	1
(A == B) ? A + B : A – B	6	2	4
(A + B) > 2 ? A – B : 0	5	3	2
(A + B) < 2 ? A – B : 0	5	3	0

Example End: Conditional Operator

A few rules govern the conditional operator. Its syntax requires that both *true_expr* and *false_expr* be given, and the logic value *z* is not allowed in *Boole_expr*. The operands in *Boole_expr* are 0-filled to match lengths before the expression is evaluated. If *Boole_expr* evaluates to *x*, the result is not necessarily *x*, too. Table 2-12 determines the result. If *true_expr* and *false_expr* have the same value, the result is determined independent of the value of *Boole_expr*.

TABLE 2-12   Resolution of ambiguity for the conditional operator

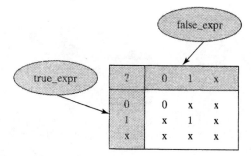

2.9.9   Exponentiation Operator

The exponentiation operator, introduced in Verilog 2001, performs arithmetic exponentiation and returns a result whose type depends on the type of the operands according to Table 2-13.

TABLE 2-13   Values returned by the exponentiation operator

Verilog-2001		
base	exponent	returned value
real, integer, or signed value	real, integer, or signed value	double-precision floating point
0	not a positive number	ambiguous
negative number	not an integer	ambiguous

Example: Exponentiation Operator

---

reg	[7: 0]	base;
reg	[2: 0]	exponent;
reg	[15: 0]	value;

...

value = base ** exponent;

...

Example End: Exponentiation Operator

2.9.10 Concatenation Operator

The concatenation operator composes a word from its operands. An unsized number may not be an operand of the concatenation operator. The concatenation operator may be nested to an arbitrary depth, and may be repeated by including a prefix that evaluates to a value.

Example: Concatenation Operator

Expression	Result
{C, B[3: 0], W, 3'b10x}	{C, B[3], B[2], B[1], B[0], W, 1'b1, 1'b0, 1'bx}
{A, B, {E, F}}	{A, B, E, F}
5{ A }	{A, A, A, A, A}

Note that the last example forms a result by repeatedly concatenating a word.

Example End: Concatenation Operator

2.9.11 Operator Precedence

Expressions are evaluated from left to right according to the operator precedence shown in Table 2-14.

2.10   Arithmetic with Signed Data Types

Verilog 1995 is limited to signed arithmetic on 32-bit integers. The *reg* and net data types are unsigned, and expressions are evaluated as signed arithmetic only if every operand is a signed variable (i.e., has type *integer*). The data types of the variables in an expression, not the

TABLE 2-14   Verilog 2001 operator precedence

Precedence	Symbol	Operator
Highest	+ − ! ~	Unary
	**	Exponentiation
	* / %	Multiply, divide, modulus
	+ −	Add, subtract
	<< >> <<< >>>	Shift
	< <= > >=	Relational
	== != === !==	Equality
	& ~&	Reduction
	^ ^~ ~^	
	| ~|	
	&&	Logical
	||	
Lowest	? :	Conditional

operators, determine whether signed or unsigned arithmetic is performed. Verilog 2001 uses the reserved keyword *signed* to declared that a *reg* or a net type variable is signed, and supports signed arithmetic on vectors of any size, not just 32-bit values.

Example: Arithmetic with Signed Variables

Figure 2-7 declares signed variables in Verilog 2001 and illustrates the results stored from arithmetic operations in Verilog 1995 and Verilog 2001.

Verilog 1995	Verilog 2001
integer m, n; **reg** [63: 0] v;	**integer** m, n; **reg signed** [63: 0] v;

...   // value stored
m = 12; // 0000_..._0000_1100
n = −4; // 1111_..._1111_1100
v = 8;   // 0000_..._0000_1000
	... // value stored
	m = 12; //0000_..._0000_1100
	n = −4; // 1111_..._1111_1100
	v = 8; // 0000_..._0000_1000

m = m / n; // result: −3	m = m / n; // result: −3
v = v / n; // result: 0	v = v / n; // result: −2

FIGURE 2-7   Arithmetic with signed data types

Example End: Arithmetic with Signed Variables

2.10.1 Signed Literal Integers

Verilog 1995 represents literal integers in three ways: an integer number (e.g., −10), an unsized radix-specified number (e.g., 'hA), and a sized radix-specified number (e.g., 64'hF). If a radix is specified, the number is interpreted as an unsigned value; if a radix is omitted, the number is interpreted as a signed value. In Verilog 2001, the symbol *s* is preappended to the base specifier to specify that a sized or unsized literal integer is signed.

Example: Declaration of Signed Variables and Literals

The following statements illustrate the declaration of signed variables and the results of arithmetic with signed variables and literals:

```
reg     signed   [63: 0]   v;        // Signed variable
...
v = 12;                              // Literal integer
...
v = v / -64'd2;                      // Stored as 0
v = v / -64'sd2;                     // Stored as -6
```

The expression v/-64'd2 divides 12 by the decimal equivalent of the two's complement of 2, e.g., by 1111...1111_1110. The expression *v/-64'sd2* forms the two's complement of 12 divided by 2.

Example End: Declaration of Signed Variables and Literals

2.10.2 System Functions for Sign Conversion

Verilog 2001 provides two new system functions for converting values to signed or unsigned values. The function **$signed** returns a signed value from the value passed in. The function **$unsigned** returns an unsigned value from the value passed in. The functions are useful because an expression returns a signed value if and only if all of its operands are signed variables. Sign conversion eliminates the need to declare an assigned value to additional variables to circumvent the restrictions of Verilog 1995.

Example: Arithmetic with Sign Conversion Functions

In the following statements, the function *$signed* returns a signed value from its argument, *sum_diff*, with the result apparent in the value stored for *signed_sum_diff*.

```
integer        v;
reg      [63: 0]  sum_diff;
...
v = -16;
sum_diff = 48;
sum_diff = sum_diff/v;                      // Returns 0
signed_sum_diff = $signed (sum_diff)/v;     // Returns -3
```

Example End: Arithmetic with Sign Conversion Functions

2.10.3 Assignment Width Extension

 Verilog 1995 has two rules for extending the bits of a word when the expression on the RHS side of an assignment statement has a smaller width than the expression on the LHS. If the expression on the RHS is *signed*, the sign-bit determines the extension to fill the LHS. If the expression on the RHS is *unsigned* (i.e. **reg, time**, and all net types), its extension is formed by filling with 0's. This can lead to inappropriate extensions when the LHS exceeds 32 bits.

Verilog 2001 has a more elaborate set of rules for extending the width of a word beyond 32 bits, as summarized in Figure 2-8. These rules differ from those for Verilog 1995, so a model that adhered to the rules of Verilog 1995 will not work in the same way as a model employing the rules of Verilog 2001.

Leftmost bit of RHS expression	Extended value	
	unsigned RHS expression	signed RHS expression
0	0	0
1	0	1
X	X	X
Z	Z	Z

FIGURE 2-8   Width extension in Verilog 2001

REFERENCES

[1] *IEEE Standard for Verilog Hardware Description Language 2001*, IEEE Std.1364-1995. Piscataway, NJ: Institute of Electrical and Electronic Engineers, 1996.
[2] *IEEE Standard for Verilog Hardware Description Language 2001*, IEEE Std.1364-2001. Piscataway, NJ: Institute of Electrical and Electronic Engineers, 2001.

PROBLEMS

1. Write a declaration of the following nets: (a) a 32-bit net having name *data_bus* and type **wire**, (b) scalar nets *clock*, *set*, and *reset*.

2. Write a declaration of the following registers: (a) a 32-bit register having name *operand_1* and type **reg**, (b) an integer having name K, (c) a 32 × 64 two-dimensional array of 16-bit words having name *Pixel_Color*.

3. Answer T (true) or F (false):
   ___ Verilog is case insensitive.
   ___ Built-in primitives describe only combinational logic.
   ___ Verilog does not have user-defined data types.
   ___ The right arithmetic shift operator is denoted by >>.

4. What characters are allowed in an identifier?

5. Write a list of declarations of primitives corresponding to the schematic in Figure P2-5.

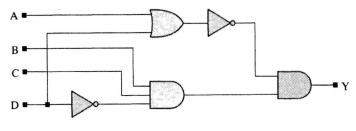

FIGURE P2-5

CHAPTER 3 — Modeling Structure with Verilog

A Verilog model of a circuit encapsulates a description of its functionality as a structural or behavioral view of its input/output relationship. A structural view could be a netlist of gates or a high-level architectural partition of the circuit into major functional blocks, such as an ALU. A behavioral view could be a simple Boolean equation model, a register-transfer level (RTL) model of a datapath, or an algorithm. We will begin by considering structural models in this chapter, and then use simulation in Chapter 4 to verify the functionality of models. Chapters 5 and 6 treat modeling and verification of sequential machines.

3.1 Design Encapsulation

Structural modeling is similar to creating a schematic. Figure 3-1 shows a gate-level schematic of a half-adder circuit, along with its complete Verilog description. A schematic consists of icons (symbols) of logic gates, lines representing wires that connect gates, and labels of gates and relevant signal names at I/O pins and internal nodes. Similarly, a Verilog *structural model* consists of a list of *declarations*, beginning with the keyword **module** and ending with the keyword **endmodule**.

    Declarations, or statements, in a structural model specify the inputs and outputs of the model and list any gates (i.e. primitives) that are instantiated and interconnected to implement the desired functionality. The identifiers *G1* and *G2* are called the optional *instance names* of the primitives, having type names ***xor*** and ***and***, respectively.

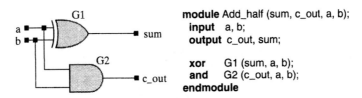

```
module Add_half (sum, c_out, a, b);
  input   a, b;
  output  c_out, sum;

  xor     G1 (sum, a, b);
  and     G2 (c_out, a, b);
endmodule
```

FIGURE 3-1   Schematic and Verilog description of a half-adder

A list of primitives describes the functionality of a design, but it has a fixed set of signal names. By itself, the list would require that the model be used only in an environment that has the same signal names. The list itself does not have a name either, but it would be helpful if it had a descriptive name by which we could identify its functionality. To circumvent these limitations, the functionality of a design and its interface to the environment are encapsulated in a Verilog module.

A module is *declared* by writing text that describes (1) its type name, (2) its functionality or structure, (3) its ports to or from the environment, and (4) its timing and other attributes of the design, such as the physical silicon area, that would be needed to implement it on a chip. All Verilog modules have the following text format:

module my_design (/* module ports go here */);
    // Declarations and functional details go here
endmodule

The keywords **module** and **endmodule** encapsulate the text that describes the module having type-name *my_design*. A module's type-name is *user defined* and distinguishes the module from declarations of other modules. The ports of the module are listed beside *my_design* in a comma-separated list enclosed by parentheses. Unlike primitives, modules do not have a restriction on the relative ordering of input and output ports in the list. The inputs and outputs can be listed in any order.

The declarations placed within a module determine whether the module will be structural, behavioral, or a combination of these. All the examples in this chapter will be structural models.

The ports of a module may be listed in any order.

3.1.1   Structural Models

A declaration of a *structural* model includes (1) a module type name, accompanied by a list of ports in parentheses,[1] (2) a list of the operational modes and sizes of the ports

---

[1] A module may have no ports, but the parentheses, though empty, are still required by the syntax of the language.

(e.g., *input*), (3) an optional list of internal wires used for connections within the module, and (4) a list of interconnected primitives or other modules, just as one would place and connect their physical counterparts on a PC board or on a schematic. The primary inputs and outputs of a physical circuit connect to its environment, and are the named ports of the model.

In operation and in simulation, signals applied at the primary inputs interact with the internal gates and/or other modules, to produce the signals at the primary outputs. A designer could apply signal generators to the inputs of the actual circuit, and observe the inputs and outputs on an oscilloscope or logic analyzer. A declared module can be referenced (instantiated) within the declaration of some other module to create more elaborate and complex structural models.

A complete Verilog structural model of a five-input and-or-invert (*AOI*) circuit is listed in Figure 3-2 to illustrate some Verilog terminology. The keywords *module* and *endmodule* enclose (encapsulate) the description.[2] The text between these keywords declares (1) the interface between the model and its environment (by declaring the port list and the mode of each port), (2) the wires that are used to connect the logic gates that model the circuit (by declaring *y1* and *y2* to have type *wire*), and (3) the logic gate primitives and the configurations of the port signals that connect them together to form the circuit (by listing the gates and their ports).

3.1.2 Module Ports

The ports of a module define its interface to the environment in which it is used. We'll use the term *mode* to indicate the direction that information (signal values) may flow through the port. A port's mode may be unidirectional (*input*, *output*) or bidirectional (*inout*). In simulation, signals generated in the environment of a module are made available through its *input* ports; signals generated within a module are made available to the environment through its *output* ports. Bidirectional (*inout*) ports accommodate

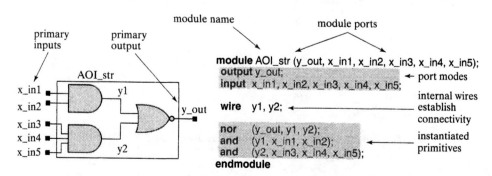

FIGURE 3-2 An and-or-invert (AOI) circuit and its Verilog structural model

---

[2]Appendix A contains a list of Verilog keywords.

a flow of information in either direction. The mode of a module port must be declared explicitly, and is not determined by the order in which a port appears in the port list; (but recall that outputs are the leftmost entries in the port list of a primitive).

   The environment of a module interacts with its ports, but does not have access to the internal description of the module's functionality. Those details are hidden from the surrounding circuitry. The listing of declarations within a Verilog module tells a simulator how to form the output of the circuit from the values of its inputs. We will discuss simulation in more detail below.

3.1.3   ANSI C Style Port Declarations

 You may have noticed that models written in the style of Verilog 1995 require a list of ports, enclosed in parentheses, and a list of statements declaring the mode and size of the ports.[3] Verilog 2001 introduced alternative, less verbose, ANSI C style declarations for the ports of modules.

Example: ANSI C Style Port Declaration

The Verilog model of a half-adder can be simplifed using the syntax of Verilog 2001 by placing the declarations of the input and output ports within the port list. Two styles follow, with the latter recommended when there are several ports.

```
module Add_half_V2001 ( output sum, c_out, input a, b);
   xor          (sum, a, b);
   and          (c_out, a, b);
endmodule
```

Alternatively,

```
module Add_half_V2001
( output      sum, c_out,
  input       a, b
);
   xor          (sum, a, b);
   and          (c_out, a, b);
endmodule
```

   Note that in the preceding code, *sum* and *c_out* are implicit scalar wires, so a separate declaration of their type is omitted.[4]

Example End: ANSI C Style Port Declaration

---

[3]Ports have a default size of 1 bit and a default type of **wire**.
[4]For clarity, models that are developed with features and syntax of Verilog 2001 will have the postfix *_V2001* appended to their names. More elaborate examples of ANSI C style for ports will be presented in Chapter 5.

3.2 Top-Down Design and Nested Modules

Complex systems are designed by systematically and repeatedly partitioning them into simpler functional units whose design can be managed and executed successfully. A high-level partition and organization of the design is sometimes referred to as an *architecture*. The individual functional units that result from the partition are expected to be easier to design and simpler to test than larger, equivalent aggregates. The divide-and-conquer strategy of top-down design enables the design of circuits having several million gates. Top-down design is used in the most modern and sophisticated design methodologies to integrate entire systems on a chip (SoC) [1]. *Nested modules are the Verilog mechanism supporting top-down design*. The instantiation of a module within the declaration of a *different*[5] module automatically creates a partition of the design.

Use nested module instantiations to create a top-down design hierarchy.

Example: Full-Adder–Structural Decomposition

A binary full-adder circuit can be formed by combining two half-adders and an *OR* gate as shown in the schematic in Figure 3-3a. The Verilog hierarchical model of the partitioned design (Figure 3-3b) contains two instances of the module *Add_half*. The

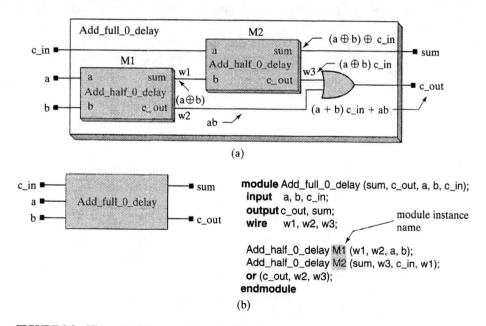

(a)

```
module Add_full_0_delay (sum, c_out, a, b, c_in);
input    a, b, c_in;
output c_out, sum;
wire     w1, w2, w3;                    module instance
                                        name

Add_half_0_delay M1 (w1, w2, a, b);
Add_half_0_delay M2 (sum, w3, c_in, w1);
or (c_out, w2, w3);
endmodule
```

(b)

FIGURE 3-3 Hierarchical decomposition of a full-adder: **(a)** gate-level schematic; **(b)** Verilog model

---

[5]Recursive functions are not supported in Verilog 1995, but are supported in Verilog 2001.

module names have been appended with *_0_delay* to indicate that their internal models propagate signals without accounting for the propagation delay of physical gates.[6]

Example End: Full-Adder–Structural Decomposition

Modules may be nested within other modules.[7] When a module is referenced by another module (i.e., when a module is listed inside the declaration of another module), a *structural hierarchy* is formed of the nesting/nested design objects. The hierarchy establishes a partition and represents relationships between the referencing and the referenced modules. The referencing module is called a *parent* module; the referenced module is called a *child* module. The module in which a child module is instantiated is its (unique) parent module. The two instances of *Add_half_0_delay* within *Add_full_0_delay* are child modules of *Add_full_0_delay*. Primitives are basic design objects. Although modules may have other modules and primitives nested within them, nothing can be instantiated (nested) within a primitive.

3.2.1   Scope of a Name

All declarations and identifiers (names) in Verilog have a *scope* (i.e., domain of definition) that is local to the module, function, task, or named procedural (***begin ... end***) block (later) in which they are declared. They have meaning only within that scope and cannot be referenced directly from outside it. In Figure 3-4, a net at the input port of *child_module* can be driven by a differently named net or register in the enclosing *parent_module*; a net or a register at the output port of *child_module* can drive a differently named net in *parent_module*. The names on either side of the hierarchical

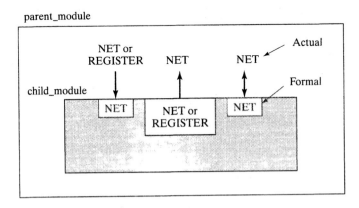

FIGURE 3-4   Scope of nets and registers

---

[6]We'll consider propagation delay in Chapter 4.
[7]Recursive nesting of a model within itself is not supported.

boundary need not match. The *formal_name* is the name given in the declaration of the instantiated module, and the *actual_name* is the name used in the instantiation of the module. The formal **input** and **inout** ports must be nets, not registers; the formal **output** port can be a net, a **reg**, or an **integer**. The actual **input** ports can be nets, **regs**, or **integers**. The actual **output** and **inout** ports must be nets.

3.2.2 Hierarchical Depth

A module hierarchy can have arbitrary depth, limited only by the capacity of the host computer's memory. Each instance of an instantiated module must be accompanied by a *module instance name* that is unique within its parent module. An instantiated primitive may be given a name, but that is not required.

The instance name of a module is required.

Example: 16-Bit Ripple-Carry Adder – Structural Decomposition

---

A 16-bit ripple-carry adder, can be formed by cascading four 4-bit ripple-carry adders in a chain in which the carry generated by a unit is passed to the carry input port of its neighbor, beginning with the least significant bit. Each 4-bit adder is declared as a cascade of full-adders. Figure 3-5 shows the partition and the ports that are associated with each unit of *Add_rca_16_0_delay_V2001*, an idealized model that ignores the propagation delay of the gates. Zero-delay models are very useful for verifying functionality (without detailed timing). By substituting other models at the lower levels of the design hierarchy later, we can account for nonzero propagation delay. For example,

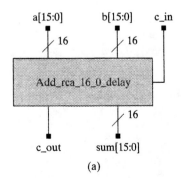

(a)

FIGURE 3-5 Hierarchical decomposition of a 16-bit, zero-delay, ripple-carry adder into a chain of four 4-bit-slice adders, each formed by a chain of full-adders: **(a)** top-level schematic symbol; **(b)** decomposition into four 4-bit adders; **(c)** full-adders and half-adders

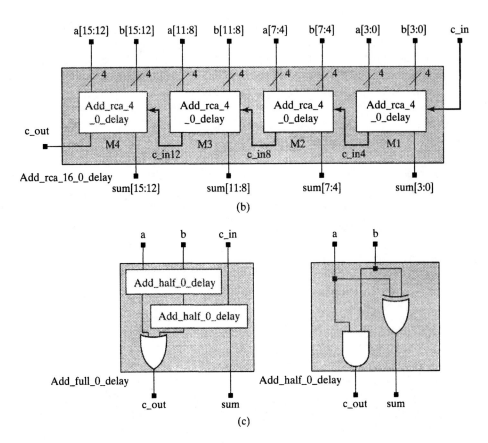

(b)

(c)

FIGURE 3-5   (Continued)

we could add unit propagation delay to the primitives in the models of the full- and half-adders, to form a 16-bit adder with unit gate delays. Unit delay models are useful because their simulation reveals the time sequence of signal changes, which can be helpful in debugging a model.

The complete text for *Add_rca_16_0_delay_V2001* is as follows:

```
module Add_rca_16_0_delay_V2001
( output [15:0]   sum,
  output          c_out,
  input  [15:0]   a, b,
  input           c_in
);

wire            c_in4, c_in8, c_in12;

Add_rca_4_0_delay_V2001 M1   (sum[3:0],   c_in4,   a[3:0],   b[3:0],   c_in);
Add_rca_4_0_delay_V2001 M2   (sum[7:4],   c_in8,   a[7:4],   b[7:4],   c_in4);
```

```
         Add_rca_4_0_delay_V2001 M3  (sum[11:8],   c_in12,   a[11:8],   b[11:8],   c_in8);
         Add_rca_4_0_delay_V2001 M4  (sum[15:12],  c_out,    a[15:12],  b[15:12],  c_in12);
      endmodule

      module Add_rca_4_0_delay_V2001
      ( output [3: 0]    sum,
        output           c_out,
        input   [3: 0]   a, b,
        input            c_in
      );
        wire             c_in2, c_in3, c_in4;
        Add_full_0_delay_V2001 M1 (sum[0],     c_in2,    a[0], b[0], c_in);
        Add_full_0_delay_V2001 M2 (sum[1],     c_in3,    a[1], b[1], c_in2);
        Add_full_0_delay_V2001 M3 (sum[2],     c_in4,    a[2], b[2], c_in3);
        Add_full_0_delay_V2001 M4 (sum[3],     c_out,    a[3], b[3], c_in4);
      endmodule

      module Add_full_0_delay_V2001 (output sum, c_out, input a, b, c_in);
        wire                         w1, w2, w3;

        Add_half_0_delay_V2001       M1 (w1, w2, a, b);
        Add_half_0_delay_V2001       M2 (sum, w3, c_in, w1);
        or                           M3 (c_out, w2, w3);
      endmodule

      module Add_half_0_delay_V2001 (output sum, c_out, input a, b);
        xor                          M1 (sum, a, b);
        and                          M2 (c_out, a, b);
      endmodule
```

Example End: 16-Bit Ripple-Carry Adder – Structural Decomposition

---

3.2.3   Design Hierarchy and Source-Code Organization

The hierarchical model for *Add_RCA_16_0_delay_V2001* illustrates how Verilog supports top-down structured design, by nesting modules within modules. Figure 3-6 shows the hierarchy for *Add_RCA_16* (a model without the *0_delay* notation). The top-level functional unit is encapsulated in *Add_RCA_16*, and contains instantiations of other functional units of lesser complexity, and so on. The lowest level of the hierarchy consists of primitives and/or modules that have no underlying hierarchical detail. All of the modules that compose a design must be placed in one or more text files which, when compiled together, completely describe the functionality of the top-level module. It does not matter how the modules are distributed across multiple source

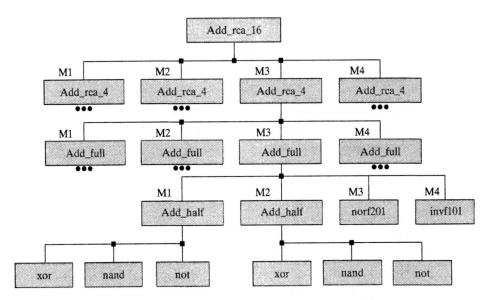

FIGURE 3-6   Design hierarchy a 16-bit ripple-carry adder

code files,[8] so long as their individual descriptions reside in a single file. A simulator will compile designated source files and extract the modules that it needs in order to integrate a complete description of any design hierarchy that is implied by the port structures and references to nested/instantiated modules.

3.2.4   Structural Connectivity

The data type *wire* connects primitives to other primitives and/or modules, and connects modules to other modules and/or primitives. By themselves, wires have no logic. *Any identifier that is referenced without having a type declaration has default-type **wire**.*[9] Consequently, the input and output ports of a module have default-type *wire* too, unless we specifically declare them to have a different type. In Figure 3-2, we explicitly declared *y1* and *y2* to have type *wire*, but did not have to do so.

An undeclared identifier has default-type wire.

---

[8]For management purposes, a design team might be required to place only one module declaration within a given source file.
[9]The default net type can be changed by a compiler directive [2].

As noted in Chapter 2, the logic value of a **wire** (net) is determined dynamically during simulation by what is connected to the wire. If a wire is attached to the output of a primitive (module), it is said to be *driven* by the primitive (module), and the primitive (module) is said to be its *driver*.

3.2.5   Options for Port Connections

The ports of an instantiated module must be connected (associated) in a manner that is consistent with the declaration of the module, but the actual and formal names of the connecting signals need not be the same, nor must they be grouped together by mode.

Connection by Position   In the model, *Add_RCA_16_0_delay*, the *formal* name of the first port of *Add_half_0_delay* (i.e., the *formal* name given in the declaration of *Add_half_0_delay*) is *sum*, but, in instance *M1*, the *actual* name of the port is *w1*. The actual ports were associated with the formal ports by their position in the port list.

Connection by Name   This mechanism for connecting ports by position works well in models having only a few ports, but when the list of ports is large, it is easier and safer to associate ports by their names, using the following convention in the port list: *.formal_name(actual_name)*. This connects *actual_name* to *formal_name*, regardless of the position of this entry in the list.

Example: Port Connection by Name

The first (M1) instantiation of *Add_half_0_delay* in *Add_full_0_delay* can be written using port name association as shown in Figure 3-7.

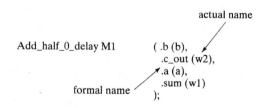

FIGURE 3-7   Formal and actual names for port association by name in module *Add_half_0_delay*

Example End: Port Connection by Name

Our next example of a structural model will be used as a point of comparison with other examples to illustrate alternative styles of design with Verilog.

Example: 2-Bit Comparator

A 2-bit comparator compares two 2-bit binary words, *A* and *B*, and asserts outputs indicating whether the decimal equivalent of word *A* is less than, greater than, or equal to that of word *B*. The functionality of the comparator is described by the following set of Boolean equations, where *A1* and *A0* are the bits of *A* and *B1* and *B0* are the bits of *B*, and denotes the complement of a literal:

A_lt_B = A1' B1 + A1' A0' B0 + A0' B1 B0

A_gt_B = A1 B1' + A0 B1' B0' + A1 A0 B0'

A_eq_B = A1' A0' B1' B0' + A1' A0 B1' B0 + A1 A0 B1 B0 + A1 A0' B1 B0'

Karnaugh map methods can be used to eliminate redundant logic from these equations and produce the generic gate-level description of the comparator shown in Figure 3-8 [3-5]. This gate-level, combinational logic implementation of the comparator can be modeled by a structural interconnection of Verilog primitives. Their aggregate behavior is that of the comparator circuit.

Following is a structural Verilog description corresponding directly to the schematic:

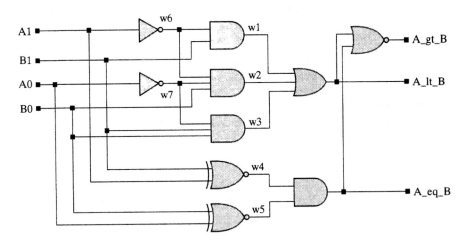

FIGURE 3-8   Schematic of a 2-bit binary comparator

```
module compare_2_str (A_gt_B, A_lt_B, A_eq_B, A0, A1, B0, B1);
output  A_gt_B, A_lt_B, A_eq_B;
input   A0, A1, B0, B1;

nor     (A_gt_B, A_lt_B, A_eq_B);
or      (A_lt_B, w1, w2, w3);
and     (A_eq_B, w4, w5);
```

```
and     (w1, w6, B1);
and     (w2, w6, w7, B0);
and     (w3, w7, B0, B1);
not     (w6, A1);
not     (w7, A0);
xnor    (w4, A1, B1);
xnor    (w5, A0, B0);
endmodule
```

A synthesis tool can automatically optimize a gate-level description, remove redundant logic, and draw the resulting schematic [3].

Example End: 2-Bit Comparator

Next, we will use the 2-bit comparator as a building block to form a structural model of a 4-bit comparator.

Example: 4-Bit Comparator

A 4-bit comparator has the ports shown in Figure 3-9, and compares 4-bit binary words and asserts outputs indicating their relative size. It would be cumbersome to write the Boolean equations for the outputs, so we will connect the outputs of two 2-bit comparators with additional logic to generate the appropriate outputs that result from comparing 4-bit words. The logic for connecting the 2-bit comparators is based on the observation that a strict inequality in the higher order bit pair determines the relative magnitudes of the 4-bit words. On the other hand, if the higher order bit pairs are equal, the lower order bit pairs determine the output. The hierarchical structure shown in Figure 3-10 implements the 4-bit comparator, and the simulation results in Figure 3-11 display the assertions of the outputs for some values of the bits of the datapaths, with $A\_bus = \{A3, A2, A1, A0\}$ and $B\_bus = \{B3, B2, B1, B0\}$ formed in the testbench for the purpose of simulation.

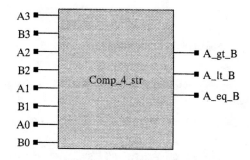

FIGURE 3-9 Block diagram symbol of a 4-bit comparator

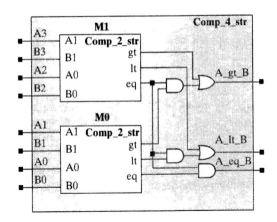

FIGURE 3-10　Hierarchical structure of a 4-bit binary comparator with nested 2-bit comparators

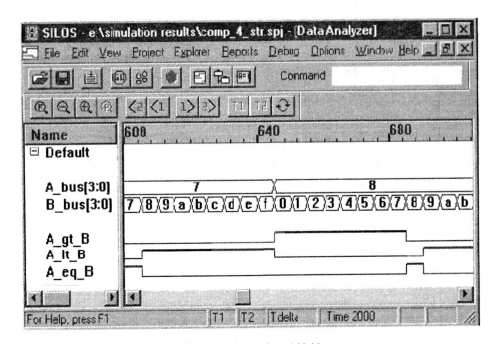

FIGURE 3-11　Simulation results for a 4-bit binary comparator

The following source code for module *Comp_4_str* has two instantiations of the module *Comp_2_str*:

```
module Comp_4_str (A_gt_B, A_lt_B, A_eq_B, A3, A2, A1, A0, B3, B2, B1, B0);
output  A_gt_B, A_lt_B, A_eq_B;
input   A3, A2, A1, A0, B3, B2, B1, B0;
wire    w1, w0;
```

```
Comp_2_str M1 (A_gt_B_M1, A_lt_B_M1, A_eq_B_M1, A3, A2, B3, B2);
Comp_2_str M0 (A_gt_B_M0, A_lt_B_M0, A_eq_B_M0, A1, A0, B1, B0);

or     (A_gt_B, A_gt_B_M1, w1);
and    (w1, A_eq_B_M1, A_gt_B_M0);
and    (A_eq_B, A_eq_B_M1, A_eq_B_M0);
or     (A_lt_B, A_lt_B_M1, w0);
and    (w0, A_eq_B_M1, A_lt_B_M0);
endmodule
```

Example End: 4-Bit Comparator

3.3   Port Names: A Matter of Style

Design teams follow elaborate rules that govern the style of their Verilog models to ensure that only constructs supported by synthesis tools are used. Other rules govern usage of uppercase and lowercase text (e.g., parameters must be uppercase), and naming conventions for parameters, signals, modules, et al., with the aim of increasing the readability and the reusability of the code [6]. At a minimum, signals should be given names that describe their use (e.g., *clock*), and modules should be given names that describe their encapsulated functionality (e.g., *comparator*). The examples in the rest of the book will generally follow a particular port-naming convention. The ports will be ordered in the following sequence: bidirectional datapath signals, bidirectional control signals, datapath outputs, control outputs, datapath inputs, control inputs, synchronizing signals (e.g., clock).

3.4   Common Error: Passing Variables through Ports

Syntax errors result from port declarations that do not conform to the rules of the language. Table 3-1 summarizes the rules that apply to nets and registers that are ports of a Verilog module.

A variable that is declared as an *input* port of a module is implicitly a net variable, within the scope of the module, and may not be declared as a register variable. A variable that is declared to be an *output* port may be a net or a register variable. An *inout* port of a module may not be a register type. A register variable may not be

TABLE 3-1   Rules for port modes with nets and registers

VARIABLE TYPE	PORT MODE		
	input	output	inout
NET VARIABLE	YES	YES	YES
REGISTER VARIABLE	NO	YES	NO

placed in an output port of a primitive gate. A variable having type *real* may not be connected to a port of a module or to a terminal of a primitive.[10]

3.5   Four-Valued Logic and Signal Resolution in Verilog

Verilog's abstract modeling constructs and the truth tables of its built-in primitives are defined for all four logic values of a primitive's inputs.[11] A simulator creates input waveforms in this four-valued logic system and generates the internal and output signals for a circuit.

The value **x** represents a condition of ambiguity in which the simulator cannot determine whether the value of the signal is 0 or 1. This happens, for example, when a wire is driven by two primitives that have opposing output values. The primitive gates that are built into Verilog are able to model this kind of contention between their input signals automatically. (See Chapter 2.) Verilog also resolves contention on nets having multiple drivers.

The logic value **z** denotes a three-state condition in which a wire is disconnected from its driver. Figure 2-4 showed the waveforms a simulator would produce in simulating an *and* primitive that is driven by signals that range over all of the possible input values. The waveforms in Figure 3-12 demonstrate how a Verilog simulator resolves

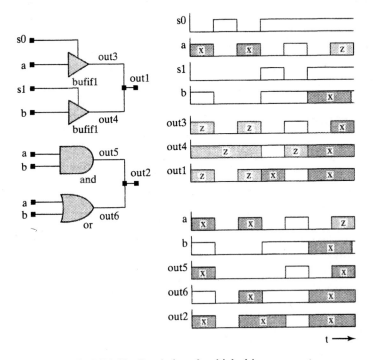

FIGURE 3-12   Resolution of multiple drivers on a net

---

[10]See the Language Reference Manual [1] for limitations on the use of operators with real operands. Verilog includes two system tasks that convert data types to transfer real data across a port boundary in a hierarchical structure: *$realtobits* and *$bitstoreal*.

[11]Appendix A describes Verilog's built-in primitives and their truth tables in Verilog's four-value logic system.

multiple drivers on a net. Notice that the three-state primitives[12] produce a value of **z** when they are not enabled, and that the value of **x** is produced when a wire is driven by opposing values. Depending on the physical technology implementing a circuit, it could be necessary to ensure that a bus does not have contending multiple drivers active at the same time.[13]

3.6   Truth Table Models of Combinational and Sequential Logic

Although Verilog's built-in primitives correspond to simple combinational logic gates, and do not include sequential parts, the language has a mechanism for declaring user-defined primitives (UDPs), which use truth tables to describe sequential behavior and/or more complex combinational complex logic. UDPs are widely used in ASIC cell libraries, because they simulate faster and require less storage than modules.

User-defined primitives are declared in a source file in the same way that a module is declared, but with the encapsulating keyword pair ***primitive ... endprimitive***. They can be instantiated like built-in primitives. A UDP has only a single output port; all the ports of a UDP must be scalars.

3.6.1   Combinational UDPs

The truth table for a combinational UDP consists of a section of columns, one for each input, followed by a colon and a final column that specifies the output. The order of the input columns must conform to the order in which the input ports are listed in the declaration. A simulator references the table whenever one of its inputs changes, searching top-down through the table for a match between the entries in the input columns of a row of the table and the logic values of the inputs to the primitive. The search terminates at the first match.

Example: Combinational UDP

The following text declares *AOI_UDP*, a truth table version of the five-input AOI circuit that was introduced in Section 3.1.3:

```
primitive AOI_UDP (y, x_in1, x_in2, x_in3, x_in4, x_in5);
   output y;
   input   x_in1, x_in2, x_in3, x_in4, x_in5;
```

---

[12]See Appendix B.
[13]Two net data types, ***wand*** and ***wor***, automatically resolve contention between multiple drivers.

```
table
// x1 x2 x3 x4 x5 : y
 0 0 0 0 0 : 1;
 0 0 0 0 1 : 1;
 0 0 0 1 0 : 1;
 0 0 0 1 1 : 1;
 0 0 1 0 0 : 1;
 0 0 1 0 1 : 1;
 0 0 1 1 0 : 1;
 0 0 1 1 1 : 0;

 0 1 0 0 0 : 1;
 0 1 0 0 1 : 1;
 0 1 0 1 0 : 1;
 0 1 0 1 1 : 1;
 0 1 1 0 0 : 1;
 0 1 1 0 1 : 1;
 0 1 1 1 0 : 1;
 0 1 1 1 1 : 0;

 1 0 0 0 0 : 1;
 1 0 0 0 1 : 1;
 1 0 0 1 0 : 1;
 1 0 0 1 1 : 1;
 1 0 1 0 0 : 1;
 1 0 1 0 1 : 1;
 1 0 1 1 0 : 1;
 1 0 1 1 1 : 0;

 1 1 0 0 0 : 0;
 1 1 0 0 1 : 0;
 1 1 0 1 0 : 0;
 1 1 0 1 1 : 0;
 1 1 1 0 0 : 0;
 1 1 1 0 1 : 0;
 1 1 1 1 0 : 0;
 1 1 1 1 1 : 0;
endtable
endprimitive
```

Example End: Combinational UDP

Example: A Two-Channel Multiplexer User-Defined Primitive

The Verilog UDP *mux_prim*, shown in Figure 3-13, describes a two-input multiplexer, and includes comments citing some basic rules for UDP models.

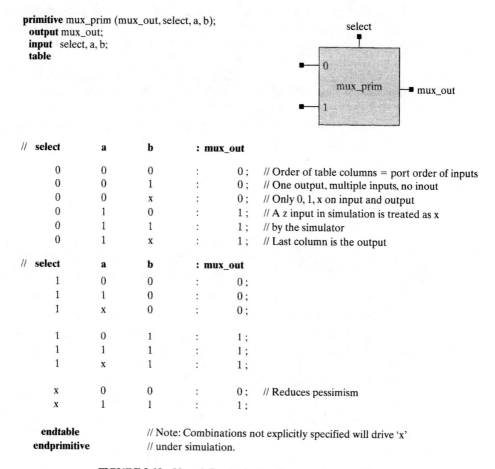

```
primitive mux_prim (mux_out, select, a, b);
   output mux_out;
   input   select, a, b;
   table
```

// select	a	b	: mux_out	
0	0	0	: 0 ;	// Order of table columns = port order of inputs
0	0	1	: 0 ;	// One output, multiple inputs, no inout
0	0	x	: 0 ;	// Only 0, 1, x on input and output
0	1	0	: 1 ;	// A z input in simulation is treated as x
0	1	1	: 1 ;	// by the simulator
0	1	x	: 1 ;	// Last column is the output

// select	a	b	: mux_out
1	0	0	: 0 ;
1	1	0	: 0 ;
1	x	0	: 0 ;
1	0	1	: 1 ;
1	1	1	: 1 ;
1	x	1	: 1 ;
x	0	0	: 0 ; // Reduces pessimism
x	1	1	: 1 ;

```
   endtable        // Note: Combinations not explicitly specified will drive 'x'
   endprimitive    // under simulation.
```

FIGURE 3-13 User-defined primitive for a two-input multiplexer

Example End: A Two-Channel Multiplexer User-Defined Primitive

A simulator will automatically assign the (default) value **x** to the output of a UDP, if its inputs have values that do not match a row of the table. An input value of **z** is treated as **x** by the simulator when searching for a match. The last two rows of the table describing the behavior of the multiplexer in Figure 3-13 reduce the pessimism that might result during simulation. If both data inputs have the same value, the output has that value, regardless of the value of the *select* input. When the value of *select* is **x** (ambiguous), the output is 0 if both inputs are 0, and 1 if both inputs are 1. If the UDP table does not include this additional detail, a simulator will propagate a value of **x** to the output when *select* is **x**. It is generally desirable to reduce the situations under which a primitive propagates a value of **x**, because ambiguity may reduce the amount of useful information that can be derived from a simulation.

The entries for the inputs in a truth table can be reduced by using a shorthand notation. The **?** symbol allows an input to take on any of the three values, 0, 1, and **x**. This allows one table row to effectively replace three rows.

Example: Short-Hand Notation for a User-Defined Primitive

The following truth table illustrates how the UDP of a two-input multiplexer could be rewritten using shorthand notation:

table

```
// Shorthand notation:
// ? represents iteration of the table entry over the values 0,1, x.
// i.e., don't care on the input

//  select      a      b      : mux_out
//     0        0      ?      :      0 ; // ? = 0,1, x shorthand notation.
//     0        1      ?      :      1 ;

//     1        ?      0      :      0 ;
//     1        ?      1      :      1 ;

//     ?        0      0      :      0 ;
//     ?        1      1      :      1 ;
```

endtable

Note how, when *select* is 0 and channel *a* is 0, the output is 0, regardless of the value of the input at channel *b*. When *select* is 1 and channel *b* is 0, the output is 0, when channel *a* is *0*, *1*, or **x**. The **?** shorthand notation substitutes 0, 1, and **x** in the table row and effectively implements a don't-care condition on the associated input.

Example End: Short-Hand Notation for a User-Defined Primitive

---

3.6.2   Sequential UDPs

The truth table for a sequential UDP is like that for a combinational UDP, but inserts a column for the present state before the column for the output. The output of a sequential UDP (i.e., the state that will be caused by the present state and inputs) is the last column of the table. The columns for the state and the next state are each preceded by a colon. The order of the input columns must conform to the order in which the input ports are listed in the declaration. The output of a sequential UDP must be declared to have type **reg**, because the value of the output is produced abstractly, by a table, and must be held in memory during simulation to correspond to the waveform of a signal whose existence is continuous for the duration of the simulation.

The output of a sequential user-defined primitive must be declared to have type reg.

Example: User-Defined Primitive for a Transparent Latch

A truth table description of a transparent latch is given next by *latch_rp*. The table describes transparent behavior and latching behavior and also deals with the possibility that, under simulation, the input *enable* might acquire the value *x*:

```
primitive latch_rp (q_out, enable, data);
    output  q_out;
    input   enable, data;
    reg     q_out;

    table
//          enable  data          state        q_out/next_state
            1       1       :      ?       :      1 ;
            1       0       :      ?       :      0 ;
            0       ?       :      ?       :      - ;
// Above entries do not deal with enable = x.
// Ignore event on enable when data = state:

            x       0       :      0       :      - ;
            x       1       :      1       :      - ;
// Note: The table entry '-' denotes no change of the output.
    endtable
endprimitive
```

Example End: User-Defined Primitive for a Transparent Latch

3.6.3 Sequential UDPs: Optional Syntax for Ports

 Verilog 2001 has optional syntax that includes the mode and type of the ports in the list of the ports of a userdefined primitive.

Example: ANSI C Syntax for a Transparent Latch UDP

Figure 3-14 displays the optional new syntax for declaring UDPs in Verilog 2001.

Verilog 1995	Verilog 2001
primitive latch_rp (q_out, enable, data);	primitive latch_rp (data);
output q_out;	output reg q_out,
input enable, data;	input enable, data;
reg q_out;	
table	table
...	...
endtable	endtable
endprimitive	endprimitive

FIGURE 3-14   Syntax options for UDPs in Verilog 2001

Example End: ANSI C Syntax for a Transparent Latch UDP

The transparent latch modeled by *latch_rp* exhibits *level-sensitive* behavior, (i.e., the output can change any time that an input changes, depending on the value of the inputs). The value of the output is determined only by the value of the *enable* and *data* inputs. In contrast, a truth table describing *edge-sensitive* behavior will be activated when an input changes. Whether the output changes depends on whether a synchronizing input has made an appropriate transition. For example, a flip-flop that is sensitive to the rising edge of its clock would have an entry of *(01)* in the corresponding column of the table. UDPs can describe behavior that is sensitive to either the positive or negative edge (transition) of a clock signal, with built-in semantics for positive (*posedge*) and negative (*negedge*) signal transitions. A falling edge (*negedge*) transition is denoted by the following signal value pairs: *(10)*, *(1x)*, and *(x0)*; rising edges are denoted by *(01)*, *(0x)*, and *(x1)*.

Example: User-Defined Primitive for a D-Type Flip-Flop

The UDP *d_prim1_V2001* in Figure 3-15 describes the behavior of an edge-sensitive D-type flip-flop. The input signal *clock* synchronizes the transfer of *data* to *q_out*.

```
primitive d_prim1_V2001
  (output reg    q_out,
   input         clock, data);
```

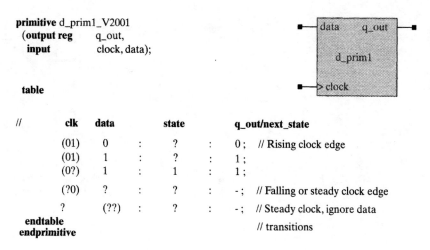

table

//	clk	data		state		q_out/next_state
	(01)	0	:	?	:	0 ; // Rising clock edge
	(01)	1	:	?	:	1 ;
	(0?)	1	:	1	:	1 ;
	(?0)	?	:	?	:	- ; // Falling or steady clock edge
	?	(??)	:	?	:	- ; // Steady clock, ignore data

endtable
endprimitive   // transitions

FIGURE 3-15   Truth table model of a D-type flip-flop

Example End: User-Defined Primitive for a Transparent Latch

The notation in the truth table for a sequential behavior uses parentheses to enclose the defining logic values of a signal whose transition affects the output (i.e., the synchronizing input signal). In the table in Figure 3-16, the *(01)* entry in the column for *clock* denotes a low-to-high transition of the signal *clock*, (i.e., a value change). Note that the row corresponding to the entry of *(?0)* for *clock* actually denotes 27 input possibilities and replaces 27 rows of entries, as there are two more ? symbols in that row. For example *(?0)* represents *(00)*, *(10)* and *(x0)*. Each of these is combined with three possibilities for the data; each of the resulting nine possibilities is combined with three possibilities for the state. In effect, this row specifies that the output should not change in any of these situations. Since the model represents the physical behavior of a rising-edge sensitive behavior, the output should not change on a falling edge, or if there is no edge at all *(00)*. If this row is omitted, the model will propagate an **x** value under simulation. Remember, it is desirable that the UDP table be as complete and unambiguous as possible.

A truth table can include both level-sensitive behavior and edge-sensitive behavior to model synchronous behavior with asynchronous set and reset conditions. Because a simulator will search the truth table from top to bottom, the level-sensitive behavior should precede the edge-sensitive behavior in the table, to give priority to the level-sensitive control signals.

Example: User-Defined Primitive for a J-K Flip-Flop

A J-K flip-flop having asynchronous preset and clear with edge-sensitive sequential behavior is described in Figure 3-16. The *preset_b* and *clear_b* inputs are active-low, and the output is sensitive to the rising edge of the clock. The signal *clock* synchronizes

primitive jk_prim_V2001
(output reg   q_out,
 input   clk, j, k, preset, clear
);

table

//	clk	j	k	pre	clr		state		q_out/next_state
// Preset Logic									
	?	?	?	0	1	:	?	:	1 ;
	?	?	?	*	1	:	1	:	1 ;
// Clear Logic									
	?	?	?	1	0	:	?	:	0 ;
	?	?	?	1	*	:	0	:	0 ;
// Normal Clocking									
//	clk	j	k	pre	clr		state		q_out/next_state
	r	0	0	0	0	:	0	:	1 ;
	r	0	0	1	1	:	?	:	- ;
	r	0	1	1	1	:	?	:	0 ;
	r	1	0	1	1	:	?	:	1 ;
	r	1	1	1	1	:	0	:	1 ;
	r	1	1	1	1	:	1	:	0 ;
	f	?	?	?	?	:	?	:	- ;
// j and k cases									
//	clk	j	k	pre	clr		state		q_out/next_state
	b	*	?	?	?	:	?	:	- ;
	b	?	*	?	?	:	?	:	- ;
// Reduced pessimism									
	p	0	0	1	1	:	?	:	- ;
	p	0	?	1	?	:	0	:	- ;
	p	?	0	?	1	:	1	:	- ;
	(?0)	?	?	?	?	:	?	:	- ;
	(1x)	0	0	1	1	:	?	:	- ;
	(1x)	0	?	1	?	:	0	:	- ;
	(1x)	?	0	?	1	:	1	:	- ;
	x	*	0	?	1	:	1	:	- ;
	x	0	*	1	?	:	0	:	- ;

endtable
endprimitive

FIGURE 3-16   User-defined primitive for a J-K flip-flop

the changes of *q_out*. Depending on the values of the *preset_b* and *clear_b* signals when the clock edge occurs, *q_out* does not change ($j = 0, k = 0$), *q_out* gets a value of 0 ($j = 0, k = 1$), *q_out* gets a value of 1, ($j = 1, k = 0$), or *q_out* is toggled ($j = 1, k = 1$).

Example End: User-Defined Primitive for a J-K Flip-Flop

3.6.4 Waveform Transition Symbols for UDPs

The table of a UDP can become very large, so additional notation has been developed to represent waveform transitions in sequential UDPs. The standard symbols are shown in Table 3-2.

TABLE 3-2   Symbols for waveform transitions in a UDP

Symbol	Interpretation
0	Logic 0
1	Logic 1
x	Unknown value
?	Iteration of an input over the values 0, 1, x
b	Iteration of the inputs over the values 0, 1
-	No change
(vw)	Input value change from v to w, where v and w can be 0, 1, x, ?, or b
*	Denotes all transitions on the input, (i.e. (??))
r	Denotes the input transition (01)
f	Denotes the input transition (10)
p	Denotes the input transitions (01), (0x), (x1), (1z), z1)
n	Denotes the input transitions (10), (1x), (x0), (1z), (z0)

3.6.5 Multiple Events

The evaluation of a primitive that is driven by multiple events occurring at the same time depends on the order in which the events are processed by the host simulator. Consider a D-type flip-flop that is initially in the state with its output equal to '0'. If the clock and the data both make a transition from '0' to '1' at the same time, the output will be '0' if the clock is evaluated first; the output will be '1' if the data is evaluated first. This "race" condition cannot be modeled in the truth table of the UDP. In practice, one would use a timing analysis tool to verify that the data changes satisfy nonzero setup conditions with respect to the clock signal.

3.6.6 Summary of Rules for UDPs

The rules for user-defined primitives are summarized in Table 3-3.

TABLE 3-3   Rules for user-defined primitives

RULES: USER-DEFINED PRIMITIVES
1. UDPs are instantiated in the same manner as predefined primitives.
2. The output of a UDP must be a single scalar.
3. The output of a combinational UDP must be a net.
4. The output of a sequential UDP must have type **reg**.
5. Each row of a UDP table may specify a transition on, at most, one input.
6. Transitions not specified by by the UDP table default to "x" in simulation.
7. All transitions which should not affect the output must be specified, otherwise they will result in assignment of "x" to the output.
8. If the output is sensitive to any edge of an input, it must be specified for all edges of that input (i.e., the table must consider them explicitly).
9. Instantiations of UDPs may include propagation delay.
10. A UDP table may not contain **inout** variables.
11. Only 0, 1, x entries are allowed entries for inputs and outputs.
12. In simulation, a "z" input value is treated as "x" in a UDP table.
13. The order of columns in a UDP table conforms to the order of the UDP port list.

3.6.7   Initialization of Sequential Primitives

A sequential UDP may be assigned an initial state within the declaration of the primitive. The declared value is assigned to the output of the primitive at the start of simulation. The initial value assigned to the output of a sequential UDP may affect the initial values of the outputs of other primitives, modules, or continuous assignments that are in the fanout of the UDP.

Example: Initialization of a Sequential User-Defined Primitive

---

The UDP *d_prim2_V2001* has the same functionality as *d_prim1_V2001* discussed earlier, but includes a declaration of an initial state for the output, *q_out*. The statement *initial q_out* = 0 declares that the initial value of *q_out* is 0. The code is as follows:

```
primitive d_prim2_V2001
(output reg      q_out;
 input           clock, data,)
 initial  q_out = 0;

 table
 // See d_prim1_V2001
 endtable
endprimitive
```

Example End: Initialization of a Sequential User-Defined Primitive

---

A sequential UDP may have only one statement assigning initial value to the output. The assignment must be made to an identifier that has been declared to be the output of the primitive, and which has been declared to be of type **reg**. Since a UDP may have only a single, scalar output, the declared initial value must be one of the following: *1*, *0*, *1'b1*, *1'b0*, or *1'bx*. No other value format specification may be used.

REFERENCES

[1] Chang, H. et al. *Surviving the System on Chip Revolution*. Boston: Kluwer, 1999.
[2] *IEEE Standard for Verilog Hardware Description Language 2001*, IEEE Std.1364-2001. Piscataway, NJ: 1996, Institute of Electrical and Electronic Engineers, 2001.
[3] Ciletti, M.D. *Modeling, Synthesis, and Rapid Prototyping with the Verilog HDL*. Upper Saddle River, NJ: Prentice Hall, 1999.
[4] Wakerly, J.F. *Digital Design Principles and Practices*, 3rd Ed. Upper Saddle River, NJ: Prentice Hall, 2000.
[5] Katz, R.H. *Contemporary Logic Design*. Redwood City, CA: Benjamin Cummings, 1994.
[6] "Verilog HDL Coding – Semiconductor Reuse Standard." Chandler, AZ: Motorola, 2001.

PROBLEMS

1. Using Verilog gate-level primitives, develop a structural model for the circuit in Figure P3-1.

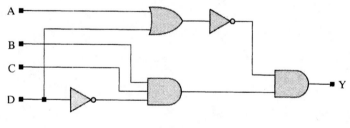

FIGURE P3-1

2. Using Verilog gate-level primitives, develop a structural model for the circuit in Figure P3-2.

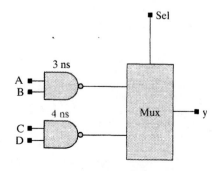

FIGURE P3-2

3. Develop UDPs for the circuits in Figure P3-1, 2.
4. What are the allowed modes (types) of module ports in Verilog?
5. Answer T(true) or F(false):

   a. The output ports of a module must be listed first in the list of ports.
   b. The type of the input port of a module must be a net.
   c. Declaring a module within another module creates a design hierarchy.
   d. All UDPs have scalar outputs.
   e. The truth table of a UDP may have multiple edge transitions in a row if the shorthand notation (??) is used.

CHAPTER 4   **Simulating Hardware with Verilog Models**

Two methods are used to verify the functionality of Verilog models: logic simulation and formal verification. A logic simulator applies stimulus patterns to a model and monitors its simulated behavior to determine whether it is correct. Formal verification tools construct elaborate mathematical proofs to verify a model's functionality without having to apply stimulus patterns. Although the use of formal methods is increasing, logic simulation is still widely used due to the difficulty of fully simulating large circuits. We will consider only logic simulation.[1]

4.1   Test Methodology

A large circuit must be tested and verified systematically to ensure that all of its logic has been exercised and found to be functionally correct. A haphazard test methodology makes debugging very difficult, creates a false sense of security that the model is correct, and risks enormous loss should a product fail as a result of an untested area of logic. In practice, design teams write an elaborate test plan that specifies the features that will be tested and the process by which they will be tested.

Example: Testing Methodology for a 16-bit Ripple-Carry Adder

The partition of a 16-bit ripple-carry adder into four bit-slices of 4 bits each was shown in Figure 3-4. Each of the 4-bit units was built as a chain of full-adders, and each full-adder

---

[1] A student version of the Silos III Verilog development environment and simulator is available for downloading at www.simucad.com.

was composed of a simple hierarchy of half-adders and glue logic. An attempt to verify the 16-bit adder by applying 16-bit stimulus patterns to its datapaths and an additional bit for its carry-in bit requires checking the results of applying 2^{33} input patterns! It would be foolhardy to attempt this if a simpler strategy can be found. Applying 2^{33} patterns consumes a lot of CPU time, and any error that might be detected would be difficult to associate with the underlying circuit. A more clever strategy is to verify that the half-adder and full-adder each work correctly. Then, the 4-bit slice can be verified exhaustively by applying only 2^9 patterns! Once these simpler design units have been verified, the 16-bit adder can be tested to work correctly for a carefully chosen set of patterns that checks the connectivity between the four units. This reduces the number of patterns and focuses the debugging effort on a much smaller portion of the overall circuitry.

Example End: Testing Methodology for a 16-bit Ripple-Carry Adder

Although modeling begins with a complex functional unit, and partitions it in a top-down fashion to enable the design of simpler units, systematic verification proceeds in the opposite direction, beginning with the simpler units and moving to the more complex units above them in the design hierarchy. A basic methodology for verifying the functionality of a digital circuit consists of building a testbench that applies stimulus patterns to the circuit and displays the resulting waveforms. The user, or software, can verify that the response is correct. The testbench, or design unit test bench (DUTB), is a separate Verilog module, having the basic organization shown in Figure 4-1. It resides at the top of a new design hierarchy, and contains a stimulus generator, a response monitor, and an instantiation of the unit under test (UUT). The stimulus generator uses Verilog statements to define the patterns that are to be applied to the circuit. During simulation, the response monitor selectively gathers data on signals within the design and

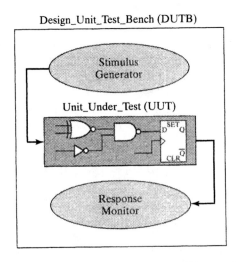

FIGURE 4-1   Organization of a testbench for verifying a unit under test

displays them in a text or graphical format. Testbenches can be very complex, containing a variety of pattern generators and additional software to perform analysis on the gathered data to detect and report functional errors.

A simulator performs three essential tasks: it (1) checks the source code, (2) reports any violations of the language's syntax,[2] and (3) simulates the behavior of the circuit under the application of input signals that are defined in the testbench [1]. Syntax errors must be eliminated before a simulation can run, but be aware that the absence of syntax errors does not imply that the functionality of the model is correct.

4.2   Signal Generators for Testbenches

A Verilog behavior is a group of statements that execute during simulation to assign value to simulation variables (signals) as though they were driven by hardware. The keyword *initial* declares a *single-pass* behavior (also known as an initial block) that begins executing when the simulator is activated, at $t_{sim} = 0$ (we use t_{sim} to denote the timebase of the simulator). The statements that are associated with the behavior are listed within the *begin . . . end* block keywords, and are called procedural statements.

Example: A Testbench for a Half-Adder

The following module, *t_Add_half_0*, has the basic structure of a testbench for verifying *Add_half_0_delay* in a simulator having a graphical user interface to display waveforms resulting from simulation:[3]

```
module t_Add_half_0 ();
  wire          sum, c_out;
  reg           a, b;

  Add_half_0_delay M1 (sum, c_out, a, b);        //UUT

  initial begin                                   // Time Out
  #100 $finish;
  end

  initial begin                                   // Stimulus patterns
  #10 a = 0; b = 0;
  #10 b = 1;
  #10 a = 1;
  #10 b = 0;
  end
endmodule
```

---

[2]Appendix C presents the formal syntax of the Verilog language.
[3]Appendix D describes some of Verilog's built-in system tasks, such as **$monitor**, which can be used to display simulation results in a text format.

Some constructs used in a testbench are introduced in *t_Add_half_0*, and will be explained in the next section. Notice that the code contains an instantiation of the UUT, *Add_half_0_delay*. The waveforms that are to be applied to the UUT are not generated by hardware, but by a Verilog behavior, declared by the keyword ***initial*** and accompanied by statements enclosed by the block statement keyword pair ***begin . . . end***. In this simple example, the user serves as the response monitor by comparing the output waveforms with their expected values.

Example End: A Testbench for a Half-Adder

When each procedural statement in the testbench *t_Add_half_0* executes, it assigns a value to a variable (e.g., b = 1) using the *procedural assignment operator*, =. Such statements are called *procedural assignments*. The time at which a procedural assignment statement executes depends on its order in the list of statements, and on an optional delay time preceding the statement (e.g., #10). The statements execute sequentially, from top to bottom and from left to right, across lines of text that may contain multiple statements.

In *t_Add_half_0*, each line is preceded by a time delay (e.g., 10 simulator time units) that is prescribed with a delay control operator (#) and a delay value, (e.g., #10). A delay control operator preceding a procedural statement suspends its execution and, consequently, postpones execution of the subsequent statements in the behavior, until the specified time interval has elapsed during simulation. A single-pass behavior expires when the last statement has executed, but the simulation does not necessarily terminate, because other behaviors might still be active.

The general structure of a testbench consists of one or more behaviors that generate waveforms at the inputs to the UUT, monitor the simulation data, and control the overall sequence of the testing activity. Note that the inputs to the UUT in *t_Add_half_0* are assigned value abstractly by a single-pass behavior and are declared by the keyword ***reg***, indicating that the variables (signals) *a* and *b* are getting their values from execution of procedural statements (just like in an ordinary procedural language, such as C, but as waveforms that evolve under the control of the simulator). Since hardware is not driving the value of an abstractly generated input, the type declaration ***reg*** ensures that the value of the variable will exist from the moment it is assigned by a procedural statement, until execution of a later procedural statement changes it. The outputs of the UUT are declared as wires. Think of them as providing the ability to observe the output ports of the UUT.

The waveforms that result from simulating *Add_half_0_delay* are shown in Figure 4-2. The cross-hatched waveform fill pattern beginning at $t = 0$ denotes the value x. In Verilog, *all nets and regs are given the value x when the simulation begins*; the simulator assigns the default logic value z (high impedance) to all nets that are not driven. These initial assigned values remain until they are changed by subsequent activity during simulation. The waveforms in Figure 4-2 are annotated at time $t_{sim} = 10, 20, 30$, and 40, to show the input events that are generated by the signal generator in the testbench and to show the events of *sum* and *c_out* that result from events on *a* and *b*.

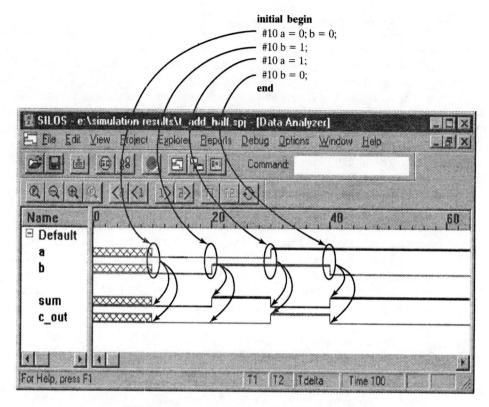

FIGURE 4-2 Simulation results for *Add_half_0_delay*

In the preceding example, the inputs to *Add_half_0_delay* are initially assigned value at time 10, when the first assignment is made. The indicated simulation time steps are dimensionless; in a later example, we will use a *timescale directive* to associate physical units with the time base for simulation.[4] Notice the correlation between the waveforms specified by the stimulus generator in the testbench, and the simulated waveforms applied to the circuit. Execution of each statement is delayed by 10 time steps, so the final statement in the stimulus generator executes at time step 40 (i.e., in this example, the delays accumulate). The testbench includes a separate behavior for a stopwatch that terminates the simulation after 100 time steps. The stopwatch executes a built-in Verilog system task, *$finish*, which surrenders control to the operating system of the host machine when time step 100 is reached. *A stopwatch is optional and not needed here, but, in general, will prevent endless execution if the testbench fails to terminate the simulation.*

A Verilog simulator assigns an initial value of x to nets and regs.

---

[4]See Appendix E for Verilog's compiler directives.

4.3 Event-Driven Simulation

An *event* is a change in the value of a signal (variable) during simulation. The single-pass behavior in *t_Add_half_0* programmed the inputs to *Add_half_0_delay* to change at prescribed times, independent of the signals in the circuit. However, the events of the outputs of the UUT, *sum* and *c_out*, depend on events at the inputs to the device, just as the signals in a physical circuit change in response to the signals at the input. Using the schedule of events at the inputs, and the structure of a circuit, a simulator creates and executes a schedule for the events at the outputs.

Logic simulators are said to be *event-driven* because their computational activity is triggered at discrete times by the propagation of events in a circuit. Event-driven simulators are inactive during the interval between events (i.e., they do not compute the values of signals), and the signals remain unchanged until the next time the events occur. So the time step of a simulator increments according to the discrete events where activity occurs. When an event occurs at an input to the UUT, the simulator schedules updating events for the internal signals and outputs of the UUT, if needed. Then the simulator rests until the next triggering event occurs at the input. All of the gates and abstract behaviors are active concurrently [2, 3], and it is the simulator's job to detect events and schedule any new events that result from their occurrence.

4.4 Testbench Template

Testbenches are an important tool in the design flow of an ASIC. Much effort is expended to develop a thorough testbench, because it is an insurance policy against failure. A test plan should be developed *before* the testbench is written. The plan, at a minimum, should specify what features will be tested and how they will be tested in the testbench. The following template serves as a starting point for developing a testbench:

```
module t_DUTB_name ();          // substitute the name of the UUT
    reg ...;                    // Declaration of register variables for primary inputs
                                // of the UUT
    wire ...;                   // Declaration of primary outputs of the UUT
    parameter    time_out =     // Provide a value
UUT_name UUT_instance_name ( UUT ports go here);

    initial $monitor ( );       // Specification of signals to be monitored and
                                // displayed as text

    initial #time_out $finish;  // Stopwatch to assure termination of simulation

    initial                     // Develop one or more behaviors for pattern
                                // generation and/or error detection

    begin
                                // Procedural statements generating waveforms
                                // to the input ports, and comments documenting
```

```
                              // the test.  Use the full repertoire of behavioral
                              // constructs for loops and conditionals.
       end
       endmodule
```

4.5   Propagation Delay

Physical logic gates have a propagation delay between the time an input changes and the time the output responds to the change. The primitives in Verilog have a default delay of 0, meaning that an event of the output is scheduled to occur in the same time step as the event of the input that caused it. Simulation is commonly done with 0 delay to quickly verify the functionality of a model. Simulation with a unit delay is often done, too, because it exposes the time sequence of signal activity, which can be masked by 0-delay simulation.

All primitives and nets have a default propagation delay of 0.

Example: Unit Delay Simulation – Half- and Full-Adders

The primitives within *Add_full* and *Add_half* are shown in the following code, with annotation that assigns a unit delay to them:

```
module Add_full (sum, c_out, a, b, c_in);
    output      sum, c_out;
    input       a, b, c_in;
    wire        w1, w2, w3;

    Add_half    M1 (w1, w2, a, b);
    Add_half    M2 (sum, w3, w1, c_in);
    or          #1 M3 (c_out, w2, w3);
endmodule

module Add_half (sum, c_out, a, b);
    output      sum, c_out;
    input       a, b;

    xor         #1 M1 (sum, a, b);
    and         #1 M2 (c_out, a, b);
endmodule
```

Note how the delay notation *#1* has been inserted before the instance name of each instantiated primitive. The effect of the delay is apparent in the simulated transitions of *sum* and *c_out* shown in Figure 4-3. Notice that the zero-delay simulation results in Figure 4-2 do not reveal whether *c_out* is formed before or after *sum*. Both, in fact,

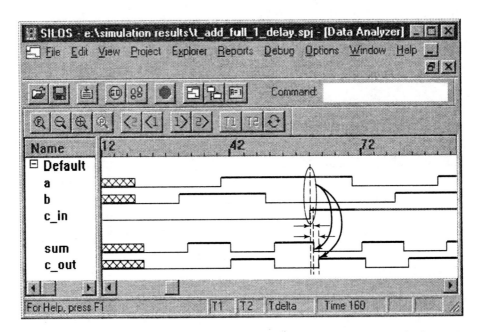

FIGURE 4-3   Results of unit-delay simulation of a 1-bit full-adder, with event propagation from *c_in* to *sum* and *c_out*

appear to change as soon as the inputs change. The results in Figure 4-3 reveal the time-ordering of the signal activity, showing that *c_out* forms after *sum*, when *c_in* changes with *a = 1* and *b = 0*, corresponding to a longer path through the internal gates of the adder.

Note that the displayed waveforms show only the final values of *sum* and *c_out*, not any intermediate note value generated at the same time stop.

Example End: Unit Delay Simulation – Half- and Full-Adders

ASICs are fabricated by assembling the logic cells from a standard-cell library on a common silicon die. The library cells are predesigned and precharacterized so that their Verilog model includes accurate timing information. Synthesis tools use this information to optimize the performance (speed) of a design.

Example: Simulation with Standard Cells

The models *Add_half_ASIC* and *Add_full_ASIC*, shown next, use parts (*norf201*, *invf101*, *xorf201*, and *nanf201*) from a standard-cell library having propagation delays corresponding to a physical CMOS process.[5] CMOS **AND** gates are commonly

---

[5]*norf201* is a two-input nor gate; *invf101* is an inverter, *xorf201* is a two-input exclusive-OR gate; and *nanf201* is a two-input NAND gate.

implemented by combining a *NAND* gate with an inverter; likewise, an **OR** gate is implemented by a **NOR** gate and an inverter. The Verilog *timescale directive* `timescale 1ns/1ps`, at the first line of the source file, directs the simulator to interpret the numerical time variables as having units of nanoseconds, with a resolution of picoseconds.[6] Here is the code for the two models:

```
`timescale 1ns / 1 ps                   module Add_half_ASIC (sum, c_out, a, b);
module Add_full_ASIC                      output        sum, c_out;
(sum, c_out, a, b, c_in);                 input         a, b;
  output        sum, c_out;               wire          c_out_bar;
  input         a, b, c_in;
  wire          w1, w2, w3;               xorf201       M1 (sum, a, b);
  wire          c_out_bar;                nanf201       M2 (c_out_bar, a, b);
                                          invf101       M3 (c_out, c_out_bar);
  Add_half_ASIC M1 (w1, w2, a, b);      endmodule
  Add_half_ASIC M2 (sum, w3, w1, c_in);


  norf201       M3 (c_out_bar, w2, w3);
  invf101       M4 (c_out, c_out_bar);
endmodule
```

The following testbench generates waveforms for the inputs to the full-adder and monitors the waveforms of *c_out* and *sum*:

```
module t_Add_full_ASIC ();
  wire          sum, c_out;
  reg           a, b, c_in;

  initial $display ("t        a b  c_in ");
  initial $display ("                         c_out");
  initial $display ("                              sum");
  initial $monitor($realtime,," %b %b %b %b %b", a, b, c_in, c_out, sum);
  initial #100 $display ("End of simulation");
  initial #101 $finish;

  initial fork
   #10 c_in = 0;
   #20 a = 0;
   #20 b = 0;
   #25 b = 1;
   #40 a = 1;
   #50 b = 0;
   #60 c_in = 1;
   #70 a = 0;
   #80 b = 1;
   #90 a = 1;
  join
   Add_full_ASIC M0 (sum, c_out, a, b, c_in);
endmodule
```

---

[6]See Appendix E for a description of timescales.

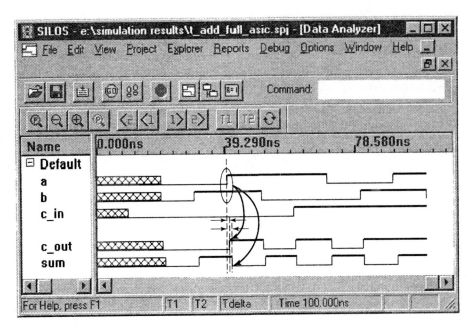

FIGURE 4-4 Results of simulating a 1-bit full-adder implemented with ASIC cells having technology-dependent propagation delays

The code produces the graphical display shown in Figure 4-4, as well as the following standard output:

t	a	b	c_in	c_out	sum
0	x	x	x	x	x
10	x	x	0	x	x
20	0	0	0	x	x
20.682	0	0	0	0	x
21.366	0	0	0	0	0
25	0	1	0	0	0
26.228	0	1	0	0	1
40	1	1	0	0	1
40.444	1	1	0	1	1
41.366	1	1	0	1	0
50	1	0	0	1	0
50.682	1	0	0	0	0
51.228	1	0	0	0	1
60	1	0	1	0	1
60.444	1	0	1	1	1
60.683	1	0	1	1	0
70	0	0	1	1	0
71.297	0	0	1	1	1
71.365	0	0	1	0	1

80	0	1	1	0	1
81.058	0	1	1	1	1
81.297	0	1	1	1	0
90	1	1	1	1	0
91.297	1	1	1	1	1

End of simulation

In the testbench code, the built-in system task *$monitor* statement establishes a mechanism that automatically prints standard output when its arguments have events (see Appendix D). The quoted string specifies the format of the output in C-like syntax, followed by a list of arguments. The system task *$realtime* prints the time at which the events occur, in real-number format.[7] The system task *$display* is used to print headers and other text. It prints only when the statement executes.

The models for *norf201*, *invf101*, *xorf201*, and *nanf201* include propagation delays based on characterization of the physical standard cells [3]. The effect of the realistic propagation delays is apparent in the waveforms produced by simulating *Add_full_ASIC*, as shown in Figure 4-4.

Example End: Simulation with Standard Cells

4.5.1 Inertial Delay

Logic transitions in a digital circuit correspond to transitions in voltage levels caused by the accumulation or dissipation of charge at a physical node/net. The physical behavior of a signal transition is said to have *inertia*, because every conducting path has some resistance, as well as capacitance, and charge on a capacitor cannot accumulate or dissipate instantly.

The propagation delay of the primitive gates in Verilog obeys an *inertial* delay model to account for the fact that charge must accumulate or dissipate in the physical circuit before a voltage level can be established, corresponding to a 0 or a 1. If an input signal is applied to a gate and then removed before sufficient charge has accumulated, the output signal will not achieve a voltage level corresponding to a transition. For example, if all of the inputs to a NAND gate are at value 1 for a long time before one of them is changed momentarily to 0, the output will not change to 1 unless the input is held to 0 for a long enough time. In Verilog, the amount of time that the input pulse must be constant, in order for the gate to make a transition, is the *inertial delay* of the gate.

Verilog uses the propagation delay of a gate as the minimum width of an input pulse that could affect the output, (i.e., *the value of the propagation delay is also used as the value of the inertial delay*). The width of a pulse must be at least as long as the propagation delay of the gate. The Verilog simulation engine detects whether the duration

---

[7]An alternative task, *$time*, prints time as an integer value, but produces output having less resolution when the physical delay values are not integer values.

of an input has been too short, and then deschedules previously scheduled outputs triggered by the leading edge of a pulse. Inertial delay has the effect of suppressing (filtering out) input pulses whose duration is shorter than the propagation delay of the gate.

Example: Inertial Delay

The input to the inverter in Figure 4-5 changes at $t_{sim} = 3$. Because the inverter has a propagation delay of 2, the effect of this change is to cause the output to be *scheduled* to change at $t_{sim} = 5$. However, for pulsewidth $\Delta = 1$, the input changes back to the initial value at $t_{sim} = 4$. The simulator cannot anticipate this activity. The effect of the two successive changes is to create a narrow pulse at the input to the inverter. Because the width of the pulse is less than the propagation delay of the inverter, the simulator deschedules the previously scheduled output event, corresponding to the leading edge of the narrow input pulse, and does not schedule the event corresponding to the trailing edge of the pulse. Descheduling is required because the simulator cannot anticipate the falling edge and must wait until it occurs. On the other hand, the pulse having $\Delta = 6$ persists long enough for the output to be affected. The simulator detects the need for descheduling by noting that a prior event is scheduled, but has not executed, when the edge corresponding to the back edge of the pulse occurs at the input. The simulator removes both events from the queue.

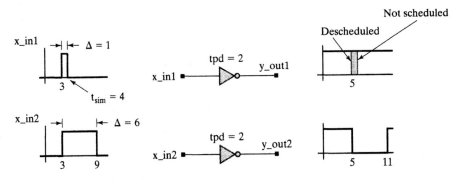

FIGURE 4-5   Event descheduling caused by an inertial delay

Example End: Inertial Delay

4.5.2   Transport Delay

The time of flight of a signal traveling a wire of a circuit is modeled as a *transport delay*. With this model, narrow pulses are not suppressed, and all transitions at the driving end of a wire appear at the receiving end after a finite time delay. In most ASICs, the physical distances are so small that the time of flight on wires can be ignored, because at the speed of light, the signal takes only .033 ns to travel a centimeter. However, Verilog can assign delay to individual wires in a circuit to model transport delay effects in circuits where it cannot be neglected, such as in a multichip hardware module or on a printed circuit board. Wire delays are declared with the declaration of a wire. For example, *wire #2 A_long_wire* declares that *A_long_wire* has a delay of two time steps. The examples in this text will not include transport delay.[8]

REFERENCES

[1] Ciletti, M.D. *Modeling, Synthesis, and Rapid Prototyping with the Verilog HDL.* Upper Saddle River, NJ: Prentice Hall, 1999.
[2] *IEEE Standard for Verilog Hardware Description Language 2001*, IEEE Std.1364-2001. Piscataway, NJ: 1996, Institute of Electrical and Electronic Engineers, 2001.
[3] Chang, H. et al. *Surviving the System on Chip Revolution.* Boston: Kluwer, 1999.

PROBLEMS

1. Develop a testbench and verify the structural model for the circuit in Figure P3-1. Use the following name for your testbench, the model, and its ports: *t_Combo_str()*, *Combo_str (Y, A, B, C, D)*. Note: The testbench will have no ports. Exhaustively simulate the circuit and provide graphical output demonstrating that the model is correct. Generate text output using the *$monitor* and *$display* tasks.
2. Develop a small set of test patterns that will (1) test a half-adder circuit, (2) test a full-adder circuit, (3) exhaustively test a 4-bit ripple-carry adder, and (4) test a 16-bit ripple-carry adder by verifying that the connectivity between the 4-bit slices are connected correctly, given that the 4-bit slices themselves have been verified.
3. Develop and verify a Verilog module that produces a 4-bit output code indicating the number of 1s in an 8-bit input word.

---

[8]For additional details, see [1].

CHAPTER 5   Modeling Behavior with Verilog

This chapter presents constructs for developing behavioral models of combinational and sequential logic, and writing and executing testbenches for simulating, monitoring, and verifying behavioral models using a simulator.

5.1   Behavioral Modeling

Behavioral models describe functionality abstractly, independently of technology. They describe the functional relationship between the inputs and outputs of a logic circuit, but do not model the propagation delays associated with signal transitions in physical hardware, which depend on the state of the technology that produced the hardware. Once a Verilog model is developed, it can be implemented in a variety of ASIC technologies and FPGAs.

Although a design can be described by gate-level models, it is more convenient to describe a design with a behavioral model and let a synthesis tool develop the physical implementation. This saves a designer time, and allows consideration of alternative designs and hardware prototypes. Structural models are used in forming architectural partitions of a design, but behavioral models are commonly used to describe the functionality of each block in the structure.

We will consider three types of behavioral models: (1) continuous assignments, (2) single-pass behaviors, and (3) cyclic behaviors. Of these, the last two execute procedural statements and are more abstract. We will present behavioral models of combinational logic, level-sensitive sequential logic, and edge-sensitive sequential logic in this chapter, and develop models for finite state machines and datapath controllers in Chapter 6.

5.2   Continuous Assignments and Boolean Equations

Continuous assignments are the Verilog counterpart of Boolean equations that describe combinational logic. Using the built-in operators discussed in Chapter 2, continuous assignments automatically and continuously monitor a syntax-compliant expression of operands and operators to schedule an update event for the value of a net. This happens, of course, during simulation. Many operators have a gate-level counterpart, *so such expressions are easily synthesized into physical circuits* [7]. Note: arithmetic equations can be described by continuous assignments too.

A continuous assignment statement is declared with the keyword ***assign***, followed by a net variable (usually having type ***wire***), an assignment operator (=), and an expression. The variable on the left-hand side (LHS) of a continuous assignment statement is said to be the *target* of the assignment.[1]

Example: Continuous Assignment

The five-input *AOI* circuit that was modeled in Chapter 3 with primitives can be described by a single continuous assignment statement, as shown in *AOI_5_CA0*:

```
module  AOI_5_CA0 (y_out, x_in1, x_in2, x_in3, x_in4, x_in5);
  input         x_in1, x_in2, x_in3, x_in4, x_in5;
  output        y_out;

  assign  y_out = ~((x_in1 & x_in2) | (x_in3 & x_in4 & x_in5));

endmodule
```

Example End: Continuous Assignment

The continuous assignment in *AOI_5_CA0* does not execute like a statement in an ordinary programming language. Instead, it declares a relationship that governs how *y_out* depends on the signals on the right-hand side (RHS) of the assignment operator during simulation. The expression assigning value to *y_out* in *AOI_5_CA0* uses the bitwise inversion operator ($\sim$), the bitwise AND operator (&), and the bitwise OR operator (|). The assignment is said to be *sensitive* to the variables in the RHS expression, because whenever a variable in the RHS changes during simulation, the RHS expression is reevaluated and the result is used to schedule an update event for the LHS.

A continuous assignment is said to describe *implicit combinational logic*, because the expression of the continuous assignment is equivalent to logic gates that implement the same function. A continuous assignment can be more compact and understandable than a schematic or a netlist of primitives.

---
[1]The target of a continuous assignment must be a net.

Because the simulator schedules an update event for the LHS whenever the value of the RHS expression changes during simulation, a continuous assignment is said to declare an *event scheduling rule* that governs *when* and *how* the value of a net will be changed during simulation.

5.2.1 Multiple Continuous Assignments

A module may contain multiple continuous assignments, and they are all active concurrently with each other and with other continuous assignments, primitives, abstract behaviors, and instantiated modules, just as all of the logic in a circuit is active concurrently.

Example: Two-Bit Comparator with Continuous Assignments

As an alternative to the structural model of the 2-bit comparator presented in Chapter 3, the model *compare_2_CA0* is described by three (concurrent) continuous assignment statements.[2] The model is equivalent to *compare_2_str*, which used primitives, but has no explicit binding to hardware or to primitive gates. The code for *compare_2_CA0* is as follows:

```
module compare_2_CA0 (A_lt_B, A_gt_B, A_eq_B, A1, A0, B1, B0);
  input   A1, A0, B1, B0;
  output A_lt_B, A_gt_B, A_eq_B;

  assign A_lt_B = (~A1) & B1 | (~A1) & (~A0) & B0 | (~A0) & B1 & B0;

  assign A_gt_B = A1 & (~B1) | A0 & (~B1) & (~B0) | A1 & A0 & (~B0);

  assign A_eq_B = (~A1) & (~A0) & (~B1) & (~B0) | (~A1) & A0 & (~B1) & B0
      | A1 & A0 & B1 & B0 | A1 & (~A0) & B1 & (~B0);

endmodule
```

One liability of continuous assignments is that complex expressions can be difficult for a reader to interpret correctly.

Example End: Two-Bit Comparator with Continuous Assignments

Note that continuous assignment statements suppress detail about the internal structure of the module, and deal only with the Boolean or arithmetic equations that describe the input–output relationships of the model. A synthesis tool will create the actual hardware realization of the assignment.

---

[2]The order in which multiple continuous assignments are listed in the source code is arbitrary, (i.e., the order of the statements does not affect the meaning of the model, and has no effect on the results of simulation). The order does not establish a precedence for their evaluation.

5.2.2   Modeling Three-State Behavior with Continuous Assignments

Continuous assignments are commonly used with the conditional operator to model three-state behavior.

Example: Continuous Assignment for Three-State Behavior

The five-input *AOI* circuit can be modified to have an additional input, *enable*, and to have a three-state output, as described by *AOI_5_CA1*:

```
module  AOI_5_CA1 (y_out, x_in1, x_in2, x_in3, x_in4, x_in5, enable);
input           x_in1, x_in2, x_in3, x_in4, x_in5, enable;
output          y_out;

assign  y_out = enable ? ~((x_in1 & x_in2) | (x_in3 & x_in4 & x_in5)) : 1'bz;

endmodule
```

Example End: Continuous Assignment for Three-State Behavior

Recall that the *conditional operator (? :)* acts like a software if-then-else switch that selects between two expressions. (See Chapter 2.) If the value of *enable* is true in *AOI_5_CA1*, the expression immediately to the right of the *?* is evaluated and used to assign value to *y_out*; otherwise, the expression to the right of the *:* is used.[3] This example also illustrates how to write models that include three-state outputs. The value of *y_out* is formed by combinational logic, while *enable* is asserted, but has the value *z* otherwise. This functionality corresponds to the equivalent logic circuit shown in Figure 5-1. Notice that the continuous assignment statement is an implicit, abstract, and compact (and possibly cryptic) representation of the structure described by an equivalent gate-level schematic or a netlist of primitives.

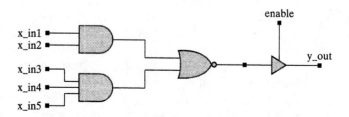

FIGURE 5-1   Equivalent circuit modeled by *AOI_5_CA1*

---

[3]The syntax of the conditional operator requires that both alternative expressions be specified.

5.2.3   Implicit Continuous Assignments

A continuous assignment may be implied by the declaration of a net. This simplified syntax eliminates the need for a separate declaration of the type of the target net and a separate declaration of the continuous assignment.

Example: Implicit Continuous Assignment

The model described by *AOI_5_CA2* declares *y_out* to be of type **wire** and associates with it a Boolean expression that determines the value of *y_out* during simulation:

```
module AOI_5_CA2 (y_out, x_in1, x_in2, x_in3, x_in4, x_in5, enable);
   input        x_in1, x_in2, x_in3, x_in4, x_in5, enable;
   output       y_out;

   wire y_out = enable ? ~((x_in1 & x_in2) | (x_in3 & x_in4 & x_in5)) : 1'bz;

endmodule
```

Example End: Implicit Continuous Assignment

5.2.4   Restrictions for Continuous Assignments

The target of a continuous assignment must be a net, and may not be a register variable. An attempt to assign value to a register variable using a continuous assignment will produce a syntax error.

5.2.5   Implicit Nets

 In Verilog 1995, an undeclared identifier will be an implicit net data type if it (1) appears in the port of an instantiated module, or (2) is connected to an instance of a primitive, or (3) appears on the LHS of a continuous assignment statement and is also declared as a port of the module containing the assignment. If the implicit net is connected to a vector port, it will inherit the size of the port; otherwise, it will be a scalar net. The default data type of an implicit net is **wire**, which can be modified by a compiler directive. If the type of the LHS of a continuous assignment is not declared explicitly and is not determined implicitly by the preceding rules, an error will result. In Verilog 2001,[4] an undeclared

---

[4]For additional features of Verilog 2001, see [1, 3].

identifier that is not a port of a module will be inferred as an implicit scalar net. Thus, continuous assignments to such nets do not require a separate declaration of the type of the net.

Example: Implicit Nets

Figure 5-2 shows a module that compiles with Verilog 2001, but not with Verilog 1995.

Verilog 1995	Verilog 2001
module Add (sum, a, b, c_in); 　**output** sum; 　**input**　a, b; 　**input**　c_in; 　**reg**　　sum; 　**assign** sum = a + b + c_in; 　**assign** match = a & b; // Error **endmodule**	**module** Add (sum, a, b, c_in); 　**output** sum; 　**input**　a, b; 　**input**　c_in; 　**reg**　　sum; 　**assign** sum = a + b + c_in; 　**assign** match = a & b; // Valid **endmodule**

FIGURE 5-2

Example End: Implicit Nets

The mechanism for implicitly declaring a net can be disabled in Verilog 2001, by including a new argument, ***none***, with the `` `default_nettype `` compiler directive. This argument requires all nets to be explicitly declared. Disabling the default assignment of type to undeclared identifiers will reveal compilation errors that arise from misspelled identifiers, but that would otherwise go undetected.

5.2.6   Propagation Delay and Continuous Assignments

Propagation (inertial) delay can be associated with a continuous assignment, so that its implicit logic has the same functionality and timing characteristics as its gate-level counterpart.

Example: Continuous Assignment with Propagation Delay

The functionality of an AOI gate structure with unit propagation delays on its implicit gates is described by module *AOI_4_CA*. Each declaration of a **wire** includes a logic

expression assigning value to the **wire**, and includes a unit time delay. The simulator reacts to a change in an RHS expression and schedules a change to update the LHS variable, subject to the propagation delay. The code is as follows:

```
module  AOI_4_CA (y_out, x_in1, x_in2, x_in3, x_in4);
   input          x_in1, x_in2, x_in3, x_in4;
   output         y_out;

   wire #1 y1 = x_in1 & x_in2;          // Bitwise and operation
   wire #1 y2 = x_in3 & x_in4;
   wire #1 y_out = ~ (y1 | y2);         // Complement the result of bitwise OR operation
endmodule
```

Example End: Continuous Assignment with Propagation Delay

5.2.7 Continuous Assignments for Modeling Transparent Latches

A latch can be modeled by a pair of continuous assignment statements with feedback. The behavior is level sensitive and will correspond to the feedback structure
of a hardware latch. Synthesis tools, however, do not accommodate this form of
feedback, even though the model can be simulated. Still, they will synthesize the behavior of a latch from a single continuous assignment, using a conditional operator
with feedback.

Example: Transparent Latch

The output of a transparent latch follows the data input while the latch is enabled, but
otherwise will hold the value it had when the enable input was deasserted. *Latch_CA*
models this functionality by a *single continuous assignment statement with feedback*:

```
module  Latch_CA (q_out, data_in, enable);
   output         q_out;
   input          data_in, enable;

   assign q_out = enable ? data_in : q_out;
endmodule
```

Figure 5-3 shows the waveforms produced by simulation of *Latch_CA*. Notice
how *q_out* follows *data_in* while *enable* is asserted, and latches *q_out* to the value of
data_in when *enable* is deasserted. The appearance of *q_out* in the RHS expression and
as the LHS target variable implies structural feedback in hardware, and will be synthesized as a latch.

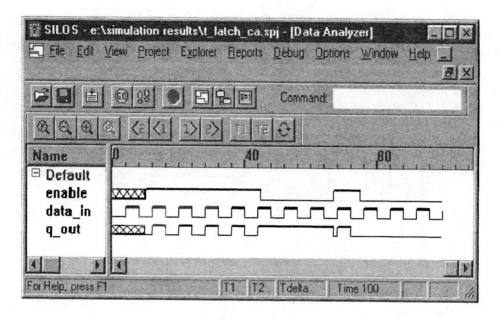

FIGURE 5-3 Simulation results for a transparent latch modeled by a continuous assignment statement with feedback

---

Example End: Transparent Latch

Example: Transparent Latch with Active-Low Reset

The following latch model, *Latch_Rbar_CA*, uses a nested conditional operator to add the functionality of an active-low reset to a transparent latch:

```
module  Latch_Rbar_CA (q_out, data_in, enable, reset_bar);
   output          q_out;
   input           data_in, enable, reset_bar;

   assign  q_out = !reset_bar ? 0 : enable ? data_in : q_out;
endmodule
```

Simulation of *Latch_Rbar_CA* produces the waveforms shown in Figure 5-4, where the actions of *enable* and *reset_bar* are apparent. Notice how *q_out* matches *data_in* while *enable* in asserted.

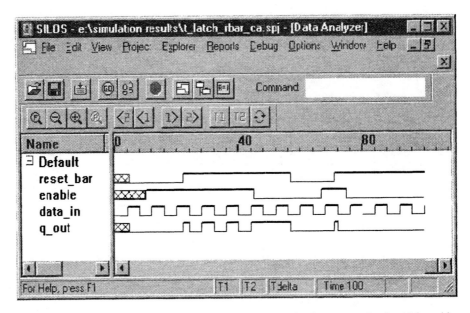

FIGURE 5-4 Simulation results for a transparent latch with active-low *reset* and active-high *enable*

Example End: Transparent Latch with Active-Low Reset

Continuous assignments are convenient for modeling level-sensitive logic, but designers writing large, complex Boolean expressions are prone to making mistakes. As noted earlier, the Boolean expressions might obscure the functionality of the design, even if they are written correctly. So, it is worthwhile to consider other language constructs that offer simpler, but more readable, alternatives that describe edge-sensitive, as well as level-sensitive, logic.

5.3   Statement Execution with Single-Pass and Cyclic Behaviors

Verilog's single-pass[5] and cyclic behaviors are abstract models of functionality. Both execute procedural statements like those found in other programming languages, but Verilog includes special constructs for modeling temporal characteristics of hardware.

Recall that the keyword *initial,* followed by a statement, declares a single-pass behavior. A single-pass behavior, also referred to as an *initial block,* executes the associated statement and then expires. The statement may be an individual statement

---

[5]Single-pass behaviors for describing signal generators in testbenches were introduced in Chapter 4.

(terminated by a semicolon), a *begin* ... *end* block statement, or a *fork* ... *join* block.[6] The statements of a *begin* ... *end* block execute sequentially, and the block expires after the last statement within it executes and reaches the keyword **end**. The statements of *fork* ... *join* execute in parallel, and the block expires after all of the statements within it execute and the keyword *join* is reached.

Cyclic behaviors are declared by the keyword *always*. Like single-pass behaviors, they execute the statement (single or block) that follows the keyword, but instead of expiring after executing its statement, an *always* behavior reexecutes the statement or block repeatedly during simulation. The flow of execution returns to the keyword *always* after reaching the semicolon that terminates an individual statement, or reaching the **end** or *join* keywords of a block statement.

Both behaviors become active at $t_{sim} = 0$, but whether they execute a statement immediately at $t_{sim} = 0$ depends on timing control constructs. Timing control constructs determine *when* a statement will execute.

5.3.1 Timing Controls in Behavioral Models

There are three mechanisms for timing control in Verilog: delay control, event control, and *wait*. When placed before a procedural statement, the delay control operator, #, postpones execution of the statement; the event control operator, @, postpones execution until an associated expression changes value, and the keyword *wait* postpones execution until an expression is true.[7]

5.3.2 Single-Pass Behavior

Single-pass behaviors[8] are declared with the keyword *initial* and are identical to cyclic behaviors, with one exception. The activity of the behavior expires (terminates) after the last statement executes. Single-pass behaviors are not supported by synthesis tools. They are used mainly in testbenches, which are not synthesized.

Example: Single-Pass Behavior—Waveform Generator

The following single-pass behavior generates the waveform shown in Figure 5-5 for a signal, *reset*. The statements within the *begin* ... *end* block execute in sequence, beginning with the assignment *reset = 0* at the start of simulation. After 10 time steps, the assignment *reset = 1* executes. Then, five time steps later, the assignment *reset = 0* executes and the behavior expires. In each case, the statements that follow the # are suspended for the indicated time.

---

[6]See Chapter 4.
[7]The wait statement is presented in Section 5.12.
[8]Formally referred to as an initial block.

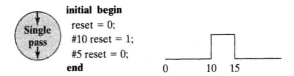

initial begin
reset = 0;
#10 reset = 1;
#5 reset = 0;
end

0   10   15

FIGURE 5-5   Waveform generated by a single-pass behavior

Example End: Single-Pass Behavior—Waveform Generator

5.3.3   Cyclic Behavior

Cyclic behaviors are abstract models of functionality. In contrast to gate-level primitives, they execute procedural statements to generate the values of variables, just like the statements of an ordinary procedural language (e.g., C) execute to retrieve, manipulate, and store variables in memory. The execution of the statements in a cyclic behavior can be unconditional or can be governed by an optional *sensitivity list*, also called an *event control expression*. Cyclic behaviors are used to model (and synthesize) both level-sensitive and edge-sensitive (synchronous) behavior (e.g., flip-flops). The sensitivity list in the full-adder in Figure 5-6 is level-sensitive.

Example: Level-Sensitive Cyclic Behavior—Full-Adder

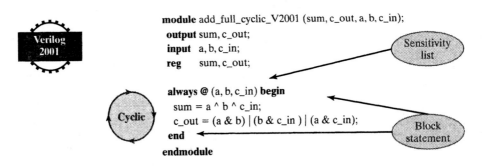

```
module add_full_cyclic_V2001 (sum, c_out, a, b, c_in);
  output sum, c_out;
  input   a, b, c_in;
  reg     sum, c_out;

  always @ (a, b, c_in) begin
    sum = a ^ b ^ c_in;
    c_out = (a & b) | (b & c_in ) | (a & c_in);
  end
endmodule
```

FIGURE 5-6   Cyclic behavioral model for a full-adder

Example End: Level-Sensitive Cyclic Behavior—Full-Adder

The cyclic behavior in *add_full_cyclic_V2001* is declared by the keyword ***always***, followed by the event control operator (@) and a sensitivity list (*(a, b, c_in)*), and a ***begin . . . end*** block statement. The comma-separated sensitivity list was included in Verilog 2001. An older, alternative form of the event control expression is given by *(a or b or c_in)*. The event control operator acts as a trigger, postponing execution of the statements that follow it, until an element of the sensitivity list changes.

The sensitivity list in *add_full_cyclic_V2001* is sensitive to the primary inputs, *a*, *b*, and *c_in*. The behavior becomes active at the beginning of simulation, but does not execute the block statement until the process is triggered by activity on a primary input. When an input has an event, the block statement executes. This is an abstract model of hardware, which forms its outputs (*sum* and *c_out*) based on the current value of the inputs to the adder.

In *add_full_cyclic_V2001*, the statements within the **begin . . . end** block statement execute sequentially, with *sum* updated before *c_out* is updated. After the last statement in the block executes, the flow of execution returns to the keyword **always** to reexecute repeatedly. In each cycle, the flow is suspended by the *event control operator*, **@**, until the sensitivity list triggers execution again. The statement following the operator cannot execute until an event is detected in the sensitivity list. This cyclic activity continues until simulation terminates.

The logic determining the values of *sum* and *c_out* in *add_full_cyclic_V2001* is level-sensitive. The values of *sum* and *c_out* are updated when the values of *a*, *b*, or *c_in* change. The functionality of *add_full_cyclic_V2001* is identical to that of the structural model of a full-adder composed of primitives or a behavioral model composed of continuous assignments. A synthesis tool will synthesize *add_full_cyclic_V2001* into equivalent combinational logic. Notice that the values of *sum* and *c_out* in *add_full_cyclic_V2001* are computed without delay, (i.e., they are updated in the same time step as the input that triggered the sensitivity list). The synthesized physical hardware will have the propagation delay of the gates that are selected to implement the logic.

A variable that is assigned value by a procedural assignment operator in a single-pass or cyclic behavior must be a declared register-type variable (i.e., not a net).

Register variables store information during simulation, but that does not necessarily imply that the synthesized circuit will have hardware registers. Notice that the variables *sum* and *c_out*, which are assigned value in Figures 5-6, have type **reg**. They hold an assigned value until it is changed, which allows them to represent continuous waveforms during simulation.

5.4   Modeling Edge-Sensitive Sequential Logic

Continuous assignment statements are limited to modeling level-sensitive behavior, (i.e., combinational logic and transparent latches). They cannot model an element having edge-sensitive behavior, such as a flip-flop. Many digital systems operate synchronously, with activity triggered by an edge of a synchronizing signal, commonly called a clock. Verilog uses edge qualifiers (**posedge**, **negedge**) with the event control operator (**@**) in sensitivity lists, modeling edge-sensitive functionality. For example, the event control expression (**posedge** clock) and the sensitivity list (**posedge** clock, **negedge** reset) are triggered by edge transitions of signals. The keywords *posedge* and *negedge* are called *event qualifiers*.[9] Event control expressions may be level and/or edge sensitive, but synthesis tools do not support mixed sensitivity (e.g., *posedge* clock **or** reset).

5.5   Procedural vs. Nonblocking Assignments

Statements using the procedural assignment operator execute in their listed order, with the storage of values occurring immediately after any statement executes and before the next statement executes. If there are data dependencies between the variables on the LHS of the statements, the order in which the assignments are listed may affect the outcome.

Example: Procedural Assignments

The shift register shown in Figure 5-7 is described by a synchronous, cyclic behavior with a list of procedural assignments:

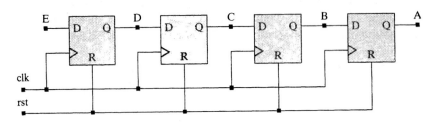

FIGURE 5-7   A 4-bit serial shift register

```
module shiftreg_PA (E, A, B, C, D, clk, rst);
 output A, B, C, D;
 input   E;
 input   clk, rst;
 reg     A, B, C, D;

 always @ (posedge clk or posedge rst) begin
  if (rst) begin A = 0; B = 0; C = 0; D = 0; end
  else begin
    A = B;
    B = C;
    C = D;
    D = E;
  end
 end
endmodule
```

---

[9]Semantically, *posedge* means a signal transition whose final value is one; *negedge* means a transition to a value of 0, in Verilog's four-valued logic.

Now consider what happens if the order of the procedural assignments in the model is reversed, as in module *shift_reg_PA_rev*:

```
module  shiftreg_PA_rev (A, B, C, D, E, clk, rst);
  output  A, B, C, D;
  input   E;
  input   clk, rst;
  reg     A, B, C, D;

  always @ (posedge clk or posedge rst) begin
    if (rst) begin A = 0; B = 0; C = 0; D = 0; end
    else begin
      D = E;
      C = D;
      B = C;
      A = B;
    end
  end
endmodule
```

In this module, the list of statements executes in sequential order, from top to bottom. The effect of the assignment made by the first procedural statement is immediate. So D changes, and the updated value is used in the second statement, and so forth. The statements execute sequentially, but at the same time step of the simulator. The list of four statements is equivalent to a single statement that assigns E to A. Synthesis tools recognize this form of expression substitution, and will synthesize a circuit consisting of a single flip-flop, as shown in Figure 5-8.

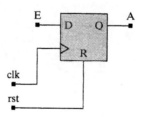

FIGURE 5-8 Circuit synthesized as a result of expression substitution in an incorrect model of a 4-bit serial shift register

Example End: Procedural Assignments

Procedural assignments are called *blocked* assignments, because a statement that makes a procedural assignment must complete execution (i.e., update memory), before the next statement in the behavior can execute. The statements that follow a procedural assignment are blocked from executing until the statement with the procedural assignment completes execution. This sets the stage for expression substitution. The preceding example demonstrates that *failure to appreciate the effects of expression substitution can lead to incorrect models.*

An alternative Verilog operator makes *concurrent procedural assignments*, also called *nonblocking assignments*, in a cyclic or single-pass behavior. Nonblocking assignments are made with the nonblocking assignment operator ($<=$), instead of the ordinary (procedural, sequential) assignment operator ($=$). Nonblocking assignment statements execute *concurrently* (in parallel) rather than sequentially, so the order in which they are listed implies no precedence of any kind, and has no effect.[10] Moreover, a simulator must implement a sampling mechanism by which all of the variables referenced by the RHS of the statements with nonblocking assignments are sampled, held in memory, and used to update the LHS variables concurrently.[11] Consequently, changes to the listed order of the nonblocking assignments do not affect the outcome of the assignments to the LHS variable, because the assignments are based on the values that were held by the RHS variables immediately before the statements executed.

Example: Nonblocking Assignments

An equivalent model of the 4-bit serial shift register shown in Figure 5-7 is as follows, with nonblocking assignment operators ($<=$):

```
module shiftreg_nb (A, E, clk, rst);
output A;
input  E;
input  clk, rst;
reg    A, B, C, D;

always @ (posedge clk or posedge rst) begin
  if (rst) begin A <= 0; B <= 0; C <= 0; D <= 0; end
  else begin
    A <= B;              //      D <= E;
    B <= C;              //      C <= D;
    C <= D;              //      B <= D;
    D <= E;              //      A <= B;
  end
end
endmodule
```

The commented nonblocking assignments in *shiftreg_nb* have reversed order and would lead to the same results in simulation, and will synthesize to the same structure.

Example End: Nonblocking Assignments

The statements in a list of nonblocking assignments execute concurrently, without dependence on their relative order. This style describes the concurrency found in actual hardware, and the register transfers that occur within synchronous machines.

---

[10]If a list of nonblocking assignments target the same variable, the last assignment in the list determines the assigned value.

[11]It is advisable to avoid having multiple behaviors assign value to the same variable, because software race conditions make the outcome indeterminate.

When a cyclic behavior executes nonblocking assignments, the simulator evaluates each of the RHS expressions before assigning values to their LHS targets. This, in general, prevents any interaction between the assignments and eliminates dependencies on their relative order. This is not the case for ordinary (i.e., sequential) procedural assignments (i.e., those using the = operator), because such statements execute in sequence, and only after the preceding statement has completed execution. If the functionality being modeled by a cyclic behavior does not depend on the sequence in which the statements are written, either blocking or nonblocking assignments can be used. However, if we are modeling logic that includes edge-driven register transfers, *it is strongly recommended that edge-sensitive, (i.e., synchronous) operations be described by nonblocking assignments, and that combinational logic be described with blocked assignments.* This practice will prevent race conditions between combinational logic and register operations.

 Modeling Tip *A variable that is assigned value by a nonblocking (<=) assignment must be a declared register variable.*

Example: Behavioral Model—D-Type Flip-Flop with Synchronous Reset

---

The keyword **always** in module *df_behav* declares a cyclic behavior corresponding to an edge-triggered flip-flop:

```
module df_behav (q, q_bar, data, set, reset, clk);
    input           data, set, clk, reset;
    output          q, q_bar;
    reg             q;

    assign  q_bar = ~ q;

    always @ (posedge clk)  // Flip-flop with synchronous set/reset
    begin
      if (reset == 0) q <= 0;
       else if (set == 0) q <= 1;
          else q <= data;
      end
endmodule
```

At every rising edge of *clk*, the behavior's procedural statements execute, computing the value of *q* and storing it in memory. A continuous assignment statement forms *q_bar* from *q*, immediately after *q* has changed. Here, too, the nonblocking, or concurrent, assignment operator (<=) is used within the cyclic behavior.

Example End: Behavioral Model—D-Type Flip-Flop with Synchronous Reset

---

In *df_behav*, the action of *reset* is synchronous, because it has no influence until the procedural statements are evaluated at the active edge of *clk*. The variable *q* retains its residual value until the next active edge of *clk*, as specified by **posedge** *clk*, because *q* was declared as a register variable of type **reg**. The Verilog keyword **posedge** qualifies the event control expression to execute its procedural statements only when a rising edge of the argument signal (e.g., *clk*) has occurred.

Example: Behavioral Model—D-type Flip-Flop with Asynchronous Reset

---

The reset action of a flip-flop can be asynchronous. The functionality modeled by *asynch_df_behav* in the following example, is sensitive to the rising edge of the clock, but also to the falling edge of *reset* and *set*, with priority given to *reset*:

```
module asynch_df_behav (q, q_bar, data, set, clk, reset );
  input        data, set, reset, clk;
  output       q, q_bar;
  reg          q;

  assign q_bar = ~q;

  always @ (negedge set or negedge reset or posedge clk)
  begin
   if (reset == 0) q <= 0;
    else if (set == 0) q <= 1;
      else q <= data;            // synchronized activity
  end
endmodule
```

Note that the last clause in the conditional statement does not decode *clk* explicitly, and executes at a rising edge of *clk* only if the asynchronous inputs are not asserted.

In general, because that *clk* and *clock* are not keywords, *so it is important to place the computational activity associated with the synchronizing signal in the last conditional clause of the if statement*. This coding discipline allows a synthesis tool to (1) correctly identify the synchronizing signal (its name and location in the event control expression are not predetermined) and (2) infer the need for a flip-flop to hold the value of *q* between the active edges of the synchronizing signal.

The cyclic behavior in *asynch_df_behav* is activated at the beginning of simulation and immediately suspends activity until triggered by its event control expression.[12] The expression is formed as an "event or" of *set, reset,* and *clk*. The Verilog language allows a mixture of level-sensitive and edge-qualified variables in an event control expression, but *synthesis tools do not support such models of behavior*. Be sure that your description is entirely edge sensitive or entirely level sensitive.

Example End: Behavioral Model—D-type Flip-Flop with Asynchronous Reset

---

[12]An event for *clk* occurs at the beginning of simulation if it is assigned a value of 1.

5.6   Multicycle Operations

Some digital machines have repetitive operations distributed over multiple clock cycles. This activity can be modeled in Verilog by a synchronous cyclic behavior having as many nested, edge-sensitive event control expressions as are needed to complete the operations.

Example: Behavioral Model—Multicycle Operations

A machine that is to form the sum of four successive samples of a datapath could store the samples in registers and then use multiple adders to form the sum, or it could use one adder to accumulate the sum sequentially. The implicit state machine *add_4cycle* adds four successive samples on a data bus [2]:

```
module add_4cycle (sum, data, clk, reset);
  output      [5: 0]   sum;
  input       [3: 0]   data;
  input                clk, reset;
  reg         [5: 0]   sum;

  always @ (posedge clk) begin: add_loop
    if (reset) disable add_loop;                  else sum <= data;
      @ (posedge clk) if (reset) disable add_loop;     else sum <= sum + data;
        @ (posedge clk) if (reset) disable add_loop;   else sum <= sum + data;
          @ (posedge clk) if (reset) disable add_loop; else sum <= sum + data;
  end
endmodule
```

The behavior in *add_4cycle* contains four event control expressions. The sum is initialized to the first sample of data in the first clock cycle. Four samples of data are accumulated after four clock cycles, before the activity flow returns to the first event control expression to await a new sequence of samples of data. Notice that the *begin* ... *end* block is given a name, **add_loop**, and the *disable* statement is included within the reset statement in each clock cycle, to ensure that the machine reinitializes properly, regardless of when reset is asserted (see Section 5.10.3).

Example End: Behavioral Model—Multicycle Operations

5.7   Cyclic Behavior without Event Control

The sensitivity list (event control expression) is optional in a cyclic behavior. In the absence of a sensitivity list, the associated statement executes repeatedly, subject to internal timing controls.

Example: Cyclic Behavior—Waveform Generator

The single-pass and cyclic behaviors produced by the following code generate the clock waveform shown in Figure 5-9:

```
initial clock = 0;

always begin
  #5 clock = ~clock;
end
```

The delay control operator is essential in this model; without it, the simulator would remain at t = 0 and cycle endlessly in a loop, forming *clock* = ~*clock* without advancing simulator time, thereby consuming the resources of the simulator and preventing other behaviors from executing.

FIGURE 5-9   Clock waveform generated by an unconditionally executing cyclic behavior

Example End: Cyclic Behavior—Waveform Generator

5.8   Modeling Level-Sensitive Sequential Logic (Transparent Latches)

A transparent latch can be modeled with cyclic behavior, as an alternative to a structural model or a continuous assignment. The recommended style uses a cyclic behavior with a nonblocking assignment operator.

Example: Cyclic Behavioral Model—Transparent Latch

```
module tr_latch_V2001
( output reg q_out,
  input enable, data
);
  always @ (enable, data)
    begin
      if (enable) q_out <= data;
    end
endmodule
```

The sensitivity list of the cyclic behavior in *tr_latch_V2001* reacts to changes in *enable* and *data*. When *enable* is asserted, the behavior is activated and *q_out* immediately gets the value of *data*. Then the activity flow returns to the **always** construct and is suspended, to await the next change of the event control expression. If *data* changes while *enable* is asserted, the cycle of *q_out* getting *data* repeats. The control flow of the **if** statement has one branch, so while *enable* is deasserted, *q_out* retains the value it had when *enable* was deasserted. While *enable* is deasserted, the events of *data* reactivate the process, but no assignment is made to *q_out*. (*Note*: The nonblocking, or concurrent, assignment operator (<=) is used within the cyclic behavior for a latch.)[13]

Example End: Cyclic Behavioral Model—Transparent Latch

Use the nonblocking assignment operator (<=) in cyclic behaviors modeling latches and edge-sensitive behavior.

5.9   More ANSI C Style Port Declarations

Chapter 3 introduced Verilog 2001's ANSI C style declarations for the ports of modules. The new syntax combines declarations of the mode and type of ports, and may include parameters in the module header. This section will present more elaborate examples.

5.9.1   Port Modes and Type Declaration

Example: ANSI C Declarations—16-bit Adder

Verilog 2001 combines the mode, type, and vector range of a port in a single declaration, as shown in Figure 5-10 . In this example, the outputs *sum* and *c_out* are declared to have type **reg**, because they are assigned value within a cyclic behavior. Also, the input ports have default type **wire**, so the declaration of type **wire** for the input ports may be omitted to further simplify the description.

---

[13]The stratified event queue (See Section 5.19) of a simulator updates the outputs of primitives, continuous assignments, and procedural assignments before updating nonblocking assignments. Thus, concurrent register transfers described by nonblocking assignments do not race with combinational logic updated by procedural assignments at the same time step. The procedural assignment operator can be used, but at the risk of simulation mismatches due to race conditions.

Verilog 1995	Verilog 2001
module Add_16 (c_out, sum, a, b, c_in); **output**　　　　c_out; **output** [15:0]　sum; **input**　[15:0]　a, b; **input**　　　　c_in; **reg**　　　　c_out; **reg**　[15:0]　sum; **wire**　[15:0]　a, b; **wire**　　　　c_in; **always @** (a **or** b **or** c_in) 　{c_out, sum} = a + b + c_in; **endmodule**	**module** Add_16 (c_out, sum, a, b, c_in); **output reg**　　　　c_out; **output reg**　[15:0]　sum; **input**　wire　[15:0]　a, b; **input**　wire　　　　c_in; **always @** (a **or** b **or** c_in) 　{c_out, sum} = a + b + c_in; **endmodule**

FIGURE 5-10　Combined declarations in Verilog 2001

Verilog 1995	Verilog 2001
module Add_16 (c_out, sum, a, b, c_in); **output**　　　　c_out; **output** [15:0]　sum; **input**　[15:0]　a, b; **input**　　　　c_in; **reg**　　　　c_out; **reg**　[15:0]　sum; **wire**　　　　a, b; **wire**　　　　c_in; **always @** (a **or** b **or** c_in) 　{c_out, sum} = a + b + c_in; **endmodule**	**module** Add_16 (**output reg**　[15:0]　sum, 　　　　　**output reg**　　　　c_out, 　　　　　**input**　　[15:0]　a, b, 　　　　　**input**　　　　c_in); **always @** (a **or** b **or** c_in) 　{c_out, sum} = a + b + c_in; **endmodule**

FIGURE 5-11　ANSI-C style port declarations in Verilog 2001

　　The optional description in Figure 5-11 places the declaration of the mode, type, and vector range of the signals in the port, rather than in separate statements.

Example End: ANSI C Declarations—16-bit Adder

5.9.2 Port Parameter List

Parameters are declared as module items in Verilog-IEEE 1364, (i.e., within the body of the module's declaration). In Verilog 2001, parameters may be declared between the module name and the port list.

Example: ANSI C Parameters

Figure 5-12 shows declarations of parameters in Verilog 1995 and Verilog 2001. The new syntax eliminates redundant declarations of the size of a port.

Verilog 1995	Verilog 2001

module Add (c_out, sum, a, b, c_in);
parameter   size = 16;
output   c_out;
output [size-1: 0]   sum;
input   [size-1: 0]   a, b;
input   c_in;
reg   c_out;
reg   [size-1: 0]   sum;
wire   [size-1: 0]   a, b;
 	
wire   c_in;
always @ (a or b or c_in)
  {c_out, sum} = a + b + c_in;
 	
endmodule
	module Add #(parameter size = 16) (c_out, sum, a, b, c_in);
	output reg c_out;
	output reg [size-1: 0] sum ;
	input wire [size-1: 0] a, b;
	input wire c_in;
	
	always @ (a or b or c_in)
	  {c_out, sum} = a + b + c_in;
	
	endmodule

FIGURE 5-12   A Verilog 2001 port declaration including the mode, type, and vector range of the signals

---

Example End: ANSI C Parameters

5.9.3 Signed Ports

Ports may be declared to be signed in two ways: by declaration with the mode of the port or by declaration of the type of the associated port variable.

Example: Signed Ports

In Figure 5-13a, a signed port is declared within the declaration of the input and output ports. In Figure 5-13b, a signed port is declared in a less verbose style within the list of ports. Signed arithmetic can be performed with signed nets, regs, and integers.

```
┌────────────────────────────────────────────────────┐
│                    Verilog 2001                      │
├────────────────────────────────────────────────────┤
│  module Add_Sub (sum_diff, a, b);                    │
│     output signed [63: 0] sum_diff;    // signed value│
│     input  signed [63: 0] a, b;        // signed value│
│     ...                                              │
│  endmodule                                           │
└────────────────────────────────────────────────────┘
```

(a)

```
┌────────────────────────────────────────────────────┐
│                    Verilog 2001                      │
├────────────────────────────────────────────────────┤
│  module Add_Sub (output reg signed  [63: 0] sum_diff,│
│                  input wire signed [63: 0] a, b);    │
│     ...                                              │
│  endmodule                                           │
└────────────────────────────────────────────────────┘
```

(b)

FIGURE 5-13

Example End: Signed Ports

5.10 Constructs for Control Flow in Behavioral Models

The behavioral constructs in Verilog are similar to those found in other programming languages: *case* statements, conditional (*if . . . else . . . if*) statements, and loops. They all control the activity flow within a behavior.

5.10.1 Case Statements

The Verilog *case* statement is similar to its counterpart in other languages (e.g., the switch statement in C). It searches from top-to-bottom to find a match between the case expression and a case item, expressed as a value in Verilog's four-value logic system. The *case* statement executes the statement associated with the first match found, and does not consider any remaining possibilities.

Example: Behavioral Model (case)—32-Bit, Four-Channel Mux

Mux_4_32_case_V2001 is a behavioral model of the four-channel, 32-bit, multiplexer shown in Figure 5-14, with three-state output. The *default* case item covers cases that might occur in simulation, and will help avoid unintentional synthesis of hardware latches if a case statement is not fully decoded. If the case items are not completely

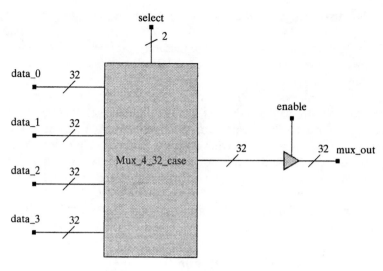

select

2

data_0   32

data_1   32

enable

32   mux_out

Mux_4_32_case   32

data_2   32

data_3   32

FIGURE 5-14   A four-channel, 32-bit multiplexer

decoded, then the default assignment would be treated as a don't-care condition in synthesis and could lead to a smaller circuit. The code is as follows:

```
module Mux_4_32_case_V2001
( output [31: 0]      mux_out,
  input  [31: 0]      data_3, data_2, data_1, data_0,
  input  [1: 0]       select,
  input               enable
);
  reg    [31: 0]      mux_int;

  assign mux_out = enable ? mux_int : 32'bz;

  always @ (data_3, data_2, data_1, data_0, select)      // Verilog 2001
    case (select)
      0:              mux_int = data_0;
      1:              mux_int = data_1;
      2:              mux_int = data_2;
      3:              mux_int = data_3;
      default:        mux_int = 32'bx;      // May execute in simulation
    endcase
endmodule
```

*Example End: Behavioral Model (**case**)—32-Bit, Four-Channel Mux*

The keyword ***always*** in *Mux_4_32_case_V2001* declares a behavior, or process (computational activity flow), that begins execution when the event control expression *(data_3, data_2, data_1, data_0, select)* changes under simulation. The behavior has a simple interpretation: Whenever a datapath input or the select bus change value, decode and update the value of an internal storage variable, *mux_int*. A continuous assignment statement is included in *Mux_4_ 32_case_V2001* to describe a three-state output under the active-high control of *enable*. (Note that *mux_int* must be a declared **reg**).

The **@** operator in *Mux_4_32_case_V2001* denotes event control, meaning that the procedural statements that follow the event control expression do not execute until an activating event occurs. When such an event occurs, the statements execute in sequence, top to bottom. When the last statement completes execution, the computational activity returns to the location of the keyword **always**, where the event control operator, **@**, suspends the behavior until the next sensitizing event occurs. Then the cycle repeats. A cyclic behavior becomes active in simulation at time 0, when the simulation begins, but in this example the activity immediately suspends until the event control expression changes. Then the **case** statement executes, and assigns value to *mux_int*, and immediately returns control to the event control operator.

5.10.2 Conditional (*if*) Statements

The conditional (*if*) statement executes a statement if a condition is true. Two other variations are supported: *if . . . else*, which executes one of two statements depending on a condition, and *the if . . . else . . . if* statement, which models more complex activity flows.

---

*Example: Behavioral Model (Nested **if**)—32-Bit, four-channel Mux*

An alternative model uses nested conditional statements (*if*) to model a multiplexer. The model *Mux_4_32_if* also includes a continuous assignment that forms a three-state output:

```
module Mux_4_32_if_V2001
( output [31: 0]      mux_out,
  input  [31: 0]      data_3, data_2, data_1, data_0,
  input  [1: 0]       select,
  input               enable
);
  reg    [31: 0]      mux_int;

  assign  mux_out = enable ? mux_int : 32'bz;

  always @ ( data_3, data_2, data_1, data_0, select)      // Verilog 2001
    if (select == 0) mux_int = data_0; else
     if (select == 1) mux_int = data_1; else
      if (select == 2) mux_int = data_2; else
       if (select == 3) mux_int = data_3; else mux_int = 32'bx;
endmodule
```

---

*Example End: Behavioral Model (Nested **if**)—32-Bit, four-channel Mux*

Example: Behavioral Model—8:3 Encoder

Two implementations of a an 8:3 encoder are shown next. Neither decodes all possible patterns of *Data* fully, but both cover the remaining outcomes with a ***default*** assignment. The result of synthesis, shown in Figure 5-15, is combinational logic. This model is intended for applications where only the indicated words of *Data* occur in operation. The default assignments will be don't-cares in synthesis and are needed to prevent synthesis of a circuit having latched outputs.[14] Following Figure 5-15 is the code for the two implementations:

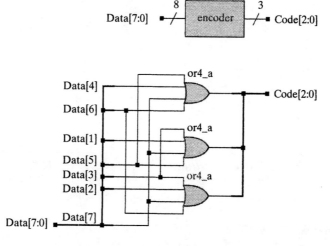

FIGURE 5-15   Result of synthesizing an encoder described by *if* statements or a **case** statement

```
module encoder_V2001
( output reg      [2: 0] Code,
  input           [7: 0] Data
);

always @ (Data)
  begin
    if (Data == 8'b00000001) Code = 0; else
    if (Data == 8'b00000010) Code = 1; else
    if (Data == 8'b00000100) Code = 2; else
    if (Data == 8'b00001000) Code = 3; else
    if (Data == 8'b00010000) Code = 4; else
    if (Data == 8'b00100000) Code = 5; else
    if (Data == 8'b01000000) Code = 6; else
    if (Data == 8'b10000000) Code = 7; else Code = 3'bx;
  end
```

---

[14]For an in-depth treatment of logic synthesis with Verilog, see [7].

```
/* Alternative description is given below

always @ (Data)
  case (Data)
    8'b00000001 : Code = 0;
    8'b00000010 : Code = 1;
    8'b00000100 : Code = 2;
    8'b00001000 : Code = 3;
    8'b00010000 : Code = 4;
    8'b00100000 : Code = 5;
    8'b01000000 : Code = 6;
    8'b10000000 : Code = 7;
    default      : Code = 3'bx;
  endcase
*/
endmodule
```

Example End: Behavioral Model—8:3 Encoder

Example: Behavioral Model—Alternative 8:3 Priority Encoder

The following code captures alternative behaviors describing an 8:3 priority encoder:[15]

```
module priority_V2001
( output reg    [2: 0]     Code,
  output                   valid_data,
  input         [7: 0]     Data
);

  assign                   valid_data = |Data; // "reduction or" operator
  always @ (Data)
    begin
      if (Data[7]) Code = 7; else
      if (Data[6]) Code = 6; else
      if (Data[5]) Code = 5; else
      if (Data[4]) Code = 4; else
      if (Data[3]) Code = 3; else
      if (Data[2]) Code = 2; else
      if (Data[1]) Code = 1; else
      if (Data[0]) Code = 0; else
                   Code = 3'bx;
```

---

[15]The *reduction or* operator is used to form the logic for valid_data. The operator forms the *or* of the bits in a word.

```
        end

/*// Alternative description is given below

always @ (Data)
  casex (Data)
     8'b1xxxxxxx   : Code = 7;
     8'b01xxxxxx   : Code = 6;
     8'b001xxxxx   : Code = 5;
     8'b0001xxxx   : Code = 4;
     8'b00001xxx   : Code = 3;
     8'b000001xx   : Code = 2;
     8'b0000001x   : Code = 1;
     8'b00000001   : Code = 0;
       default     : Code = 3'bx;
  endcase
*/
endmodule
```

The result of synthesizing the circuit is shown in Figure 5-16. Notice that the conditional (*if*) statement has an implied priority of execution and that the *casex* statement, combined with *x* in the case items, also implies priority. The *casex* statement ignores *x* and *z* in bits of the *case item* (e.g., *Data[6]*) and the *case expression* (*Data*); they are

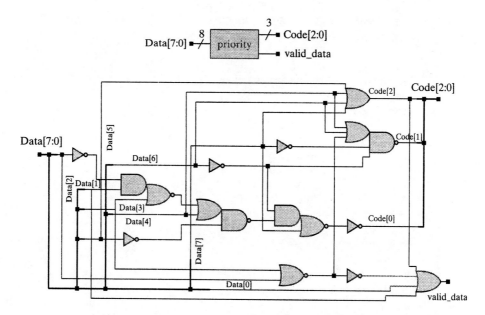

FIGURE 5-16   Circuit synthesized for **priority**, an 8:3 priority encoder

treated as don't-cares. The default assignments in both styles provide flexibility to the logic optimizer of a synthesis tool.

Example End: Behavioral Model—Alternative 8:3 Priority Encoder

Example: Behavioral Model—3:8 Decoder

A 3:8 decoder is described by the following alternative behaviors:

```
module decoder_V2001
( output reg      [7: 0] Data,
  input           [2: 0] Code
);
    always @ (Code)
    begin
      if (Code == 0) Data = 8'b00000001; else
      if (Code == 1) Data = 8'b00000010; else
      if (Code == 2) Data = 8'b00000100; else
      if (Code == 3) Data = 8'b00001000; else
      if (Code == 4) Data = 8'b00010000; else
      if (Code == 5) Data = 8'b00100000; else
      if (Code == 6) Data = 8'b01000000; else
      if (Code == 7) Data = 8'b10000000; else
                     Data = 8'bx;
    end
/* Alternative description is given below
    always @ (Code)
    case (Code)
      0             : Data = 8'b00000001;
      1             : Data = 8'b00000010;
      2             : Data = 8'b00000100;
      3             : Data = 8'b00001000;
      4             : Data = 8'b00010000;
      5             : Data = 8'b00100000;
      6             : Data = 8'b01000000;
      7             : Data = 8'b10000000;
      default       : Data = 8'bx;
    endcase
    */
endmodule
```

The decoders synthesize to the circuit in Figure 5-17.

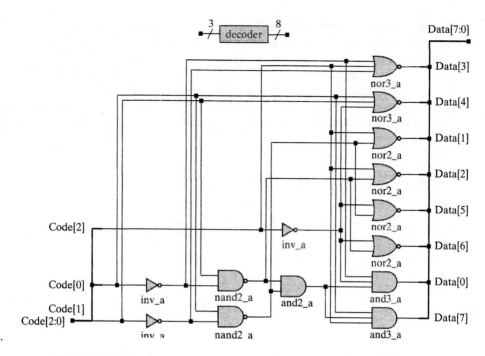

FIGURE 5-17   Circuit synthesized for **decoder**, a behavioral model of a 3:8 decoder

---

Example End: Behavioral Model—3:8 Decoder

5.10.3 Loops Constructs for Modeling Repetitive Algorithms

An algorithm for modeling the behavior of a digital machine may execute some or all
of its steps repeatedly in a given machine cycle, depending on whether the steps executed unconditionally or not. Verilog has four loop constructs: *for*, *repeat*, *forever*, and
while. Each type of loop may be disabled by using the keyword *disable* to terminate
the activity of a named block statement.

for **Loops**   A **for** loop has the form

> **for** (initial_statement; control_expression; index_statement)
>   statement_for_execution;

At the beginning of execution of a *for* loop, *initial_statement* executes once,
usually to initialize a register variable (i.e., an *integer* or a *reg*) that controls the
loop. If *control_expression* is true, the *statement_for_execution* will execute.[16] *After*

---

[16]Statement_for_execution can be a single statement or a block statement (i.e., **begin . . . end**).

the *statement_for_execution* has executed, *the index_statement* will execute, usually to increment a counter. Then the activity flow will return to the beginning of the ***for*** statement and check the value of the *control_expression* again. If *control_expression* is false, the loop terminates and the activity flow proceeds to whatever statement immediately follows the *statement_for_execution*. Note: The value of the register variable governed by *control_expression* in the ***for*** loop may be changed in the body of the loop during execution. Consequently, the number of iterations may be determined dynamically.

Example: Behavioral Model—Majority Circuit (for Loop)

A majority circuit asserts its output if a majority of the bits of an input word is asserted. The description in *Majority_4b* is suitable for a 4-bit datapath and uses a ***case*** statement to decode the bit patterns. However, this model is hardwired and becomes cumbersome for long wordlength. The parameterized alternative, *Majority_V2001*, uses a ***for*** loop to count the asserted bits in *Data*. A final procedural assignment asserts *Y* after the loop has completed execution, provided that *count* exceeds the value defined by the parameter *majority*. The parameters in *Majority_V2001* provide flexibility in sizing *Data* and *count* and in setting an assertion threshold, *majority*. Figure 5-18 shows a segment of simulation results for *Majority_V2001*. The code for that module, as well as that for *Majority_46*, follows the figure:

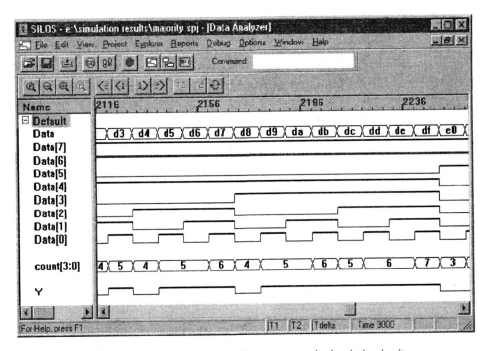

FIGURE 5-18 Simulation results for a parameterized majority circuit

```
module  Majority_4b (Y, A, B, C, D);
 input   A, B, C, D;
 output  Y;
 reg     Y;
 always @ (A or B or C or D) begin
  case ({A, B, C, D})
    7, 11, 13, 14, 15:      Y = 1;
    default                 Y = 0;
  endcase
 end
endmodule

module Majority_V2001
# (parameter     size = 8,
                 max = 3,
                 majority = 5
)
( input          [size-1: 0]        Data,
  output reg     [max-1: 0]         Y
);
  reg            [max-1: 0]         count;
  integer                          k;

  always @ (Data) begin
  count = 0;
  for (k = 0; k < size; k = k + 1) begin
    if (Data[k] == 1) count = count + 1;
  end
    Y = (count >= majority);
  end
endmodule
```

---

*Example End: Behavioral Model—Majority Circuit (**for** Loop)*

Disabling Loops   The ***disable*** statement is used to prematurely terminate a named block of procedural statements, thereby terminating the activity of a loop if the named block is associated with the loop. The effect of executing the ***disable*** is to transfer the activity flow to the statement that immediately follows the named block or task in which ***disable*** was encountered during simulation.

---

*Example: **for** Loop with **disable***

The model *find_first_one_V2001* finds the location of the first 1 in a 16-bit word (assumed to contain a 1). When ***disable*** executes, the activity flow exits the ***for*** loop, proceeds to ***end***, and then returns to the ***always*** to await the next event on *trigger*. At that time, *index_value* holds the value at which *A_word* is 1. Here is the code:

```
module find_first_one_V2001
( output reg     [3: 0]     index_value,
  input          [15: 0]    A_word,
  input                     trigger
);
always @ (trigger)
  begin: search_for_1      // Named block
    index_value = 0;         // Redundant
    for (index_value = 0; index_value < 15; index_value = index_value + 1)
      if (A_word[index_value] == 1) disable search_for_1;
  end
endmodule
```

---

*Example End: for Loop with **disable***

---

repeat Loops   The **repeat** loop executes a statement or block of statements a speci-fied number of times. When the activity flow within a behavior reaches the **repeat** keyword, an expression is evaluated once to determine the number of times that the statement is to be executed. If the expression evaluates to x or z, the result will be treated as 0 and the *statement* will not be executed, (i.e., the execution skips to the next statement in the behavior). Otherwise, the execution repeats for the specified number of times, unless it is prematurely terminated by a ***disable*** statement within the activity flow.

---

*Example: **repeat** Loop*

A **repeat** loop is used in the following fragment of code to initialize a memory array:

```
...
word_address = 0;
repeat (memory_size)
  begin
    memory [ word_address] = 0;
    word_address = word_address + 1;
  end
...
```

---

*Example End: **repeat** Loop*

---

forever Loops   The **forever** loop causes unconditional repetitive execution of state-ments, subject to the ***disable*** statement, and is a convenient construct for describing clocks in testbenches.

Example: Clock Generator (*forever* Loop)

Clock generators are used in testbenches of synchronous circuits. A flexible clock generator will be parameterized for a variety of applications. The following code produces the symmetric waveforms in Figure 5-19 under simulation:

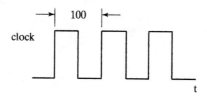

FIGURE 5-19   Clock waveforms implemented with a *forever* loop

```
parameter half_cycle = 50;

initial
  begin: clock_loop        // Note: clock_loop is a named block of statements
    clock = 0;
    forever
     begin
       #half_cycle clock <= 1;
       #half_cycle clock <= 0;
     end
  end

initial
  #350 disable clock_loop;
```

In the preceding code, the loop mechanism *forever* executes until the simulation terminates. This example also illustrates how the activity of an *initial* behavior may continue for the duration of a simulation, without expiring. The *disable* statement terminates execution after 3,500 time steps by disabling the named block *clock_loop*.

An alternative clock generator that cycles for the duration of the simulation is given by the following code:

```
initial begin
  clock = 0;
  forever #half_cycle clock <= ~ clock;
end
```

Example End: Clock Generator (*forever* Loop)

while Loops   A Verilog *while* loop has the form

```
while (expression) statement;
```

When the *while* statement is encountered during the activity flow of a cyclic or single-pass behavior, *statement*[17] executes repeatedly while a Boolean *expression* is true. When the *expression* is false, the activity flow skips to whatever statement follows *statement*. For example, the statement that follows increments a synchronous counter while *enable* is asserted by an external agent. Termination of a *while* loop is determined dynamically during simulation.

Example: **while** *Loop*

```
initial begin
  count = 0;
  while (enable) #5 count = count + 1;
end
```

Example End: **while** *Loop*

In many situations, loops can be constructed using any of the four basic looping mechanisms of Verilog, but be aware that some EDA synthesis tools will synthesize only the *for* loop. Also, notice that *always* and *forever* are not the same construct, though both are cyclic. The *always* construct declares a concurrent behavior; the *forever* loop is a computational activity flow mechanism, and is used only *within* a behavior. The execution of a *forever* loop is not necessarily concurrent with any other activity flow. Another significant distinction is that *forever* loops can be nested, while cyclic and single-pass behaviors cannot. Finally, a *forever* loop executes only when it is reached within a sequential activity flow. An *always* behavior becomes active and can execute at the beginning of simulation.

5.11 Initialization of Variables in Simulation

Variables of type *wire* and *reg* are initialized to a default value[18] of *x* in the first cycle of simulation. Integer and time variables are initialized to 0; *real* and *realtime* variables are initialized to the default value 0.0. In Verilog 1995, a separate declaration of a behavior must be used to override the default initial value of a register variable.

 Verilog 2001 combines the declaration of an initial value with the declaration of the type of a *reg, integer, time, real*, or *realtime* variable that is declared at the module level (i.e., a variable declared elsewhere, such as in a task, may not be declared to have an initial value). A *wire* remains at its default value until the *wire* is driven to a different value in simulation. A *wire* may inherit an initial value from a continuous assignment.

---

[17]*Statement* can be a single statement or a block statement (i.e., **begin. ... end**).
[18]Recall that the default net type can be overridden by a compiler directive.

Verilog 1995	Verilog 2001

module Clk_gen (clock);
  parameter   delay = 5;
  output   clock;
  reg   clock;
 	
  initial begin
   clock = 0;
   forever #delay clock = ~clock;
  end
 	
endmodule
	module Clk_Gen #(**parameter** delay = 5) (**output** clock);
	  reg clock = 0);
	
	  initial forever #delay clock = ~clock;
	
	endmodule

FIGURE 5-20

Verilog 1995	Verilog 2001

module Clk_gen (clock);
  parameter   delay = 5;
  output   clock;
  reg   clock;
 	
  initial begin
   clock = 0;
   forever #delay clock = ~clock;
  end
 	
endmodule
	module Clk_Gen # (**parameter** delay = 5) (**output reg** clock = 0);
	
	  initial forever #delay clock = ~clock;
	
	endmodule

FIGURE 5-21

An example of initialization of a variable in Verilog 2001 is given in Figure 5-20. An initial value may be assigned to a variable as part of an ANSI C style of a port declaration, as shown in Figure 5-21.

5.12 Named Events

In addition to the data type families of nets and registers, Verilog has an abstract type called a *named event*. Declared by the keyword ***event***, a named event provides a high-level abstract mechanism of communication and synchronization within and between modules [1]. The occurrence of the event itself is determined explicitly by a procedural statement using the event-trigger operator, $->$. Named events are not supported by synthesis tools.

Example: Named Event

In module Flop_event, the abstract event *up_edge* is triggered when *clock* has a positive edge transition. A second behavior detects the event of *up_edge* and assigns value to the flip-flop's output, subject to an asynchronous *reset* signal. Admittedly, this is not a recommended way to model a flip-flop, but it illustrates the use of named events. Named events can be triggered remotely, across hierarchical boundaries in a testbench, via the mechanism of hierarchical dereferencing [1, 2]. Here is the code for Flop_event:

```
module  Flop_event (clock, reset, data, q, q_bar);
  input   clock, reset, data;
  output q, q_bar;
  reg     q;
  event  up_edge;

  assign q_bar = ~q;
  always @ (posedge clock) -> up_edge;
  always @ (up_edge or negedge reset)
    begin
      if (reset == 0) q <= 0; else q <= data;
    end
endmodule
```

If *up_edge* was triggered remotely, e.g., in some_module, it could be referenced by its hierarchical pathname, say *Top.some_module.upedge.*

Example End: Named Event

A named event must be declared before it is used. No hardware needs to be specified to hold the value of the named event (i.e., no **reg** is needed.), or to transmit the value to another module (i.e., no net is needed). Thus, a suspended behavioral (procedural) statement in one module can resume execution on the basis of behavior that occurs in another module, or in another behavioral statement within the same module, with no need for additional data objects supporting the transaction.

5.13   wait Statement

The *wait* construct models level-sensitive behavior by suspending (but not terminating) the activity flow in a behavior, until an *expression* is TRUE. If *expression* evaluates to TRUE when the statement is encountered, the execution is not suspended. If *expression* is FALSE, the simulator suspends the activity thread that contains the *wait*, and establishes a monitoring mechanism that observes a condition *expression*. Other processes may execute while the process with the *wait* is suspended. When the condition *expression* becomes TRUE, execution resumes with the *statement_or_null* that is associated with **wait**. Synthesis tools do not support the *wait* construct, but it may be useful in testbenches.

---
*Example: **wait** Statement*

When the activity flow of the behavior within *example_of_wait* reaches the **wait** statement, *enable* is evaluated to determine whether it is TRUE or FALSE. If it is TRUE, the activity flow continues. Otherwise it suspends operation until *enable* becomes TRUE. The following is the code:

```
module example_of_wait ( );
...
  always
    begin
...
      wait (enable) register_a = register_b;
      #10 register_c = register_d;
...
    end
endmodule
```

---
*Example End: **wait** Statement*

5.14 Design Management with Functions, Tasks, and Parameters

Verilog models are a legacy of their author. Whether a model is useful to anyone else depends on the correctness and clarity of the description. Even a correct model has limited utility if its credibility is compromised by poor documentation and style. Verilog has two types of subprograms that can improve the clarity of a description by encapsulating and organizing code: tasks and functions. Tasks create a hierarchical organization of the procedural statements within a Verilog behavior; functions replace an expression. Tasks and functions let designers manage a smaller segment of code. Both constructs facilitate a readable style of code, with a single identifier conveying the meaning of many lines of code. Encapsulation of Verilog code into tasks or functions hides the details of an implementation from the outside world. Overall, tasks and functions improve the readability, portability, and maintainability of a model.

5.14.1 Functions

Verilog functions are declared within a parent module and can be referenced in any valid expression, for example in the RHS of a continuous assignment statement. A function is implemented by an expression and returns a value at the location of the function's identifier. Functions may implement only combinational behavior, (i.e., they compute a value immediately on the basis of the value of the parameters that are passed into the function). Consequently, they may not contain timing controls (no delay control (**#**), event control (**@**), or *wait* statements), and may not invoke a task. They may, however, call other functions.

A function may contain a declaration of inputs and local variables. The value of a function is returned by its name when the expression calling the function is executed. Consequently, a function may not have any declared output or inout port (argument), but must have at least one input argument. The execution, or evaluation, of a function takes place in zero time, (i.e., in the same time step that the calling expression is evaluated by the host simulator). The definition of a function implicitly defines an internal register variable having the same name, range, and type as the function itself; this variable must be assigned value within the function body by assigning value to the identifier of the function.

Example: Behavioral Model –Improved Readability with Functions

The Verilog model *arithmetic_unit* uses functions with descriptive names to make the source code more readable:

```
module arithmetic_unit_V2001
( output          [4: 0] result_1,
  output          [3: 0] result_2,
  input           [3: 0] operand_1, operand_2
);

  assign result_1 = sum_of_operands (operand_1, operand_2);
  assign result_2 = largest_operand (operand_1, operand_2);

  function [4: 0] sum_of_operands;
    input [3: 0] operand_1, operand_2;

    sum_of_operands = operand_1 + operand_2;
  endfunction

  function [3: 0] largest_operand;
    input [3: 0] operand_1, operand_2;

    largest_operand = (operand_1 >= operand_2) ? operand_1 : operand_2;
  endfunction
endmodule
```

The combinational circuit synthesized from *arithmetic_unit_V2001* is shown in Figure 5-22.

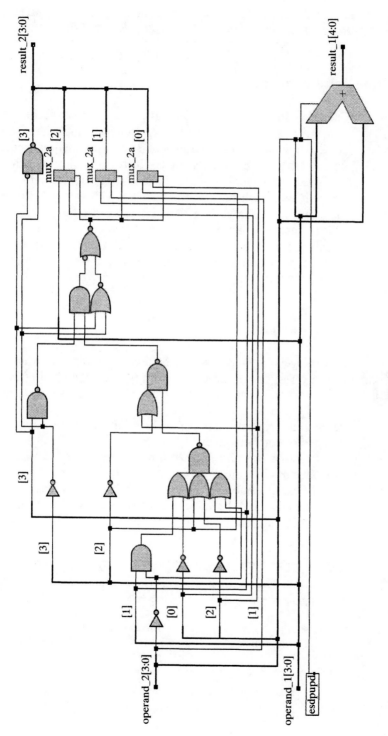

FIGURE 5-22 Circuit synthesized from *arithmetic_unit*.

Example End: Behavioral Model –Improved Readability with Functions

5.14.2 Recursive Functions

Functions in Verilog 1995 are static, and may not include delay constructs (i.e., **#, @**, or **wait**). Functions effectively implement combinational logic equivalent to an expression. Because a function executes in zero time, there is no possibility for concurrent calls to the same function. However, subsequent calls to a function overwrite its memory space. If a function calls itself recursively, each call will overwrite the memory of the previous call. In Verilog 2001, a function can be declared **automatic**, which causes distinct memory to be allocated each time a function is called. The memory is released when the function exits. The classic example of recursion in Figure 5-23 compares a recursive implementation in Verilog 2001 with an invalid description in Verilog 1995.

5.14.3 Constant Functions

In Verilog 1995, functions may be used only in places where a nonconstant expression can be used, which restricts their utility. For example, the widths and depths of arrays can be hard wired by fixed numbers, defined by parameters, which are constants. Although parameters can be defined in terms of other parameters, this mechanism for scaling a design can be cumbersome.

Verilog 2001 supports *constant functions*, which can be called wherever a constant is required. Constant functions are evaluated at elaboration time, and do not depend on the values of variables at simulation time. Only constant expressions may be passed to a constant function, not the value of a net or register variable. Consequently, a constant function may reference only parameters, localparams,[19] locally declared

Verilog 1995	Verilog 2001
function [63: 0] Bogus **input** [31:0] N; **if** (N == 1) Bogus = 1; **else** Bogus = N * Bogus (N-1); **endfunction**	**function automatic** [63: 0] factorial **input** [31:0] N; **if** (N == 1) factorial = 1; **else** factorial = N * factorial (N-1); **endfunction**

FIGURE 5-23   A recursive function in Verilog 2001

---

[19]See Section 5.16.2.

variables, and other constant functions. The parameters that are used by a function must be declared before the function is called, and the memory used by a function is released after the function has been elaborated.

Avoid using ***defparam***[20] statements to redefine the parameters within a function, because the value returned may differ between simulators. The parameters within an instance of a module can be redefined unambiguously by the # construct. Constant functions may not call system functions and tasks and may not use hierarchical path references.

5.14.4 Signed Functions

 Functions in Verilog 1995 may be called any place that an expression can be used. The value returned by a function is signed if and only if the function is declared to be an integer. With the reserved keyword ***signed***, Verilog 2001 allows signed arithmetic to be performed on returned values of a vector. Figure 5-24 identifies the possible types of a function in Verilog 1995 and Verilog 2001. Remember that the data types of the variables in an expression, not the operators, determine whether signed or unsigned arithmetic is performed. Signed arithmetic is performed only when all of the operands are signed variables.

5.14.5 Tasks

Tasks are declared within a module, and they may be referenced only from within a cyclic or single-pass behavior. A task can have parameters passed to it, and the results of executing the task can be passed back to the environment. When a task is called, copies of the parameters in the environment are associated with the inputs, outputs,

Example	Returned Value	Verilog 1995	Verilog 2001
function sum	single bit	x	x
function [31:0] sum	unsigned vector of 32 bits	x	x
function integer sum	signed vector of 32 bits	x	x
function real sum	64-bit double-precison	x	x
function time sum	unsigned 64-bit vector	x	x
function signed [63:0] sum	signed 64-bit vector		x

FIGURE 5-24   Types of functions in Verilog 2001

---

[20]See Section 5.16.1.

and inouts within the task, according to the order in which the inputs, outputs, and inouts are declared. The variables in the environment are also visible to the task. Additional, local variables may be declared within a task. A word of caution: a task can call itself, but the memory supporting the variables of a task is shared by all calls. The language does not support recursion, so anticipate side effects.[21]

A task must be named, and may include local declarations of any number or combination of the following: *parameter, input, output, inout, reg, integer, real, time, realtime,* and *event.* The arguments of the task retain the type they hold in the environment that invokes the task. For example, if a wire bus is passed to the task, it may not have its value altered by an assignment statement within the task. All the arguments to the task are passed by value—not by a pointer to the value. When a task is invoked, its formal and actual arguments are associated in the order in which the task's ports have been declared (i.e., positional association).

Example: Behavioral Model - Task

The synchronous adder, *adder_task*, contains a user-defined task that adds two 4-bit words and a carry bit:

```
module adder_task (c_out, sum, clk, reset, c_in, data_a, data_b, clk);
  output              c_out;
  output     [3: 0]   sum;
  input      [3: 0]   data_a, data_b;
  input               clk, reset;
  input               c_in;

  reg                 c_out;
  reg        [3: 0]   sum;

  always @ (posedge clk or posedge reset)
    if (reset)     {c_out, sum} <= 0; else
    add_values (c_out, sum, data_a, data_b, c_in);

  task add_values;
    output          c_out;
    output  [3: 0]  sum;
    input   [3: 0]  data_a, data_b;
    input           c_in;

    begin
      {c_out, sum} <= data_a + (data_b + c_in);
    end
  endtask
endmodule
```

---

[21]Verilog 2001 adds automatic tasks and functions, which allocate unique storage to each call of a task or function, thereby supporting recursion. See Section 5.14.6.

The circuit produced by the synthesis tool is in Figure 5-25.

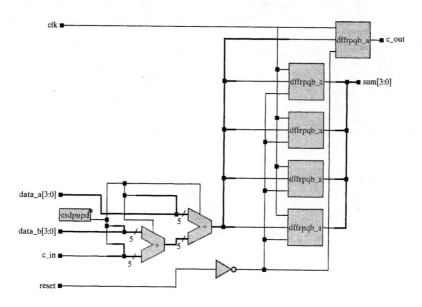

FIGURE 5-25   Circuit synthesized from *adder_task*

Example End: Behavioral Model - Task

5.14.6 Reentrant Tasks

Tasks in Verilog 1995 are allocated static memory that persists for the duration of simulation. The memory space of a task is shared by all calls to the task. Task variables retain their value between calls. Tasks may be called from multiple concurrent behaviors, setting up the possibility that data may be overwritten and compromised before a given call to a task is complete. As noted in [1, 3], designers work around this problem by placing the same task in multiple modules, isolating their memory space, but this wastes resources and complicates maintenance of the code.

Verilog 2001 supports *reentrant tasks* with dynamic allocation and deallocation of memory during simulation each time a task is called. The keyword **automatic** designates a task having dynamic memory allocation. Such tasks are not static, and their allocated memory is not shared. Because the memory allocated for an automatic task is released when the task completes execution, models using such tasks must not reference data generated by the task after the task exits. This imposes restrictions on the style of code that may use automatic tasks (See [1, 3]).

Verilog 1995	Verilog 2001
function [16: 0] sum_FA; **input** [15: 0] a, b; **input** c_in; sum_FA = a + b + c_in; **endfunction**	**function** [16: 0] sum_FA **(input** [15: 0] a, b, **input** c_in); sum_FA = a + b + c_in; **endfunction**

(a)

Verilog 1995	Verilog 2001
task sum_FA; **output** [16: 0] sum_FA; **input** [15: 0] a, b; **input** c_in; sum = a + b + c_in; **endtask**	**task** sum_FA **(output** [16: 0] sum, **input** [15: 0] a, b, **input** c_in); sum = a + b + c_in; **endtask**

(b)

FIGURE 5-26   Syntax for declarations of (a) functions and (b) tasks in Verilog 1995 and Verilog 2001

5.14.7 ANSI C Style Declarations of Functions and Tasks

The syntax of Verilog 1995 for declaring functions and tasks separates the arguments of a function or task from its name and associates inputs and outputs with their order in separately made declarations.

Verilog 2001 provides an optional ANSI C style that associates the arguments with the name, using the same syntax as that for modules. Examples of the new syntax for functions and tasks are shown in Figure 5-26.

The type of the inputs and outputs of a function or task is inferred to be **reg** (i.e., a vector of bits), unless specified by a declaration within the function of task. Verilog 2001 allows the type to be declared within the port of the function or task, as shown in Figure 5-27.

5.15   Parameter Redefinition

Parameters make models more configurable, readable, extendable, and portable. Declared by the keyword *parameter*, parameters in Verilog 1995 are run-time constants, and their value can be changed only before simulation, during elaboration. There are

Verilog 1995	Verilog 2001

function real sum_Real;
  input   real   a, b;
 	
  sum_Real = a + b;
 	
endfunction
	function real sum_Real (input real a, b);
	
	  sum_Real = a + b;
	
	endfunction

(a)

Verilog 1995	Verilog 2001

task sum_Real;
  output real   sum;
  input real   a, b;
 	
  sum = a + b;
 	
endtask
	task sum_Real
	  (output real sum, input real a, b);
	
	  sum = a + b;
	
	endtask

(b)

FIGURE 5-27   Declarations of type for (a) functions and (b) tasks in Verilog 1995 and Verilog 2001

two mechanisms for redefining the value of a parameter: indirectly (remotely), using the keyword *defparam*, and implicitly, by *in-line redefinition*.

In-line, or direct, substitution overrides the value of the parameter on a module instance basis.

Example: In-line Parameter Redefinition

The parameters declared within the *G2* instance of *modXnor* are overridden by including #(4, 5) in the instantiation of the module. The code is as follows:

```
module modXnor (y_out, a, b);
   parameter                    size = 8, delay = 15;
   output          [size-1:0]   y_out;
   input           [size-1:0]   a, b;
   wire            [size-1:0]   #delay y_out = a ~^ b;        // bitwise xnor
endmodule

module Param ();
   wire            [7:0]        y1_out;
   wire            [3:0]        y2_out;
   reg             [7:0]        b1, c1;
   reg             [3:0]        b2, c2;
   modXnor G1 (y1_out, b1, c1);              // Uses default parameters
   modXnor #(4, 5) G2 (y2_out, b2, c2);      // Overrides default parameters
endmodule
```

The values given in the instantiation replace the values of *size* and *delay* that were given in the declaration of *modXnor*. The replacement is made in the order that the parameters were originally declared. This method can be cumbersome if the edited value is near the end of a long list.

Example End: In-line Parameter Redefinition

Indirect substitution uses hierarchical dereferencing to override the value of a parameter in a module. Declaring a separate module in which the **defparam** statement is used with the hierarchical pathname of the parameters that are to be overridden does this most conveniently. (*Note*: This feature can be misused because it allows annotation from anywhere within a design hierarchy, creating the possibility of accidental changes.)

Example: Indirect Parameter Redefinition

In *hdref_param* the values of *size* and *delay* in instance *G2* of *modXnor* are overridden by the statements in module *annotate*:

```
module hdref_Param;              // a top level module
    wire          [7:0] y1_out;
    wire          [3:0] y2_out;
    reg           [7:0] b1, c1;
    reg           [3:0] b2, c2;

    modXnor       G1 (y1_out, b1, c1),
                  G2 (y2_out, b2, c2);   // instantiation
endmodule

module annotate;                 // a separate "annotation" module
    defparam
    hdref_Param.G2.size = 4,      // parameter assignment by
    hdref_Param.G2.delay = 5;     // hierarchical reference name
endmodule

module modXnor (y_out, a, b);
    parameter              size = 8, delay = 15;
    output     [size-1:0]  y_out;
    input      [size-1:0]  a, b;
    wire       [size-1:0]  #delay y_out = a ~^ b;   // bitwise xnor
endmodule
```

Example End: Indirect Parameter Redefinition

The declaration redefining a parameter with the **defparam** keyword can be placed anywhere in the design hierarchy, and it redefines the value of a parameter at any location in the design hierarchy, via hierarchical dereferencing of path names. This can compromise readability and poses the risk that parameters can be changed inadvertently from any location in the design, since parameters are not fixed constants. Inline redefinition requires that text adhering to the syntax #(value_1, value_2, ..., value_m) be inserted after the instance name of a module, to redefine parameters declared within the module. The order of the sequence of value_1, value_2 ... must correspond to the order of the sequence in which the parameters are declared within the module. This is cumbersome when the modules contain several parameters, not all of which are to be redefined. Because the parameters are not explicitly named in this syntax for redefinition, the practice is prone to error, and renders the model less readable.

Verilog 1995 also supports *specparams* (*specify parameters*), which may be declared and used only within *specify ... endspecify* blocks[22] within a module. A *specparam* is local to the block in which it is declared, and may be used only within the block. A standard delay format (SDF) file can redefine the value of a *specparam*. The risk, again, is that specparams could mistakenly be redefined.

A parameter inherits its size and type from the final value assigned to it during elaboration, before simulation, which need not be the same type that was assigned to the parameter when it was declared in its parent module. For example, the value assigned to a parameter could be an unsized integer (at least 32 bits), a sized integer, a real (floating point) number, or a string. Other parameters can be operands in the expression that declares the value of a parameter. Thus, in Verilog 1995, the size and type of a parameter can be changed when the parameter is redefined, which could produce undesirable side effects, because the operations performed in an expression depend on the size and type of its operands. Figure 5-28 displays the rules used by Verilog 1995 to determine the arithmetic performed by the operands in an expression.

Verilog 1995	
Operands	Operation
All operands are signed integers	Signed arithmetic
An operand is unsigned	Unsigned integer arithmetic
At least one operand is a real value	Floating point arithmetic

FIGURE 5-28   Rules for arithmetic in Verilog 1995

---

[22]Specify blocks are used to declare input-output paths across a module, assign delay to those paths, and declare timing checks (for example, the setup time of a flip-flop) to be performed on signals [2]. We will not consider timing checks in this introductory text.

Verilog 2001				
Specified by Declaration			Subject to Redefinition	Redefinition Rule
Sign	Range	Type		
No	No	No	Yes	Same as Verilog 1995[1]
Yes	Yes	No	No	Parameter is signed / Size is specified by the range
Yes	No	No	Inherits size	Parameter is signed / Size is inherited from last redefinition
No	Yes	No	No	Parameter is unsigned / Size is fixed by range
		Yes	Yes	Parameter retains type

[1]In Verilog 1995, a parameter inherits the vector size and type of the last parameter redefinition.

FIGURE 5-29   Rules for arithmetic in Verilog 2001

Verilog 2001 provides explicit definition of the size and data type of a parameter. Figure 5-29 shows the rules for determining how the size and type of a parameter are redefined in Verilog 2001, by an expression having arithmetic operators. When the sign, size, or type of a parameter is explicitly declared, it cannot be overridden by a subsequent parameter value redefinition.

5.15.1 Parameter Redefinition by Name Association

Verilog 2001 provides *explicit in-line redefinition* of parameters on a module-instance basis by name association. The syntax for redefining the parameters of an instantiated module is as follows:

```
module_name
instance_name
    #(.parameter_name (parameter_value), ...) (port_connections);
```

This feature of Verilog 2001 explicitly identifies the redefined parameters. The redefinition does not depend on the order in which the parameters are defined in the associated module. Consequently, the code is self-documenting and more readable than its counterpart in Verilog 1995.

5.15.2 Local Parameters

Verilog 2001 introduces local parameters (keyword, *localparam*), whose value cannot be directly redefined from outside the module in which they are declared.[23] Figure 5-30 compares parameters, specify parameters, and local parameters. Although a *localparam*

| | | Verilog 2001 | | |
| | | Verilog 1995 | | |
		parameter	specparam	localparam
Location of declaration	Module item	yes	no	yes
	Task item	yes	no	yes
	Function item	yes	no	yes
	Specify block	no	yes	no
Method of direct redefinition	By a defparam	yes	no	no
	Redefined in-line	yes	no	no
	SDF files	no	yes	no
Method of indirect redefinition by assignment of value	From another parameter	yes	yes	yes
	From a localparam	yes	yes	no
	From a specparam	no	yes	no
Allowed reference	Within a module	yes	no	yes
	Within a specify block	no	yes	no

FIGURE 5-30   Parameters in Verilog 1995 and Verilog 2001

---

[23]It might be desirable to protect, for example, the state assignment codes from inadvertent change.

cannot be directly redefined, it can be indirectly redefined by assigning it the value of another parameter, which can be changed by the methods described.

5.15.3 A Comparison of Styles for Behavioral Modeling

We have already seen how a 2-bit comparator can be described by a gate-level structure and by a Boolean equation-based behavioral model. Next, we present simpler and more readable alternatives that also use continuous assignments, and then we contrast modeling styles based on (1) continuous assignments, (2) Register Transfer Logic (RTL), and (3) behavioral algorithms.

Before considering alternative behavioral models, note that a register variable may be assigned value only by a procedural statement, a user-defined sequential primitive, a task, or a function. A reg variable may never be the output of a predefined primitive gate or the target of a continuous assignment. An attempt to assign value to a wire (explicit or implicit) by a procedural assignment, nonblocking assignment, or an ***assign . . . deassign*** procedural continuous assignment (See Section 5.17), will produce a syntax error.

5.15.4 Continuous Assignment Models

A modeling style based on continuous assignments describes level-sensitive behavior. Continuous assignments execute concurrently with each other, with gate-level primitives, and with all of the behaviors in a description.

Example: 32-bit Comparator

It is not feasible to write the Boolean equations that compare 32-bit words, but continuous assignments using the built-in operators of Verilog provide a solution. We include a parameter declaration to size the wordlength of the datapath. This model is readable, understandable, compact, and extendable to datapaths of arbitrary size:

```
module compare_32_CA (A_gt_B, A_lt_B, A_eq_B, A, B);
   parameter      word_size = 32;
   input          [word_size-1: 0]    A, B;
   output         A_gt_B, A_lt_B, A_eq_B;

   assign         A_gt_B = (A > B),           // Note: list of multiple assignments
                  A_lt_B = (A < B),
                  A_eq_B = (A == B);
endmodule
```

Example End: 32-bit Comparator

5.15.5 Dataflow/RTL Models

Dataflow models of combinational logic describe concurrent operations on signals, usually in a synchronous machine, where computations are initiated at the active edges of a clock and are completed in time to be stored in a register at the next active edge. At each active edge, the hardware registers read and store the data inputs that were formed as a result of the previous clock edge, and then propagate new values to be stored in registers at the next edge. Dataflow models for synchronous machines are also referred to as register transfer level (RTL) models, because they describe register activity in a synchronous machine [2, 4-5]. RTL models are written for a specific architecture, (i.e., the registers, datapaths, and machine operations and their schedule are known *a priori*). RTL models are popular in industry because they are easily synthesized by modern tools for electronic design automation (EDA). The next example illustrates an RTL model of a synchronous circuit, an autonomous linear feedback shift register that executes concurrent transformations on a datapath, under the synchronizing control of its only input, a clock signal.

Example: RTL Model—Linear Feedback Shift Register (LFSR)

Linear feedback shift registers (LFSRs) are commonly used in data compression circuits, implementing a signature analysis technique called cyclic redundancy check (CRC) [6]. Autonomous LFSRs are used in applications requiring pseudorandom binary numbers.[24] For example, an autonomous LFSR can be a random pattern generator, providing stimulus patterns to a circuit. The response to these patterns can be compared with the circuit's expected response, thereby revealing the presence of an internal fault. The autonomous LFSR shown in Figure 5-31 has binary tap coefficients $C_1, \ldots, C_N$ that determine whether $Y(0)$ is fed back to a given stage of the register. The structure shown has $C_N = 1$ because $Y[N]$ is connected directly to the input of the leftmost stage. In general, if $C_{N-j+1} = 1$, then the input to stage j is formed as the *exclusive-or* of $Y[j-1]$ and $Y[N]$, for $j = 2, \ldots N$. Otherwise, the input to stage j is the output of stage $j-1$, (i.e., Y[j] <= Y[j-1]). The vector of tap coefficients determines the coefficients of the *characteristic polynomial* of the LFSR, which characterize its cyclic nature [6]. The characteristic polynomial determines the period of the register, (i.e., the number of cycles before a pattern repeats).

The following Verilog code describes an eight-cell autonomous LFSR with a synchronous (edge-sensitive) cyclic behavior, using an RTL style of design:

---

[24]LFSRs are also used as fast counters when only the terminal count is needed.

```verilog
module Auto_LFSR_RTL_V2001
#( parameter          Length = 8,
                      initial_state = 8'b1001_0001,        // 91h
    parameter [Length: 1]  Tap_Coefficient = 8'b1100_1111
)
(output  reg [1: Length]  Y,
  input                   Clock, Reset
);

  always @ (posedge Clock)
    if (!Reset) Y <= initial_state;        // Active-low reset to initial state
      else begin
        Y[1] <= Y[8];
        Y[2] <= Tap_Coefficient[7] ? Y[1] ^ Y[8] : Y[1];
        Y[3] <= Tap_Coefficient[6] ? Y[2] ^ Y[8] : Y[2];
        Y[4] <= Tap_Coefficient[5] ? Y[3] ^ Y[8] : Y[3];
        Y[5] <= Tap_Coefficient[4] ? Y[4] ^ Y[8] : Y[4];
        Y[6] <= Tap_Coefficient[3] ? Y[5] ^ Y[8] : Y[5];
        Y[7] <= Tap_Coefficient[2] ? Y[6] ^ Y[8] : Y[6];
        Y[8] <= Tap_Coefficient[1] ? Y[7] ^ Y[8] : Y[7];
      end
  end
endmodule
```

Each bit of the register is assigned value concurrently with the other bits; the order of the listed nonblocking assignments is of no consequence. The movement of data through the register under simulation is shown in binary and hexadecimal format in Figure 5-32, for the initial state and three cycles of the clock. Notice that this model is not fully parameterized, because the register transfers are correct only if *Length* = 8.

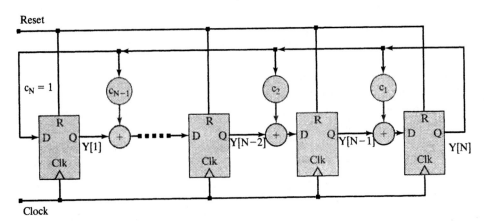

FIGURE 5-31   Linear feedback shift register with modulo-2 (exclusive-or) addition

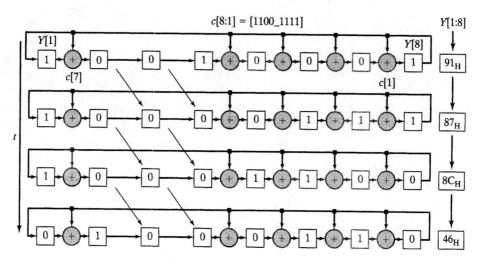

FIGURE 5-32 Data movement in a linear feedback shift register with modulo-2 (exclusive-or) addition

---

Example End: RTL Model—Linear Feedback Shift Register (LFSR)

5.15.6 Algorithm-Based Models

A behavioral model described by a circuit's input/output algorithm is more abstract than an RTL description. The algorithm prescribes a sequence of procedural assignments within a cyclic behavior. The outcome of executing the statements determines the values of storage variables and, ultimately, the output of the machine. The algorithm described by the model does not have explicit binding to hardware, and it does not have an implied architecture of registers, datapaths, and computational resources. This style is most challenging for a synthesis tool, because it must perform what is referred to as *architectural synthesis*, which extracts the resources (e.g., determines actual requirements for processors, datapaths, and hardware memory) and scheduling requirements that support the algorithm, and then maps the description into an RTL model whose logic can be synthesized.

Not all algorithms can be implemented in hardware. Nonetheless, this descriptive style is useful and attractive, because it is abstract, and eliminates the need for an *a priori* architecture. Also, the description can be very readable and understandable. The key distinction to remember is that the assignment statements in a dataflow (RTL) model execute concurrently (in parallel) and operate on explicitly declared registers in the context of a specified architecture; the statements in an algorithmic model execute sequentially, without an explicit architecture.

Example: Behavioral Model—Comparator (Algorithmic Model)

The cyclic behavior in *compare_2_algo_V2001* is activated whenever any bit of *A* or *B* changes. The algorithm first initializes all register variables to 0, a precaution that will prevent the synthesis of unwanted latches. Then the algorithm traverses a decision tree to determine which of the three outputs to assert. The nonasserted outputs will retain the value that was assigned to them at the beginning of the sequence. The code is as follows:

```
module compare_2_algo_V2001
( output reg      A_lt_B, A_gt_B, A_eq_B,
  input  [1: 0]   A, B
);
    always @ (A, B)          // Level-sensitive behavior
      begin
        A_lt_B = 0;
        A_gt_B = 0;
        A_eq_B = 0;
        if (A == B)          A_eq_B = 1;    // Note: parentheses are required
        else if (A > B)      A_gt_B = 1;
        else                 A_lt_B = 1;
      end
endmodule
```

Example End: Behavioral Model—Comparator (Algorithmic Model)

Figure 5-33 shows the gate-level schematic obtained by synthesizing[25] *compare_2_algo_V2001* and targeting the implementation to generic gates. Notice that

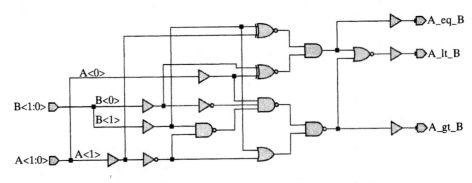

FIGURE 5-33 Synthesis results derived from *compare_2_algo*

---

[25]With Synopsys' Design Compiler. Note that the tool represents vector ranges by the braces $\diamond$ rather than [ ].

the algorithm has register variables to support its execution, but does not need hardware memory because it actually describes and synthesizes to combinational logic.

5.16   Instance Generation

Verilog 1995 supports structural modeling with declarations of arrays of instances of primitives and modules. The *generate . . . endgenerate* construct in Verilog 2001 extends this feature to replicate distinct copies of net declarations, register variable declarations, parameter redefinitions, continuous assignments, *always* behaviors, *initial* behaviors, tasks, and functions.[26] Verilog 2001 introduces a new kind of variable, denoted by the keyword *genvar*, which declares a nonnegative integer[27] that is used as an index in the replicating *for* loop associated with a *generate . . . endgenerate* block. The index of the *for* loop of a *generate . . . endgenerate* block must be a *genvar* variable, and the initializing statement and the loop update statement must both assign value to the same *genvar* variable. The contents of the *for* loop of a *generate . . . endgenerate* statement must be within a named *begin . . . end* block. The name of the block is used to build a unique name for each generated item.

Example: Generation of a 32-Bit Adder

The model described by *Add_CLA_V2001* generates a 32-bit adder from copies of an 8-bit adder, with instance names *M[0].ADD, M[1].ADD, M[2].ADD*, and *M[3].ADD*. A separate generate statement connects the internal carry chain of the adder by generating continuous assignments. Notice that the entire model is parameterized, so redefining the value of *size* to 64 will generate and connect eight copies of the 8-bit slice adder, *Add_cla_8*. This leads to a more compact description than instantiating eight individual 8-bit adders. Additionally, manual replication of structural items does not lead to a parameterized model, which ultimately limits the utility of the model. Here is the code:

```
module Adder_CLA_V2001
  #(parameter          size = 32)
  ( input   [size -1: 0]   a, b,
     input                 c_in,
     output [size -1: 0]   sum,
     output                c_out
  );
```

---

[26]A *generate ... endgenerate* block may not include port declarations, constant declarations, or specify blocks.
[27]A variable of type *genvar* may be declared within a module or within the *generate ... endgenerate* block; it may not be assigned a negative value, an *x* value, or a *z* value.

```
wire    [size/8 -1: 0]      c_o, c_i;
assign                      c_i[0] = c_in;
assign                      c_out = c_o[size/8 -1];

generate
  genvar j;
  for (j = 1; j <= 3; j = j+ 1)
  begin: j
    assign c_i[j] = c_o[j-1];
  end
endgenerate

generate
  genvar k;
  for (k = 0; k <= size/8 -1; k = k + 1)
  begin: M
    Add_cla_8 ADD (sum[((k+1)*8 -1) -: 8], c_o[k], a[((k+1)*8 -1) -:8], b[((k+1)*8 -1)
    -: 8], c_i[k]);
  end
endgenerate
endmodule
```

Example End: Generation of a 32-Bit Adder

Example: Generation of a Pipeline

In *generated_array_pipeline_V2001*, **generate** statements are used to generate a parameterized pipeline of words:

```
module generated_array_pipeline_V2001
#(parameter              width = 8,
                         length = 16
)
( input  [width -1: 0]   data_in,
  input                  clk, reset,
  output[width -1: 0]    data_out
);
  reg   [width -1: 0]    pipe    [0: length -1];
  wire  [width -1: 0]    d_in    [0: length -1];

  assign d_in[0] = data_in;
  assign data_out = pipe[width-1];

generate
  genvar k;
  for (k = 1; k <= length-1; k = k+1) begin: W
   assign d_in[k] = pipe[k-1];
  end
```

```
      endgenerate
    generate
      genvar j;
      for (j = 0; j <= length-1; j = j+ 1)
        begin: stage
          always @ (posedge clk or negedge reset)
            if (reset == 0) pipe[j] <= 0; else pipe[j] <= d_in[j];
        end
    endgenerate
    endmodule
```

Example End: Generation of a Pipeline

The replication of items by a generate block can be controlled by *if* statements and *case* statements.

Example: Conditional Generation

Add_RCA_or_CLA_if_V2001 uses an *if* statement to determine whether a ripple-carry adder or a look-ahead adder is instantiated, depending on the width of the data-path. *Add_RCA_or_CLA_case_V2001* uses a *case* statement to determine the instantiation. Here is the code for the two modules:

```
module Add_RCA_or_CLA_if_V2001
#(parameter size = 8)
( input   [size -1: 0]  a, b,
  input                  c_in,
  output [size -1: 0]    sum,
  output                 c_out
);

  generate
    if (size < 9) Add_rca #(size) M1 (sum, c_out, a, b, c_in);
      else Add_cla #(size) M1 (sum, c_out, a, b, c_in);
  endgenerate
endmodule



module Add_RCA_or_CLA_case_V2001
#(parameter size = 8)
( input   [size -1: 0]  a, b,
  input                  c_in,
  output [size -1: 0]   sum,
  output                 c_out
);

  generate
    case (1)
```

```
    size < 9:          Add_rca #(size) M1 (sum, c_out, a, b, c_in);
    default:           Add_cla #(size) M1 (sum, c_out, a, b, c_in);
 endgenerate
 endmodule
```

In the *case* statement the Boolean value of the expression **size** $< \;$ **9** is compared to 1 (TRUE).

Example End: Conditional Generation

5.17 Procedural Continuous Assignment

There are two constructs for procedural continuous assignments, which declare dynamic bindings to nets or registers in a model. Ordinarily, a continuous assignment remains in effect for the duration of a simulation. A *assign ... deassign* procedural continuous assignment (PCA) is made by a procedural statement to establish an alternative binding, (i.e., dynamically substitute the right-hand side expression). PCAs using the keyword *assign* are utilized to model the level-sensitive behavior of combinational logic, transparent latches, and asynchronous control of sequential parts.[28] The PCA remains in effect until it is removed by the (optional) *deassign* keyword or until another procedural continuous assignment is made.

Example: **assign** *. . .* **deassign** *Procedural Continuous Assignment*

The following four-channel mux uses the *assign ... deassign* PCA to bind the output to a selected datapath:

```
module mux4_PCA (a, b, c, d, select, y_out);
   input         a, b, c, d;
   input [1:0]   select;
   output        y_out;
   reg           y_out;

   always @ (select)
      if (select == 0) assign y_out = a; else
      if (select == 1) assign y_out = b; else
      if (select == 2) assign y_out = c; else
      if (select == 3) assign y_out = d; else assign y_out = 1'bx;
endmodule
```

Example End: **assign** *. . .* **deassign** *Procedural Continuous Assignment*

---

[28]*PCAs* are not widely supported by synthesis tools. Restrict usage to testbenches and models that are intended only for simulation efficiency [2].

The *force . . . release* form of a PCA applies to register variables, as well as to nets, and overrides *assign . . . deassign* continuous assignments. The *force . . . release* construct is used primarily within testbenches to inject logic values or logic into a design [2].

Example:force . . . release Procedural Continuous Assignment

In synchronous operation, the value of the *data* input of a D-type flip-flop transfers to the *q* output at the synchronizing edge of *clock*, (e.g., at the rising edge or the falling edge of the synchronizing signal). If either the *preset* or the *clear* signal is asserted, this (synchronous) clocking action is ignored and the output is held at a constant value. Following is a Verilog model of this behavior for active-low *preset* and *clear*:

```
module FLOP_PCA (q, qbar, data, preset, clear, clock);
    output      q, qbar;
    input       data, preset, clear, clock;
    reg         q;

    assign      qbar = ~q;

    always @ (negedge clock) q <= data;

    always @ (clear or preset) begin
      if (!clear) assign q = 0;
        else if (!preset) assign q = 1;
          else deassign q;
      end
endmodule
```

Note that the assigned PCA has immediate effect. While *preset* or *clear* is asserted, the ordinary synchronous behavior is ignored. If both *clear* and *reset* are deassigned, the synchronous activity commences with the next active edge of the clock after the deassignment executes. Note: This model is not intended for synthesis.

Example End:force . . . release Procedural Continuous Assignment

---

5.18 Intra-Assignment Delay

When a timing control operator (**# or @**) appears in front of a procedural statement in a behavioral model, the delay is referred to as a blocking delay, and the statement that follows the operator is said to be blocked. The statement that follows a blocked statement in the sequential flow cannot execute until the preceding statement has completed execution. Verilog supports another form of delay in which a timing control is placed to the right-hand side of the assignment operator, within an assignment statement. This type of delay, called intra-assignment delay,[29] evaluates the right-hand side expression of the assignment and then schedules the assignment to occur in the future, at a time determined by the timing control. Ordinary delay control postpones the execution of a statement; intra-assignment delay postpones the occurrence of the assignment that results from executing a statement. A statement in a list of blocked procedural assignments, (i.e. those using the = operator), must complete before the statement after it, can execute.

Example: Intra-Assignment Delay
_____

When the first statement in the following code is encountered in the sequential activity flow below, the value of *B* is sampled and is scheduled to be assigned to *A* five time units later:

```
...
A = #5 B;
C = D;
...
```

The statement does not complete execution until the assignment occurs. After the assignment to *A* is made, the next statement can execute (*C=D*). Thus, *C* gets *D* five time units after the first statement is encountered in simulation.

Example End: Intra-Assignment Delay
_____

Intra-assignment delay control (#) has the effect of causing the right-hand side expression of an assignment to be evaluated immediately when the procedural statement is encountered in the activity flow. However, the assignment that results from the statement is not executed until the specified delay has elapsed. Thus, referencing and evaluation are separated in time from the actual assignment of value to the target register variable.

Intra-assignment delay can also be implemented with the event control operator and an event expression. In this case, the execution of the statement is scheduled subject to the occurrence of the event specified in the event expression.

Example: Event Control Expression with Intra-Assignment Delay
_____

In the following description, *G* gets *ACCUM* when *A_BUS* changes:

```
...
G = @ (A_BUS) ACCUM;
C = D;
...
```

---

[29]Intra-assignment delay is not supported by synthesis tools.

As a result of the intra-assignment delay, the procedural assignment to *G* cannot complete execution until *A_BUS* changes. The statement *C=D* is blocked until *G* gets value. The value that *G* gets is the value of *ACCUM* when the statement is encountered in the activity flow. This may differ from the actual value of *ACCUM* when *A_BUS* finally has activity and triggers the assignment.

Example End: Event Control Expression with Intra-Assignment Delay

---

5.19 Simulation, Endless Loops, and Race Conditions

An event at the input of a primitive causes the simulator to schedule an updating event for its output. Likewise, an event in the RHS expression of a continuous assignment statement causes the scheduling of an event for the assignment's target variable. In both cases, scheduling is governed by any propagation delay associated with the primitive or continuous assignment, which has the effect of scheduling the output/target event to occur at a future time step of the simulator, rather than in the current time step.

Simulators behave differently, though, when a cyclic behavior is activated. The associated statements execute sequentially, in the same time step, until the simulator encounters (1) a delay control operator (#), (2) an event control operator (@), (3) a *wait* construct,[30] or (4) the last statement of the behavior. The first three have the effect of suspending the execution of the behavioral statement until a condition is satisfied; the last possibility causes the activity to restart from the first statement of the behavior.

Models for primitives and continuous assignments cannot suspend themselves. They execute immediately. Cyclic behaviors can suspend themselves. When they do, their activity can cause other behaviors, primitives, and continuous assignments to be activated. But until an active behavior is suspended, the rest of the world waits for it to suspend. A consequence of this is that a cyclic or single-pass behavior having a loop that does not include a mechanism for suspension of its activity will execute endlessly and consume the attention of the simulator. Good modeling will prevent this from happening, otherwise; reach for the *off* button.

If multiple behaviors are activated at the same time step, the order in which the simulator executes them is indeterminate. Care must be taken to avoid having such behaviors assign value to the same register, because the outcome of the assignments will be indeterminate. Synthesis tools will warn you of such features in your model. If the outputs of multiple primitives, continuous assignments, and procedural assignments are scheduled to be updated in the same time step, the order in which they are updated is indeterminate [1, 2]. Multiple concurrent behaviors (i.e., ***always*** or ***initial*** blocks) may assign value to the same register variable at the same time step. A simulator must determine the outcome of these multiple assignments, and distinguish between blocking

---

[30]A *wait* statement is not synthesized by the leading synthesis tools. It may be used in a testbench, or a model that will not be synthesized.

(=) and nonblocking (<=) assignments. The activity of a simulator is triggered by an event, (i.e. a change in the value of a net, a register variable, or the triggering of an abstract event). The processing steps of the simulator are organized to determine the order in which assignments to variables occur in simulation. Consequently, an event queue manages the assignments to registers when nonblocking and blocking assignments are made simultaneously to the same target variable (i.e., in the same time step).

At a given time step, the simulator will (1) evaluate the expressions on the RHS of all the assignments, in order to register variables in statements that are encountered at that time step, (2) execute the blocking assignments to registers, (3) execute nonblocking assignments that do not have intra-assignment timing controls (i.e., they execute in the current time step), (4) execute a past procedural assignment whose timing controls have scheduled an assignment for the current simulator time, and (5) advance the simulator time (t_{sim}). The language reference manual for Verilog refers to this organization of the simulation activity as a stratified event queue. That is, the queue of pending simulation events is organized into five different regions, as shown in Table 5.1.

The first region of the stratified event queue, the active region, consists of events that are scheduled to occur at the current simulation time, and which have top priority for execution. These events result from (1) evaluating the RHS of nonblocking assignments, (2) evaluating the inputs of a primitive and changing the output, (3) executing a procedural (blocked) assignment to a register variable, (4) evaluating the RHS of a continuous assignment and updating the LHS, (5) evaluating the RHS of a procedural continuous assignment and updating the LHS, and (6) evaluating and executing *$display* and *$write* system tasks. Any procedural assignments blocked by a #0 delay control are placed in the inactive queue and execute after the active queue is empty, in the next simulation cycle at the current time step of the simulator. The activity of the active queue is dynamic. When it becomes empty, the contents of the inactive queue are moved to the active queue, and the process continues.

The order of processing events in the active queue is not specified by the LRM and is tool dependent. For example, if an input to a module at the top level of the design hierarchy has an event at the current simulation time, as prescribed by a testbench, the event would reside in the active area of the queue. Now, suppose that the input to the module is connected to a primitive having zero propagation delay and whose output is changed by the event on the input port. This event would be scheduled to occur at the current simulation time, and would be placed in the active area of the queue. If a behavior is activated by the module input, and if the behavior generates an event by means of a nonblocking assignment, that event would be placed in the nonblocking assignment update area of the queue. Events that were scheduled to occur at the current simulation time, but which originated in nonblocking assignments at an earlier simulation time, would also be placed in the nonblocking assignment update area. The monitor area contains events that are to be processed after the active, inactive, and nonblocking assignment update events, such as the *$monitor* task. The last area of the stratified event queue builds a queue consisting of events that are to be executed in the future. Given this organization of the event queue, *the simulator executes all of the active events in a single simulation cycle.* As it executes, it may add events to any of the

TABLE 5-1   Stratified event queue for event-driven simulation

Class of Event	Time of Occurrence	Order of Processing
Active Event ■ Evaluate RHS of nonblocking assignments ■ Evaluate inputs to primitives and update their outputs ■ Execute blocking assignments ■ Update continuous assignments ■ Update procedural continuous assignments ■ Execute **$display** and **$write** statements	Current t_{sim}	In any order
Inactive	Current t_{sim} with #0 blocking assignments	In any order after all active events
Nonblocking Assignment Update	Evaluated during previous or present t_{sim} to be assigned at t_{sim}	In any order after all active and inactive events
Monitor	Current t_{sim}	After all active, inactive, and nonblocking assignment update events
Future Active and Nonblocking Assignment Update	A Future Simulation Time	

Simulation cycle: the processing of all of the events in the active event queue. An explicit #0 delay control requires that the executing process be suspended and added as an inactive event for the current simulation time, so that the process is resumed in the next simulation cycle (IEEE 1364).

regions of the queue, but it may only delete events from the active region. After the active region is empty, the events in the inactive region are activated, (i.e. they are added to the active region and a new simulation cycle begins). After the active region and the inactive region are empty, the events in the nonblocking assignment update area of the queue are activated, and a new simulation cycle begins. After the monitor events have executed, the simulator advances time to the next time at which an event is scheduled to occur. Whenever an explicit #0 delay control is encountered in a behavior, the associated process is suspended, and added as an inactive event for the current simulation time. The process will be resumed in the next simulation cycle at the current time.

In addition to the structure imposed by the stratified event queue, the simulator must adhere to the rule that the relative ordering of blocking and nonblocking assignments at the same simulation time will be such that the nonblocking assignments will be scheduled after the blocking assignments, with the exception that blocking assignments that are triggered by nonblocking assignments will be scheduled after the nonblocking assignments that are already scheduled. As a word of caution, the *$display* task executes immediately when it is encountered in the sequential activity flow of a behavior. The *$monitor* task executes at the end of the current simulation cycle, (i.e., after the nonblocking assignments have been updated). Thus, in the following code, *execute_display* assigns value to a and b, samples the current RHS of a and b, displays the current values of a and b, and then updates a and b:

```
initial begin: execute_display          initial begin: execute_monitor
  a = 1;                                   c = 1;
  b = 0;                                   d= 0;
  a <= b;                                  c <= d;
  b <= a;                                  d <= c;
  $display ("display: a = %b b= %b", a, b);  $monitor ("monitor: c = %b d= %b", c, d);
end                                      end
```

Observe that the values of a and b at the end of the behavior are not the values that were displayed, (i.e., *$display* executes before the nonblocking assignments). On the other hand, *execute_monitor* assigns value to c and d, samples c and d, updates c and d, and then prints the values of c and d. The values of c and d when the behavior expires are the same as the values that were printed. The standard output is

$display: a = 1 b = 0
$monitor: c = 0 d = 1

REFERENCES

[1] *IEEE Standard for Verilog Hardware Description Language 2001,* IEEE Std.1364-2001. Piscataway, NJ: Institute of Electrical and Electronic Engineers, 2001.

[2] Ciletti, M.D. *Advanced Digital Design with the Verilog HDL.* Upper Saddle River, NJ: Prentice Hall, 2003.

[3] Sutherland, S. *Verilog 2001*. Boston: Kluwer, 2002.

[4] Lee, S., *Design of Computers and Other Complex Digital Devices*. Upper Saddle River, NJ: Prentice Hall, Inc., 2000.

[5] Mano, M. M., and Kime, C. R., *Logic and Computer Design Fundamentals*. Upper Saddle River, NJ: Prentice Hall, Inc., 1997.

[6] Abramovici, M. et al., *Digital Systems Testing and Testable Design*. Rockville, MD: Computer Science Press, 1990.

[7] Ciletti, M.D. *Modeling, Synthesis, and Rapid Prototyping with the Verilog HDL*. Upper Saddle River, NJ: Prentice Hall, 1999.

PROBLEMS

1. Using a single continuous assignment, develop and verify a behavioral model implementing a Boolean equation describing the logic of the circuit below. Use the following names for the testbench, the model, and its ports: *t_Combo_CA()*, and *Combo_CA (Y, A, B, C, D)*, respectively. (*Note*: The testbench will have no ports). Simulate the circuit exhaustively, and provide graphical and text output demonstrating that the model is correct.

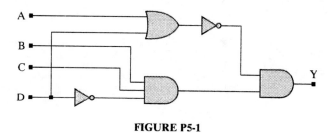

FIGURE P5-1

2. Write a testbench and verify that *Latch_CA* (See Figure 5-3) correctly models a transparent latch.

3. Write and verify a behavioral model of JK-type flip-flop having active-low asynchronous reset.

4. Explain why the following code fragment will execute endlessly:

```
reg [3: 0] K
for (K=0; K<=15; K = K+1) begin
...
end
```

Recommend an alternative description.

5. Develop and verify an 8-bit ALU having input datapaths *a* and *b*, output datapath {*c_out*, *sum*}, and an operand *Oper*, and having the functionality indicated in Figure P5-5.

Operand	Function
Add	a + b
Subtract	a + ~b + 1
Or_ab	{1'b0, a | b}
And_ab	{1'b0, a & b}
not_ab	{1'b0, (~a) & b}
exor	{1'b0, a ^ b}
exnor	{1'b0, a ~^ b}

FIGURE P5-5

CHAPTER 6 — # Modeling Finite-State Machines and Datapath Controllers with Verilog

Finite-state machines are widely used in digital systems, and are readily modeled with Verilog. This chapter presents common styles for describing and modeling finite-state machines, with attention to synthesizable models. State transition graphs, algorithmic state machine (ASM) charts, and algorithmic state machine and datapath (ASMD) charts will be used to develop Verilog models of state machines.

6.1   Finite-State Machines

Unlike combinational logic, whose output is an immediate function of only its present inputs, sequential logic depends on the history of its inputs. This dependency is expressed by the concept of *state*. The future behavior of a sequential machine is completely characterized by its input and its present state. At any time, the state of a system is the minimal information needed, together with the inputs to the system, to determine the future of the system. For example, knowing the number of 1's that will appear at the input of a machine that counts 1's in a serial bit stream is not enough information to determine the count at any time in the future. The present count must also be known. Thus, the state of the counter is its present count.

Sequential machines are widely used in applications requiring prescribed sequential activity. For example, the outputs of a sequential machine control the synchronous datapath and register operations of a computer. All sequential machines have the general feedback structure shown in Figure 6-1, where the next state of the machine is formed from the present state and the present input. Combinational logic

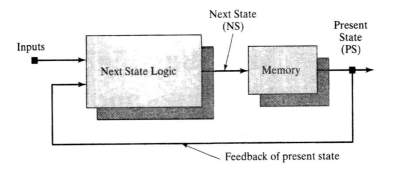

FIGURE 6-1   Block diagram of a sequential machine

forms the next state (NS) from the primary inputs and the stored value of the present state (PS). A state register (memory) holds the value of the present state (*PS*), and the value of the next state is formed from the inputs and the content of the state register. In this structure the state transitions are asynchronous.

The state transitions of an asynchronous sequential machine are unpredictable. Most ASIC circuits are designed for fast, synchronous operation, because race conditions are very problematic for asynchronous machines, and get worse as the physical dimensions of devices and signal paths shrink. Synchronous machines overcome race issues by having a clock period that is sufficient to stabilize the signals in the circuit. In an edge-triggered clocking scheme, the clock isolates a storage register's inputs from its output, thereby allowing feedback without race conditions. In fact, synchronous machines are widely used, because timing issues are reduced to (1) assuring that setup and hold timing constraints[1] are satisfied at flip-flops (for a given system clock), (2) assuring that clock skew,[2] induced by the physical distribution of the clock signal to the storage elements, does not compromise the synchronicity of the design, and (3) providing synchronizers at the asynchronous inputs to the system.

The state transitions of an edge-triggered flip-flop-based synchronous machine are synchronized by the active edge (i.e., rising or falling) of a common clock. State changes give rise to changes in the outputs of the combinational logic that determine the next state, and the outputs of the machine. Clock waveforms may be symmetric or asymmetric. Figure 6-2 illustrates features of an asymmetric clock waveform, (i.e. the length of the interval in which the clock is low is not equal to the length of the interval in which the clock is high). Register transfers are all made at either the rising or the falling edge of the clock, and input data is synchronized to change between the active edges.

The period of the clock must be long enough to allow all transients activated by a transition of the clock to settle at the outputs of the next-state combinational logic before the next active edge occurs. This establishes a lower bound on the cycle time (period) of the clock of a sequential machine. The inputs to the state register's flip-flops must remain stable for a sufficient time before and after the active edge of the clock. The constraint

---

[1]Setup constraints require the data to be stable in an interval before the active edge of the clock; hold constraints require the data to be stable in an interval after the active edge.
[2]Clock skew refers to the condition wherein the active edge of the clock does not occur at exactly the same time at every flip-flop.

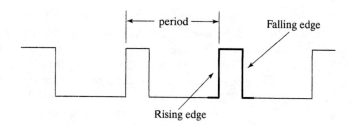

FIGURE 6-2 Waveform of an asymmetric clock signal

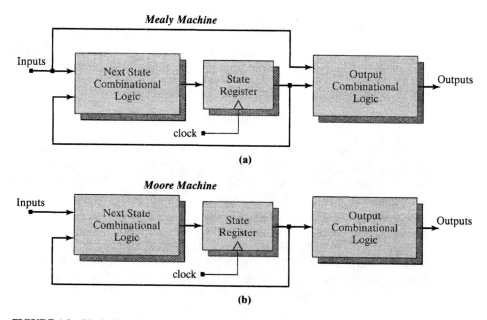

FIGURE 6-3 Block diagram structures of finite-state machines: **(a)** a Mealy machine, and **(b)** a Moore machine

imposed before the clock establishes an upper bound on the longest path through the circuit, which constrains the latest allowed arrival of data. The constraint imposed after the clock establishes a lower bound on the shortest path through the combinational logic that is driving the storage device, by constraining the earliest time at which data from the previous cycle could be overwritten. Together, these constraints ensure that valid data is stored. Otherwise, timing violations may occur at the inputs to the flip-flops and cause a condition of metastability, with the result that invalid data are stored [1, 2].[3]

The set of states of a practical sequential machine is always finite, and the number of possible states is determined by the number of bits that represent the state. A machine whose state is encoded as an *n-bit* binary word can have up to 2^n states. We will use the term *finite-state machine* (FSM) to refer to a clocked, sequential machine having one of the two structures shown in Figure 6-3. Synchronous (i.e.,

---

[3]For a discussion of Verilog's built-in system tasks for timing verification, see [2].

---

clocked) FSMs have widespread application in digital systems, for example, as data-path controllers in computational units and processors. Synchronous FSMs are characterized by a finite number of states and by clock-driven state transitions.

There are two fundamental types of FSMs: Mealy and Moore. The next state and the outputs of a Mealy machine depend on the present state and the inputs; the next state of a Moore machine depends on the present state and the inputs, but the output depends on only the present state. In both machines, the next state and outputs are formed by combinational logic.

6.2 State Transition Graphs

Finite-state machines can be described and designed systematically with the aid of timing diagrams [1], state tables, state graphs [3], and ASM charts[4]. Our focus will be on developing Verilog behavioral models of FSMs from state transition graphs (STGs) and ASM charts.

An STG, or diagram, of an FSM is a directed graph in which the labeled nodes, or vertices, correspond to the machine's states, and the directed edges, or arcs, represent possible transitions under the application of an indicated input signal, when the system is in the state from which the arc originates. The vertices of the state transition graph of a Mealy machine are labeled with the states. The edges of the graph are labeled with (1) the input that causes a transition to the indicated next state, and (2) with the output that is asserted in the present state for that input. The graph for a Moore-type machine is similar, but its outputs are indicated in each state vertex, instead of on the arcs.

For an STG to be valid, each of its vertices must represent a unique state, each arc must represent a transition from a given state to a next state under the action of the indicated input, and each arc leaving a node must correspond to a unique input. In general, the Boolean conditions associated with the inputs on the set of arcs leaving a node must sum to 1 (i.e., the graph must account for all possible transitions from a node), and each branching condition associated with assertions of the input variables in a given state must correspond to one and only one arc, (i.e., the machine may exit a node on only one arc).[4] (See [4] for guidelines for construction of state transition graphs). The state transitions represented by the STG of a synchronous machine are understood to occur at the active edges of a clock signal, based on the values of the state and inputs that are present immediately before the clock.

Given an STG for a synchronous machine, the design task is to write Verilog cyclic behaviors describing the next state and the output logic. The design of the machine specifies the logic that forms the inputs to the flip-flops from the state and the external inputs to the machine. This logic will be combinational, and will be minimized by a synthesis tool. At each active edge of the clock, the inputs to the state-holding flip-flops become the state for the next cycle of the clock.

---

[4]The chart can be simplified by showing only the transitions that leave a state, omitting arcs that begin and end at the same state, and by omitting return arcs that are activated by a reset signal.

6.3 Explicit Finite-State Machines

Explicit state machines have an explicitly declared state register and explicit logic that governs the evolution of the state under the influence of the inputs. Explicit machines can be described by two cyclic behaviors: a level-sensitive behavior describing the next state and output logic, and an edge-sensitive behavior synchronizing the transitions of the state.

Example: Explicit Finite-State Machine—BCD-to-Excess-3 Code Converter

---

A serially transmitted binary-coded decimal (BCD) word, B_{in}, is to be converted into an Excess-3 encoded serial bit stream, B_{out}. An Excess-3 code word is obtained by adding 3_{10} to the decimal value of the BCD word and taking the binary equivalent of the result. Table 6-1 shows the decimal digits, their 4-bit BCD code words, and their Excess-3 encoded counterparts. An Excess-3 code is self-complementing [1, 5, 6]. That is to say, the 9's complement[5] of an Excess-3 encoded word is obtained in hardware by complementing the bits of the word (i.e., taking the 1's complement of the word). For example, the Excess-3 code for 6_{10} is 1001_2; its bitwise complement is 0110_2, which is the code for 3_{10}. This feature of the Excess-3 code makes it possible to easily implement a diminished radix[6] complement scheme for subtracting numbers that are encoded in a BCD form. This is similar to subtracting signed binary words by adding the 2's complement of the minuend to the subtrahend. The 2's complement is formed by adding 1 to the 1's (diminished radix) complement of the minuend. Thus, the 10's complement of 6_{10} can be obtained by bitwise complementing 1001_2, the Excess-3 code of 6_{10}, and adding 1 to the result: $0110_2 + 0001_2 = 0111_2$, which decodes to 4_{10}.

A BCD-to-Excess-3 code converter for a serial bit stream can be implemented as a Mealy finite-state machine. Figure 6-4 shows a serial bit stream, B_{in}, entering the converter and the corresponding serial stream of Excess-3 encoded bits, B_{out}, leaving

TABLE 6-1   BCD and Excess-3 code words

Decimal Digit	8-4-2-1 Code (BCD)	Excess-3 Code
0	0000	0011
1	0001	0100
2	0010	0101
3	0011	0110
4	0100	0111
5	0101	1000
6	0110	1001
7	0111	1010
8	1000	1011
9	1001	1100

---

[5]The 9's complement of a binary number a is the binary value a' such that $a + a' = 9$.
[6]The radix 9 is the diminished radix for a base 10 (decimal) system.

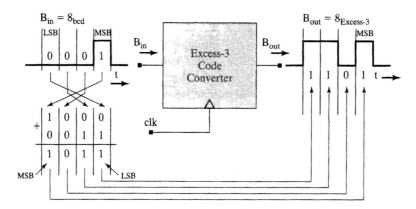

FIGURE 6-4   Input/output bit streams in a BCD to Excess-3 serial code converter

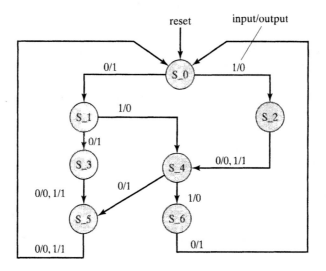

FIGURE 6-5   State transition graph for a BCD to Excess-3 serial code converter implemented as a Mealy-type FSM

the machine. Note that the bits of B_{in} are transmitted in sequence, with the LSB first. Consequently, care must be taken to interpret the waveforms of B_{in} and B_{out} correctly. The order of the bits in the waveforms is shown progressing from right to left (with increasing time), with the LSB at the left and the MSB at the right. The pattern of bits in the waveform must be reversed, as shown in Figure 6-4, to form the binary values of the transmitted and received words.

The state transition graph[7] of a serial code converter that implements the code in Table 6-1 is shown in Figure 6-5, with an asynchronous reset signal that transfers the

---

[7]The state transition graph of a *completely specified* machine with n inputs must have 2^n arcs leaving each node, and the number of its states must be a power of 2. Otherwise, some bit patterns will be unused in the hardware implementation.

machine to state S_0 whenever it is asserted, independently of the clock. The machine's action commences in S_0 with the first clock edge after reset and continues indefinitely, repeating the addition of 0011_2 to successive 4-bit slices of the input stream. The LSB of the word is the first bit in the sequence of input samples, and the first bit generated for the output word.

Manual design of a D-type flip-flop realization of an FSM consists of the following steps: (1) construct an STG for the machine, (2) eliminate equivalent states, (3) select a state code, (e.g., a binary code), (4) encode the state table, (5) develop Boolean equations describing the inputs of the D-type flip-flops that hold the state bits, and (6) using K-maps, optimize the Boolean equations (see [2] for details). In general, the number of flip-flops used to represent the state of the machine must be sufficient to accommodate a binary representation of the number of states, (i.e., a machine having 12 states requires at least four flip-flops). For a given set of flop-flops, it is then necessary to assign a unique binary code to each state. This problem is difficult because the number of possible codes grows exponentially with the number of available flip-flops. The choice ultimately matters, because it can have an impact on the complexity of the logic required to implement the machine. Our model uses a simple (sequential) 3-bit binary code to encode the seven states of the machine.

The schematic that results from manual design of the code converter [2] is shown in Figure 6-6, with three positive edge-triggered flip-flops storing the state bits. The simulation results in Figure 6-7 illustrate the input-output waveforms and the state transitions of the machine. The annotation of the displayed waveforms shows the bit stream of the encoded word produced by the converter for $B_{in} = 0100_2$, where the LSB is asserted first and the MSB is last in the time sequence. Since the output of a Mealy machine depends on the input, as well as the state, the transitions of B_{in} affect the waveform of B_{out}. We have aligned the transitions of B_{in} to occur on the inactive

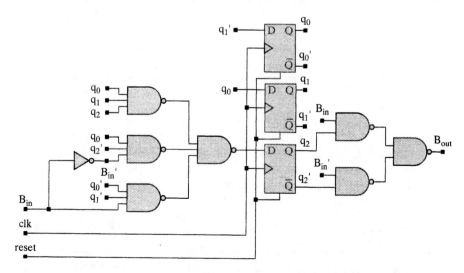

FIGURE 6-6   Circuit for a Mealy-type FSM implementing a BCD to Excess-3 code converter

edge of the clock. This is a recommended practice, which ensures that the data is stable before the active edge of the clock. Since the input of a Mealy machine can cause the output of the machine to change its value, the *valid* output of a Mealy machine is taken to be the value of the output immediately *before* the active edge of the clock. The value of B_{out} immediately before an active edge of the clock depends on the value of B_{in} immediately before the clock, and is the valid output of this machine.[8] Thus, the input bit stream 0100_2 generates the output bit stream 0111_2. The waveforms of B_{in} and B_{out} in Figure 6-7 are annotated with bubbles to mark corresponding values of the BCD and Excess-3 encoded bits.

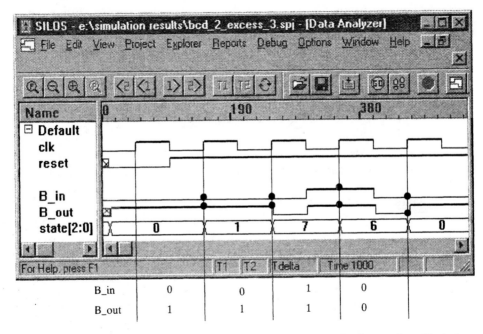

FIGURE 6-7   Simulation results for a BCD to Excess-3 code converter implemented as a Mealy-type FSM, with annotation marking corresponding input and output values[9]

As an alternative to manual design, we develop, from the STG, an explicit state machine model, *BCD_to_Excess_3b_V2001*, having two cyclic behaviors.[10] An edge-sensitive behavior describes the state transitions, and a level-sensitive behavior describes the next state and the output logic. We then verify that *BCD_to_Excess_3b_V2001* has the same functionality as the manual design. The code is as follows:

Use two cyclic behaviors to describe an explicit state machine: a level-sensitive behavior describing the combinational logic for the next state and the outputs, and an edge-sensitive behavior synchronizing the state transitions.

```verilog
module BCD_to_Excess_3b_V2001 (output reg B_out, input B_in, clk, reset_b);
  parameter      S_0 = 3'b000,              // State assignment
                 S_1 = 3'b001,
                 S_2 = 3'b101,
                 S_3 = 3'b111,
                 S_4 = 3'b011,
                 S_5 = 3'b110,
                 S_6 = 3'b010,
                 dont_care_state = 3'bx,
                 dont_care_out = 1'bx;

  reg      [2: 0]    state, next_state;
  always @ (posedge clk, negedge reset_b)
    if (reset_b == 0) state <= S_0; else state <= next_state;

  always @ (state, B_in) begin
    B_out = 0;
    case (state)
      S_0: if (B_in == 0) begin next_state = S_1; B_out = 1; end
           else if (B_in == 1) begin next_state = S_2; end

      S_1: if (B_in == 0) begin next_state = S_3; B_out = 1; end
           else if (B_in == 1) begin next_state = S_4; end

      S_2: begin next_state = S_4; B_out = B_in; end

      S_3: begin next_state = S_5; B_out = B_in; end

      S_4: if (B_in == 0) begin next_state = S_5; B_out = 1; end
           else if (B_in == 1) begin next_state = S_6; end

      S_5: begin next_state = S_0; B_out = B_in; end

      S_6: begin next_state = S_0; B_out = 1; end
      /* Omitted for BCD_to_Excess_3b_V2001 version
         Included for BCD_to_Excess_3c_V2001 version
      default: begin next_state = dont_care_state; B_out = dont_care_out; end
      */
    endcase
  end
endmodule
```

Note that the assignments in the edge-sensitive behavior in *BCD_to_Excess_3b_V2001* are nonblocking, and those in the level-sensitive behavior are blocked (procedural) assignments. The Verilog language specifies that nonblocking assignments and blocking assignments that are scheduled to occur in the same time step of simulation execute in a particular order. The nonblocking assignments are sampled first, at the beginning of the time step (before any assignments are made), then the blocked assignments are executed. After the blocked assignments are executed, the nonblocking assignments are completed by assigning, to the left-hand side of the statements, the values that were determined by the sampling at the beginning of the time step. This mechanism ensures that nonblocking assignments execute concurrently, independent of their order, and that race conditions cannot propagate through blocked assignments and thereby affect the nonblocking assignments. Nonblocking assignments describe concurrent synchronous register transfers in hardware.

 Use the procedural assignment operator (=) in the level-sensitive cyclic behavior(s) describing the combinational logic of a finite-state machine.

Note that *B_out* is initialized to 0 in the cyclic behavior for the output logic. This is a precaution against inadvertently forgetting to assign value to *B_out* in all branches of the activity flow, which would cause a latch to be synthesized. *B_out* is assigned by exception, simplifying the logic by eliminating the need for deassertions.

Matching simulation between a behavioral model and a synthesized circuit does not guarantee that an implementation of the circuit is correct. The waveforms in Figure 6-8 were obtained by simulating *BCD_to_Excess_3b_V2001*; they match those in Figure 6-7 for the manually-designed gate-level model. However, note that *BCD_to_Excess_3b_V2001* does not include a ***default*** assignment in its ***case*** statement. This leads to latches in the synthesized circuit shown in Figure 6-9a. On

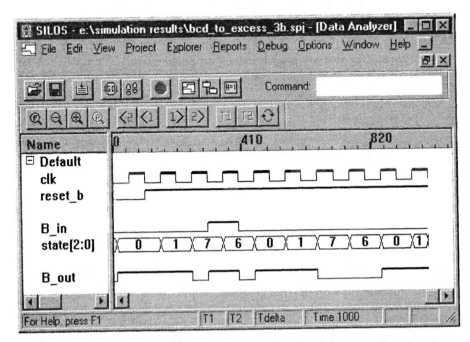

FIGURE 6-8 Results obtained from simulation of *BCD_to_Excess_3b_V2001*, a Verilog behavioral model of a BCD to Excess-3 code converter

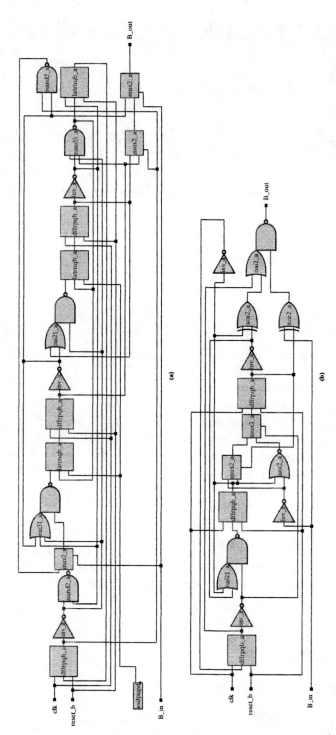

FIGURE 6-9 ASIC circuits synthesized from **(a)** *BCD_to_Excess_3b_V2001* and **(b)** *BCD_to_Excess_3c_V2001*. Note that *BCD_to_Excess_3b_V2001* has latched circuitry due to omission of **default** assignments in the **case** statement

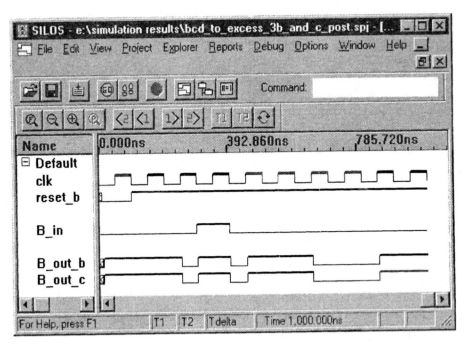

FIGURE 6-10 Postsynthesis simulation of the ASIC circuits synthesized from *BCD_to_Excess_3b_V2001* and *BCD_to_Excess_3c_V2001*.

the other hand, with don't-care default assignments to *next_state* and *B_out*, *BCD_to_Excess_3c_V2001* synthesizes to the circuit in Figure 6-9b, without latches. Figure 6-10 shows the simulation results for both circuits. The waveforms of both circuits match those of the manual design (Figure 6-7), because the testbench exercises the circuit over only the allowable input sequences. The don't-care assignments of *BCD_to_Excess_3c_V2001* give greater flexibility to the synthesis tool than the implied latch structure of *BCD_to_Excess_3b_V2001, thus it is advisable to include default assignments in all case statements.*

Use the nonblocking assignment operator (<=) in the edge-sensitive cyclic behavior describing the state transitions and the register transfers of the datapath of a sequential machine.

Example End: Explicit Finite-State Machine – BCD-to-Excess-3 Code Converter

If all possible states listed as a case item in a *case* statement are not decoded in the level-sensitive behavior describing the next state and output logic of a state machine, the combinational logic describing the next state and the output will be synthesized as the outputs of latches, the circuit may have more hardware than needed, and it may not function as intended.

Decode all possible states in a level-sensitive behavior describing the combinational next state and output logic of an explicit finite-state machine.

Synthesis tools impose some additional restrictions on how state machines can be modeled. The state register of an explicit state machine must be assigned value as an aggregate, (i.e., bit-select and part-select assignments to the state register variable are not allowed by a synthesis tool). The entire register must be assigned value. Asynchronous control signals (e.g., *set* and *reset*) must be scalars in the event control expression of the behavior. Lastly, for synthesis, the value that is assigned to the state register must be either a constant (e.g., *state_reg = start_state*) or a variable that evaluates to a constant after static evaluation (i.e., the state transition diagram must specify a fixed relationship). The description of *BCD_to_Excess_3b_V2001* satisfies these constraints.

A behavior describing the synchronous activity of an explicit state machine may contain only one clock-synchronized event control expression. This rule applies whether the same or another behavior describes the machine's next state and output logic. The description of an explicit state machine will also include an explicitly declared state register variable of type **reg**. Only one such register may be identified for a machine, which implies that each assignment to the state register must assign value to the whole register, rather than to a bit select or a part select. The constraints on procedural assignments to the same register ensure that it is possible to associate a fixed-state transition diagram with the behavior.

6.4   Algorithmic State Machine Charts for Modeling Finite-State Machines

Many sequential machines implement algorithms (i.e., multistep sequential computations) in hardware. A machine's activity consists of a synchronous sequence of operations on the registers of its datapaths, usually under the direction of a controlling state machine. State transition graphs (STGs) indicate the transitions that result from inputs that are applied when a state machine is in a particular state, but STGs do not directly display the evolution of states under application of input data. Fortunately, there is an alternative format for describing a sequential machine.

Algorithmic state machine (ASM) charts are an abstraction of the functionality of a sequential machine, and are a key tool for modeling their behavior [1 – 4, 7]. They are similar to software flowcharts, but display the time sequence of computational activity (e.g., register operations) as well as the sequential steps that occur under the influence of the machine's inputs. An ASM chart focuses on the *activity* of the machine, rather than on the contents of all the storage elements. Sometimes it is more convenient, and even essential, to describe the state of a machine by the activity that unfolds during its operation, rather than the data that is produced by the machine. For example, instead of describing a 16-bit counter by its contents, we can view it as a datapath unit and describe its activity, (e.g., counting, waiting, etc.). ASM charts can be very helpful in describing the behavior of sequential machines, and in designing a state machine to control a datapath.

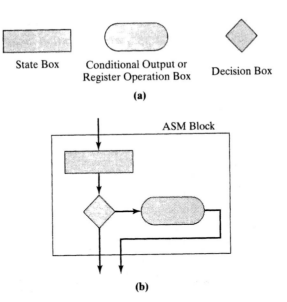

FIGURE 6-11   Algorithmic state machine charts: **(a)** symbols, and **(b)** an ASM block

An ASM chart is organized into blocks having an internal structure formed from the three fundamental elements shown in Figure 6-11a: a *state box*, a *decision box* and a *conditional box*. State boxes are rectangles; conditional boxes are rectangles with round corners; and decision boxes are diamond shaped. The basic unit of an ASM chart is an *ASM block*, shown in Figure 6-11b. A block contains one state box, and an optional configuration of decision diamonds and conditional boxes placed on directed paths leaving the block. An ASM chart is composed of interconnected ASM blocks; the state box represents the state of the machine between synchronizing clock events.

Both types of state machines, (i.e., Mealy and Moore), can be represented by ASM charts. The outputs of a Moore-type machine are usually listed inside a state box. The value of the variables in the decision boxes determine the possible paths through the block under the action of the inputs.

Example: ASM Chart for a Vehicle Speed Controller

The ASM chart in Figure 6-12 for a vehicle speed controller has a Mealy-type output, indicating that the taillights of the vehicle are illuminated when the brake is applied.

The blocks of an ASM chart represent the states of a sequential machine. Given an ASM chart, equivalent information can be expressed by a state transition graph, but with less clarity about the activity of the machine.

Conditional outputs (Mealy outputs) are placed in a conditional box on an ASM chart. These boxes are sometimes annotated with the register operations that occur with the state transition in more general machines having datapath registers as well as a state register, but we will avoid that practice in favor of the ASMD charts that will be discussed next. The decision boxes along a path in an ASM chart imply a priority

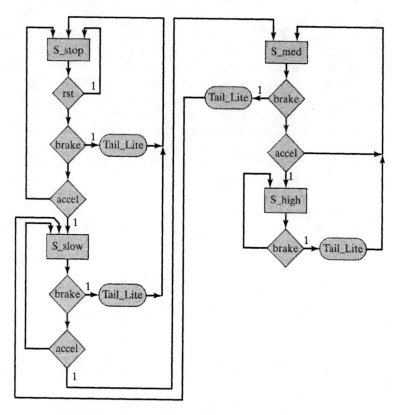

FIGURE 6-12   An ASM chart for a vehicle speed controller

decoding of the decision variables. For example, in Figure 6-12, the brake has priority over the accelerator. Only paths leading to a change in state are shown, and if a variable does not appear in a decision box on a path leaving a state, then it is understood that the path is independent of the value of the variable. (The accelerator is not decoded in state *S_high* in Figure 6-12.)

Example End: ASM Chart for a Vehicle Speed Controller

ASM charts can become cluttered, so we sometimes place only the asserted value of a decision variable on the corresponding path, and do not label paths with deasserted decision variables, unless the omission would lead to confusion. We also may omit showing default transitions and assertions that return to the same state, and paths that return to the reset state when a reset signal is asserted. An *asynchronous* reset signal is indicated by a labeled path entering a reset state, but not emanating from another state. A *synchronous* reset signal will be denoted by a decision diamond placed on the path leaving the reset state. The diamond will have an exit path that returns to the reset state if the reset signal is asserted.

6.5   ASMD Charts

One important use of a state machine is to control register operations on a datapath in a sequential machine that has been partitioned into a controller and a datapath. *We modify the ASM chart of the controller to link it to the datapath that is controlled by the machine.* The chart is modified by annotating each of its paths to indicate the concurrent register operations that occur, in the associated datapath unit, when the state of the controller makes a transition along the path. ASM charts that have been linked to a datapath in this manner are called *Algorithmic State Machine and Datapath* (ASMD) charts. ASMD charts are motivated by the finite-state machine datapath paradigm (FSMD) introduced elsewhere as a universal model that represents all hardware design [8].

ASMD charts help clarify the design of a sequential machine by separating the design of its datapath from the design of the controller, while maintaining a clear relationship between the two units. Register operations that occur concurrently with state transitions are annotated on a path of the chart, rather than in conditional boxes on the path, or in state boxes, because these registers are not part of the controller. The outputs generated by the controller are the signals that control the registers of the datapath and effect the register operations that annotate the ASMD chart.

Example: ASMD Chart for a Pipeline Datapath and Controller

The architecture and ASMD chart in Figure 6-13 describe the behavior of *pipe_2stage*, a two-stage pipeline that acts as a 2:1 decimator with a parallel input and output. Decimators are used in digital signal processors to move data from a high clock rate datapath to a lower clock rate datapath. They convert data from a parallel format to a serial format. In the example shown here, entire words of data can be transferred into the pipeline at twice the rate at which the content of the pipeline must be dumped into a holding register or consumed by some processor. The content of the holding register, *R0*, can be shifted out serially, to accomplish an overall parallel-to-serial conversion of the data stream.

The ASMD chart indicates that the machine has synchronous reset to *S_idle*, where it waits until *rst* is deasserted and *En* is asserted. Note that transitions that would occur from the other states to *S_idle* under the action of *rst* are not shown. With *En* asserted, the machine transitions from *S_idle* to *S_1*, accompanied by concurrent register operations that load the MSB of the pipe with *Data* and move the content of *P1* to the LSB (*P0*). At the next clock, the state goes to *S_full*, and now the pipe is full. If *Ld* is asserted at the next clock, the machine moves to *S_1*, while dumping the pipe into a holding register *R0*. If *Ld* is not asserted, the machine enters *S_wait* and remains there until *Ld* is asserted, at which time it dumps the pipe and returns to *S_1* or to *S_idle*, depending on whether *En* is asserted too. The data rate at R_o is one-half the rate at which data is supplied to the unit from an external datapath.

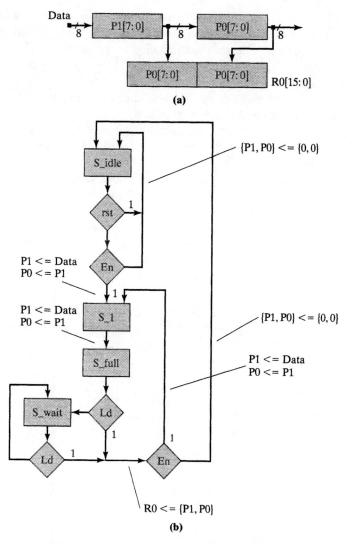

FIGURE 6-13 Two-stage pipeline register: **(a)** pipeline architecture, and **(b)** ASMD chart

---

Example End: ASMD Chart for a Pipeline Datapath and Controller

---

Note that the ASMD chart in Figure 6-13 is not fully developed. The conditional outputs that interface the controller and the datapath, and cause the indicated operations on the datapath, must be added to complete the chart.[11] Thus, the design of a

---

[11]See problem 29 at the end of the chapter.

datapath controller (1) begins with an understanding of the sequential register operations that must execute on a given datapath architecture, (2) defines an ASM chart describing a state machine that is controlled by primary input signals or status signals
from the datapath, (3) forms an ASMD chart by annotating the arcs of the ASM chart
with the datapath operations associated with the state transitions of the controller, (4)
annotates the state of the controller with unconditional output signals, and (5) includes
conditional boxes for the signals that are generated by the controller to control the
datapath. If signals report the status of the datapath to the controller, these are placed
in decision diamonds too, to indicate that there is feedback linkage between the machines. This decomposition of effort leads to separately verifiable models for the controller and the datapath. The final step in the design process is to integrate the verified
models within a parent module, and verify the functionality of the overall machine. The
complete ASMD chart for the pipeline controller is shown in Figure 6-14.

For convenience, the register operations of ASMD charts can be written with
Verilog's operators, which correspond to common hardware operations. Note the

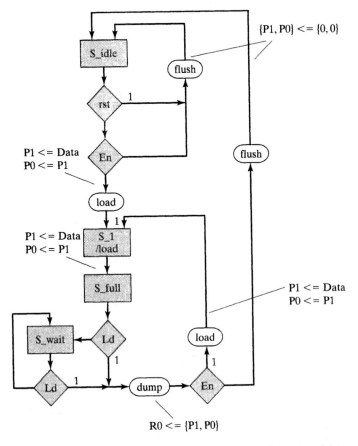

FIGURE 6-14   Two-stage pipeline register: ASMD chart with control signals and datapath register
operations

concatenation and nonblocking assignment operators in Figures 6-13 and 6-14. Datapath register operations made with a nonblocking assignment operator are concurrent, so the register transfers denoted by $R0 <= \{P1, P0\}$ and $\{P1, P0\} <= 0$ are concurrent and do not race.

6.6 Behavioral Models of Implicit State Machines

An implicit FSM does not represent the value of its state by an explicitly declared register variable (*reg*). Instead, the state is defined implicitly by the evolution of activity within a cyclic (*always ...*) behavior. Implicit FSMs may contain multiple clock-synchronized event control expressions within the same behavior, and are considered to be a more general style of design than explicit FSMs. But these machines have a significant limitation: Each state may be entered from only one other state, because states are determined by the evolution of the behavior from clock cycle to clock cycle, and a clock cycle can be entered only from the immediately preceding clock cycle. *Any sequential machine having an identical activity flow in every cycle is a one-cycle implicit state machine, and its activity can be described by one state: running.* The simplest example of such a machine is a D-type flip-flop. Counters and shift registers, for example, may also be modeled as implicit state machines.

A cyclic behavior that has multiple edge-sensitive event control expressions synchronized by a common clock describes an implicit finite-state machine. Typically, an implicit state machine can be described with fewer statements than a corresponding explicit machine, which must have an elaborate, explicit state transition graph. The STG of an implicit machine is implicit and could be constructed from the behavioral description if necessary.

Synthesis tools infer the existence of an implicit FSM when a cyclic (*always*) behavior has more than one embedded, clock-synchronized event control expression. The multiple event control expressions within an implicit finite state machine separate the activity of the behavior into distinct clock cycles of the machine.

Example: Two-Cycle Implicit Finite-State Machine

The following cyclic behavior has register assignments to *reg_a* and *reg_c* in the first clock cycle and to *reg_g* and *reg_m* in the second clock cycle:

```
always @ (posedge clk)    // Synchronized event before first assignment
  begin
   reg_a< = reg_b;                 // Executes in first clock cycle
   reg_c <= reg_d;                 // Executes in first clock cycle.
   @ (posedge clk)                 // Begins second clock cycle.
     begin
      reg_g <= reg_f;              // Executes in second clock cycle.
      reg_m <= reg_r;              // Executes in second clock cycle.
     end
  end
```

Note that both cycles must execute before the activity flow returns to the beginning of the behavior. Note also that the event control expressions that are imbedded within the behavior are not accompanied by the **always** keyword, which declares a behavior and cannot be nested. The role of these embedded event control expressions is to suspend execution of the simulation until the active edge of the clock.

Example End: Two-Cycle Implicit Finite-State Machine

The states of an implicit FSM are not enumerated *a priori*. Each edge-sensitive transition determines a state transition. A synthesis tool will use this information to determine the size of a physical register that will be synthesized to represent the state (the synthesized circuit will contain registers designated as *multiple wait states*). The tool will also extract and optimize the combinational logic that governs the state transitions in the physical machine.

Example: Implicit Finite-State Machine Model of a Counter

A counter can be viewed as having a single (equivalent) state **running**, eliminating the need for a state register and requiring only a datapath register to hold the count. Two ASMD charts are shown in Figure 6-15, one (a) for a machine with asynchronous reset, and the other (b) for a machine having synchronous reset. The action of *reset_* is to drive the state to *S_running* and flush the register holding *count*. *reset_* is shown as an asynchronous entry into *S_running* in (a). For synchronous reset action, a decision diamond for *reset_* is shown in (b) on the path leaving *S_running* to remind us that the machine ignores *up_dwn* if *reset_* is asserted.

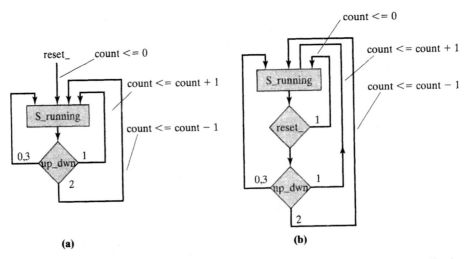

(a)   (b)

FIGURE 6-15   A simplified ASMD chart for a 4-bit binary counter: **(a)** with asynchronous active-low reset, and **(b)** synchronous active-low reset

The Verilog model[12] of the counter can be derived from the ASMD chart by noting that, at every clock edge, the machine either increments the count, decrements the count, or leaves the count unchanged. The cyclic behavior shown in *Up_Down_Implicit1_V2001* describes the decision tree for the state changes and the operations on the datapath register, while suppressing the details of the signals that will control the hardware datapath:

```
module Up_Down_Implicit1_V2001
( output reg [2: 0] count, input [1: 0] up_dwn, input clock, reset_);

  always @ (negedge clock, negedge reset_)
    if (reset_ == 0)                                    count <= 3'b0; else
      if (up_dwn == 2'b00 || up_dwn == 2'b11) count <= count; else      // redundant
        if (up_dwn == 2'b01)                           count <= count + 1; else
          if (up_dwn == 2'b10)                         count <= count –1;

endmodule
```

Example End: Implicit Finite-State Machine Model of a Counter

---

Example: Behavioral Model—Universal Shift Register

A 4-bit universal shift register is an important unit of digital machines employing a bit-slice architecture, with multiple identical slices of a 4-bit shift register chained together with additional logic to form a wider and more versatile datapath [7]. Its features include synchronous reset, parallel inputs, parallel outputs, bidirectional serial input from either the LSB or the MSB, and bidirectional serial output to either the LSB or the MSB. In the serial-in, serial-out mode, the machine can delay an input signal for four clock ticks, and act as a unidirectional shift register. In the parallel-in, serial-out mode, it operates as a parallel-to-serial converter; in the serial-in, parallel-out mode, it operates as a serial-to-parallel converter. Its parallel-in, parallel-out mode, combined with shift operations, allows it to perform any of the operations of less versatile unidirectional shift registers. The code is as follows:

```
module Universal_Shift_Reg_V2001
( output reg    [3: 0]   Data_Out,
  output                 MSB_Out, LSB_Out,
  input        [3: 0]   Data_In,
  input                 MSB_In, LSB_In, s1, s0, clk, rst
);

assign MSB_Out = Data_Out[3];
assign LSB_Out = Data_Out[0];

always @ (posedge clk) begin
  if (rst) Data_Out <= 0;
  else  case ({s1, s0})
    0:   Data_Out <= Data_Out;                  // Hold
    1:   Data_Out <= {MSB_In, Data_Out[3:1]};   // Serial shift from MSB
```

---

[12]The style of this model combines a state machine and datapath in a single cyclic behavior.

```
2:      Data_Out <= {Data_Out[2: 0], LSB_In};     // Serial shift from LSB
3:      Data_Out <= Data_In;                      // Parallel Load
  endcase
end
endmodule
```

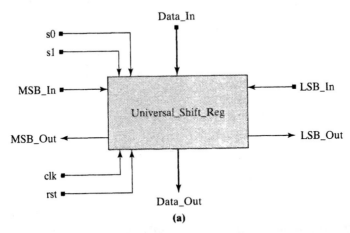

(a)

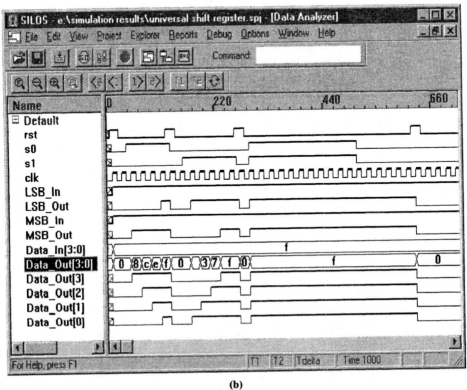

(b)

FIGURE 6-16   4-bit universal shift register: **(a)** block diagram symbol, and **(b)** simulation results verifying the 4-bit universal shift register

We can anticipate that the gate-level machine will consist of four D-type flip-flops with steering logic to manage the datapaths supporting the specified features. The block diagram symbol and simulation results verifying the functionality of the model are shown in Figure 6-15. The waveforms for *Data_Out* illustrate the right-shift, left-shift, and load operations.

Example End: Behavioral Model—Universal Shift Register

REFERENCES

[1] Wakerly, J.F. *Digital Design Principles and Practices*, 3d ed. Upper Saddle River, NJ: Prentice Hall, 2000.
[2] Ciletti, M.D. *Advanced Digital Design with the Verilog HDL*. Upper Saddle River, NJ: Prentice Hall, 2003.
[3] Katz, R.H. *Contemporary Logic Design*. Redwood City, CA: Benjamin Cummings, 1994.
[4] Roth, C.H. Jr. *Fundamentals of Logic Design*, 4th ed. St. Paul: West, 1992.
[5] Tinder, R.F. *Engineering Digital Design*, 2d ed. San Diego: Academic Press, 2000.
[6] Breeding, K.J. *Digital Design Fundamentals*. Upper Saddle River, NJ: Prentice-Hall, 1989.
[7] Clare, C.R. *Designing Logic Systems Using State Machines*. New York: McGraw-Hill, 1971.
[8] Gajski, D. et al. "Essential Issues in Codesign," in Staunstrup, J., and Wolf, W., eds., *Hardware/Software Co-Design: Principles and Practices*. Boston: Kluwer, 1997.

PROBLEMS

1. Develop and verify a Verilog model of a 4-bit binary synchronous counter having the following specifications: negative edge-triggered synchronization, synchronous load and reset, parallel load of data, active-low enabled counting.

2. Write a testbench and verify the functionality of a synchronous 3-bit *up_down_counter* having signals *counter_on* (enables the counting action), *load* (loads an initial count from an external datapath), *up_down* (determines the direction of counting), and *reset* (active high).

3. Write a parameterized and portable Verilog model of an 8-bit ring counter that can be controlled to move in either direction (from MSB to LSB or visa versa).

4. For an 8-bit datapath, develop a Verilog model for the sequential machine represented by the ASMD chart in Figure P6-4. Note: the machine has synchronous reset, and the action of *rst* drives the state to *S_idle* from every state. The register operations and state transitions are to be synchronized to the rising edge of the clock.

5. Develop and verify a model for the speed controller described by the ASM chart in Figure 6-2.

6. Develop and verify a Verilog model of the partitioned pipeline machine described by the ASMD chart in Figure 6-14.

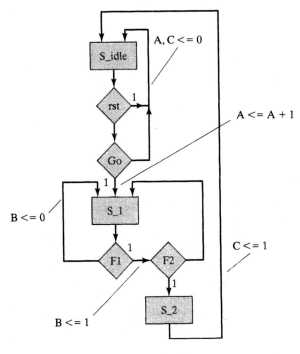

FIGURE P6-4

Verilog 2001 Keywords

Verilog 2001 keywords are predefined, lowercase, nonescaped identifiers that define the language constructs. An identifier may not be a keyword, and an escaped identifier is not treated as a keyword. In this text, Verilog keywords are printed in boldface.

always	endfunction	join	pullup
and	endgenerate	large	pulsestyle_ondetect
assign	endmodule	liblist	pulsestyle_onevent
automatic	endprimitive	localparam	rcmos
begin	endspecify	macromodule	real
buf	endtable	medium	realtime
bufif0	endtask	module	reg
bufif1	event	nand	release
case	for	negedge	repeat
casex	force	nmos	rnmos
casez	forever	nor	rpmos
cell	fork	noshowcancelled	rtran
cmos	function	not	rtranif0
config	generate	notif0	rtranif1
deassign	genvar	notif1	scalared
default	highz0	or	showcancelled
defparam	highz1	output	signed
design	if	parameter	small
disable	ifnone	pmos	specify
edge	initial	posedge	specparam
else	inout	primitive	strength
end	input	pull0	strong0
endcase	instance	pull1	strong1
endconfig	integer	pulldown	supply0

supply1	tri	use	wire
table	tri0	vectored	wor
task	tri1	wait	xnor
time	triand	wand	xor
tran	trior	weak0	
tranif0	trireg	weak1	
tranif1	unsigned	while	

APPENDIX B Verilog Primitives

Verilog has a set of 26 primitives for modeling the functionality of combinational and switch-level logic. The output terminals of an instantiated primitive are listed first in its primitive terminal list. The input terminals are listed last. The *buf*, *not*, *notif0*, and **notif1** primitives ordinarily have a single data input, and possibly a control input, but may have multiple scalar outputs. The other primitives may have multiple scalar inputs, but have only one output. In the case of the three-state primitives, (*bufif1*, *bufif0*, *tranif0*, *rtranif0*, *tranif1*, and *rtranif1*), the control input is the last input in the terminal list. If the inputs and outputs of a primitive are vectors, the output vector is formed on a bitwise basis from the input's vector. When a vector of primitives is instantiated, the ports may be vectors.

Primitives may be instantiated with propagation delay, and may have strength assigned to their output net(s).[1] Their input/output functionality in Verilog's four-valued logic system is defined by the truth tables shown below, where the symbol *L* represents *0* or *z*, and the symbol *H* represents *1* or *z*. These additional symbols accommodate simulation results in which a signal can have a value of *0* or *z*, or a value of *1* or *z*, respectively.

B.1 Multi-Input Combinational Logic Gates

The truth tables of Verilog's combinational logic gates are shown next for two inputs, but the gates may be instantiated with an arbitrary number of scalar inputs.

---

[1]Strengths are used only in switch-level models and do not synthesize.

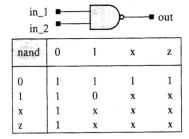

and	0	1	x	z
0	0	0	0	0
1	0	1	x	x
x	0	x	x	x
z	0	x	x	x

FIGURE B-1   Truth table for bitwise-and gate (*and*).
Terminal order: (out, in_1, in_2)

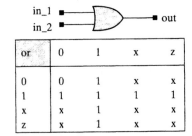

nand	0	1	x	z
0	1	1	1	1
1	1	0	x	x
x	1	x	x	x
z	1	x	x	x

FIGURE B-2   Truth table for bitwise-nand gate (*nand*).
Terminal order: (out, in_1, in_2)

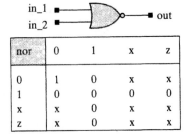

or	0	1	x	z
0	0	1	x	x
1	1	1	1	1
x	x	1	x	x
z	x	1	x	x

FIGURE B-3   Truth table for bitwise-or gate (*or*).
Terminal order: (out, in_1, in_2)

nor	0	1	x	z
0	1	0	x	x
1	0	0	0	0
x	x	0	x	x
z	x	0	x	x

FIGURE B-4   Truth table for bitwise-nor gate (*nor*).
Terminal order: (out, in_1, in_2)

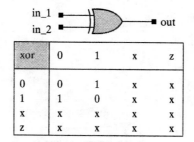

FIGURE B-5   Truth table for bitwise exclusive-or gate (*xor*).
Terminal order: (out, in_1, in_2)

xor	0	1	x	z
0	0	1	x	x
1	1	0	x	x
x	x	x	x	x
z	x	x	x	x

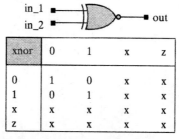

FIGURE B-6   Truth table for bitwise exclusive-nor gate (*xnor*).
Terminal order: (out, in_1, in_2)

xnor	0	1	x	z
0	1	0	x	x
1	0	1	x	x
x	x	x	x	x
z	x	x	x	x

B.2   Multioutput Combinational Gates

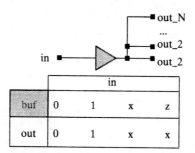

FIGURE B-7   Truth table for bitwise buffer (*buf*).
Terminal order: (out_1, out_2, . . ., out_N, in)

buf	in			
	0	1	x	z
out	0	1	x	x

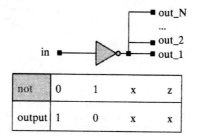

FIGURE B-8   Truth table for bitwise inverter (*not*).
Terminal order: (out_1, out_2, . . ., out_N, in)

not	0	1	x	z
output	1	0	x	x

B.3   Three-State Gates

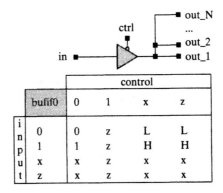

FIGURE B-9   Truth table for bitwise three-state buffer (*bufif0*) gate with active-low enable.
Terminal order: (out_1, out_2, . . ., out_N, in, ctrl)

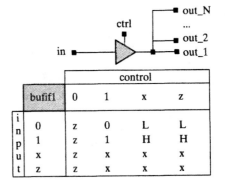

FIGURE B-10   Truth table for bitwise three-state buffer (*bufif1*).
Terminal order: (out_1, out_2, . . ., out_N, in, ctrl)

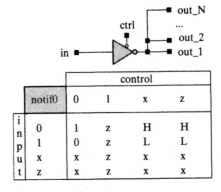

FIGURE B-11   Truth table for bitwise three-state inverter (*notif0*) with active-low enable.
Terminal order: (out_1, out_2, . . ., out_N, in, ctrl)

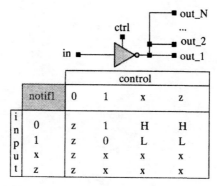

	control			
notif1	0	1	x	z
input 0	z	1	H	H
1	z	0	L	L
x	z	x	x	x
z	z	x	x	x

FIGURE B-12   Truth table for bitwise three-state inverter (*notif1*).
Terminal order: (out_1, out_2, ..., out_N, in, ctrl)

B.4   Mos Transistor Switches

The **cmos**, **rcmos**, **nmos**, **rnmos**, **pmos**, and **rpmos** gates may be accompanied by a delay specification having one, two, or three values. A single value specifies the rising, falling,

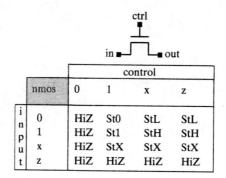

	control			
nmos	0	1	x	z
input 0	HiZ	St0	StL	StL
1	HiZ	St1	StH	StH
x	HiZ	StX	StX	StX
z	HiZ	HiZ	HiZ	HiZ

FIGURE B-13   nmos pass transistor switch (*nmos*).
Terminal order: (out, in, ctrl)

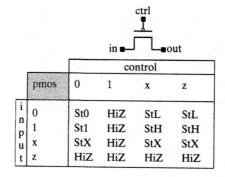

	control			
pmos	0	1	x	z
input 0	St0	HiZ	StL	StL
1	St1	HiZ	StH	StH
x	StX	HiZ	StX	StX
z	HiZ	HiZ	HiZ	HiZ

FIGURE B-14   pmos pass transistor switch (*pmos*).
Terminal order: (out, in, ctrl)

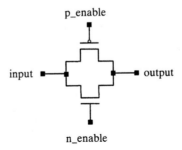

cmos	control	input			
n_enable	p_enable	0	1	x	z
0	0	St0	St1	StX	HiZ
0	1	HiZ	HiZ	HiZ	HiZ
0	x	StL	StH	StX	HiZ
0	z	StL	StH	StX	HiZ
1	0	St0	St1	StX	HiZ
1	1	St0	St1	StX	HiZ
1	x	St0	St1	StX	HiZ
1	z	St0	St1	StX	HiZ
x	0	St0	St1	StX	HiZ
x	1	StL	StH	StX	HiZ
x	x	StL	StH	StX	HiZ
x	z	StL	StH	StX	HiZ
z	0	St0	St1	StX	HiZ
z	1	StL	StH	StX	HiZ
z	x	StL	StH	StX	HiZ
z	z	StL	StH	StX	HiZ

FIGURE B-15   CMOS transmission gate (*cmos*).
Terminal order: output, input, n_enable, p_enable

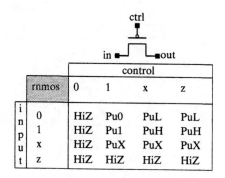

FIGURE B-16 High-resistance nmos pass transistor switch (*rnmos*). Terminal order: (out, in, ctrl)

ctrl

in ●—[ ]—● out

rnmos	control			
	0	1	x	z
input 0	HiZ	Pu0	PuL	PuL
input 1	HiZ	Pu1	PuH	PuH
input x	HiZ	PuX	PuX	PuX
input z	HiZ	HiZ	HiZ	HiZ

FIGURE B-17 High-resistance pmos pass transistor switch (*rpmos*). Terminal order: (out, in, ctrl)

rpmos	control			
	0	1	x	z
input 0	Pu0	HiZ	PuL	PuL
input 1	Pu1	HiZ	PuH	PuH
input x	PuX	HiZ	PuX	PuX
input z	HiZ	HiZ	HiZ	HiZ

and turnoff delay (i.e., to the *z* state) of the output. A pair of values specifies the rising and falling delays, and the smaller of the two values determines the delay of transitions to *x* and *z*. A triple of values specifies the rising, falling, and turnoff delay, and the smallest of the three values determines the transition to *x*. Delays of transitions to *L* and *H* are the same as the delay of a transition to *x*.[2]

---

[2]See Ciletti, M. D., *Modeling Synthesis and Rapid Prototyping with the Verilog HDL*, for a discussion of the rules governing the strength of nets driven by switch-level primitives.

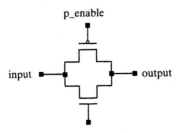

rcmos	control	input			
n_enable	p_enable	0	1	x	z
0	0	Pu0	Pu1	PuX	HiZ
0	1	HiZ	HiZ	HiZ	HiZ
0	x	PuL	PuH	PuX	HiZ
0	z	PuL	PuH	PuX	HiZ
1	0	Pu0	Pu1	PuX	HiZ
1	1	Pu0	Pu1	PuX	HiZ
1	x	Pu0	Pu1	PuX	HiZ
1	z	Pu0	Pu1	PuX	HiZ
x	0	Pu0	Pu1	PuX	HiZ
x	1	PuL	PuH	PuX	HiZ
x	x	PuL	PuH	PuX	HiZ
x	z	PuL	PuH	PuX	HiZ
z	0	Pu0	Pu1	PuX	HiZ
z	1	PuL	PuH	PuX	HiZ
z	x	PuL	PuH	PuX	HiZ
z	z	PuL	PuH	PuX	HiZ

FIGURE B-18 High-resistance cmos transmission gate (*rcmos*).
Terminal order: output, input, n_enable, p_enable

B.5 Mos Pull-Up/Pull-Down Gates

The pull-up (***pullup***) and pull-down (***pulldown***) gates place a constant value of 1 or 0 with strength *pull*, respectively, on their output. This value is fixed for the duration of simulation, so no delay values may be specified for these gates. The default strength of these gates is *pull*. (*Note*: The ***pulldown*** and ***pullup*** gates are not to be confused with ***tri0*** and ***tri1*** nets. The latter are nets providing connectivity and may have multiple drivers; the former are functional elements in the design. The ***tri0*** and **tri1** nets may have multiple drivers. The net driven by a ***pullup*** or ***pulldown*** gate may also have multiple drivers. Verilog's ***pullup*** and ***pulldown*** primitives can be used to model pull-up and pull-down devices in electrostatic-discharge circuitry tied to unused inputs on flip-flops.

FIGURE B-19   Pull-up device.
Terminal order: (out)

FIGURE B-20   Pull-down device.
Terminal order: (out)

B.6 Mos Bidirectional Switches

Verilog includes six predefined, bidirectional switch primitives: ***tran***, ***rtran***, ***tranif0***, ***rtranif0***, ***tranif1***, and ***rtranif1***. Bidirectional switches provide a layer of buffering on bidirectional signal paths between circuits. A signal passing through a bidirectional switch is not delayed, (i.e., output transitions follow input transitions without delay).

(*Note*: The ***tran*** and ***rtran*** primitives model bidirectional pass gates and may not have a delay specification. These bidirectional switches pass signals without delay. The *rtranif0*, *rtranif1*, *tranif1*, and *rtranif1* switches are accompanied by a delay specification, which specifies the turn-on and turnoff delays of the switch; the signal passing through the switch has no delay. A single value specifies both delays, a pair of values (turn-on, turnoff) specifies both delays, with the turnon being the first item and turnoff being the second item. The default delay is zero.)

FIGURE B-21   Bidirectional switch (*tran*).
Terminal order: (in_out1, in_out2)

FIGURE B-22   Resistive bidirectional switch (*rtran*).
Terminal order: (in_out1, in_out2)

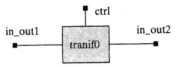

FIGURE B-23   Three-state bidirectional switch (*tranif0*).
Terminal order: (in_out1, in_out2, ctrl)

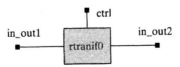

FIGURE B-24   Resistive three-state bidirectional switch (*rtranif0*).
Terminal order: (in_out1, in_out2, ctrl)

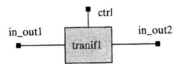

FIGURE B-25   Three-state bidirectional switch (*tranif1*).
Terminal order: (in_out1, in_out2, ctrl)

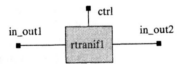

FIGURE B-26   Resistive three-state bidirectional switch (*rtranif1*).
Terminal order: (in_out1, in_out2, ctrl)

Verilog 2001 Language

The syntax of the Verilog language conforms to the following Bakkus-Naur Form (BNF) of formal syntax notation.

1. White space may be used to separate lexical tokens.
2. *Name* ::= starts off the definition of a syntax construction item. Sometimes *Name* contains embedded underscores (_). Also, the symbol ::= may be found on the next line.
3. The vertical bar, |, introduces an alternative syntax definition, unless it appears in bold.
4. *Name* in bold text is used to denote reserved keywords, operators, and punctuation marks required in the syntax.
5. [item] is an optional item that may appear once or not at all.
6. {item} is an optional item that may appear once, more than once, or not at all. If the braces are in bold, then they are part of the syntax.
7. *Name1_name2* is equivalent to the syntax construct item *name2*. The *name1* (in italics) imparts some extra semantic information to name2. However, the item is defined by the definition of *name2*.
8. The notation |... is used in the nonappendix text to indicate that there are other alternatives; due, however, to space or expediency, they are not listed here.

C.1   Source text

C.1.1   Library source text

```
library_text ::= { library_descriptions }
library_descriptions ::=
```

```
            library_declaration
            | include_statement
            | config_declaration
library_declaration ::=
            library library_identifier file_path_spec [ { , file_path_spec } ]
            [ -incdir file_path_spec [ { , file_path_spec } ] ;
file_path_spec ::= file_path
include_statement ::= include < file_path_spec > ;
```

C.1.2   Configuration source text

```
config_declaration ::=
            config config_identifier ;
            design_statement
            { config_rule_statement }
            endconfig
design_statement ::= design { [library_identifier. ] cell_identifier } ;
config_rule_statement ::=
            default_clause liblist_clause
            | inst_clause liblist_clause
            | inst_clause use_clause
            | cell_clause liblist_clause
            | cell_clause use_clause
default_clause ::= default
inst_clause ::= instance inst_name
inst_name ::= topmodule_identifier{ .instance_identifier }
cell_clause ::= cell [ library_identifier. ] cell_identifier
liblist_clause ::= liblist [ { library_identifier } ]
use_clause ::= use [ library_identifier . ] cell_identifier [ : config ]
```

C.1.3   Module and primitive source text

```
source_text ::= { description }
description ::=
            module declaration
            | udp_declaration
module_declaration ::=
            { attribute_instance } module_keyword module_identifier [module_parame-
            ter_port_list ]
                    [ list_of_ports ] ; { module_item }
                    endmodule
            | { attribute_instance } module_keyword module_identifier [ module_parame-
            ter_port_list ]
                    [ list_of_port_declarations ] ; { non_port_module_item }
                    endmodule
module_keyword ::= module | macromodule
```

C.1.4 Module parameters and ports

module_parameter_port_list ::= # (parameter_declaration { , parameter_declaration })
list_of_ports ::= (port { , port })
list_of_port_declarations ::=
    (port_declaration { , port_declaration})
    | ( )
port ::=
    [port_expression]
    | . port_identifier ([port_expression]))
port_expression ::=
    port_reference
    | { port_reference { , port_reference } }
port_reference ::=
    port_identifier
    | port_identifier [constant_expression]
    | port_identifier [range_expression]
port_declaration ::=
    {attribute_instance } inout_declaration
    | {attribute_instance } input_declaration
    | {attribute_instance } output_declaration

C.1.5 Module items

module_item ::=
    module_or_generate_item
    | port_declaration;
    | { attribute_instance } generated_instantiation
    | { attribute_instance } local_parameter_declaration
    | { attribute_instance } parameter_declaration
    | { attribute_instance } specify_block
    | { attribute_instance } specparam_declaration
module_or_generate_item ::=
    { attribute_instance } module_or_generate_item_declaration
    | { attribute_instance } parameter_override
    | { attribute_instance } continuous_assign
    | { attribute_instance } gate_instantiation
    | { attribute_instance } udp_instantiation
    | { attribute_instance } module_instantiation
    | { attribute_instance } initial_construct
    | { attribute_instance } always_construct
module_or_generate_item_declaration ::=
    net_declaration
    | reg_declaration
    | **integer**_declaration
    | real_declaration
    | time_declaration

```
            | realtime_declaration
            | event_declaration
            | genvar_declaration
            | task_declaration
            | function_declaration
non_port_module_item ::=
            { attribute_instance } generated_instantiation
            | { attribute_instance } local_parameter_instantiation
            | { attribute_instance } module_or_generate_item
            | { attribute_instance } parameter_declaration
            | { attribute_instance } specify_block
            | { attribute_instance } specparam_declaration
parameter_override ::= defparam list_of_param_assignments ;
```

C.2   Declarations

C.2.1   Declaration types

C.2.1.1 Module parameter declarations

```
local_parameter_declaration ::=
            localparam [ signed ] [ range ] list_of_param_assignments ;
            | localparam integer list_of_param_assignments ;
            | localparam real list_of_param_assignments ;
            | localparam realtime list_of_param_assignments ;
            | localparam time list_of_param_assignments ;
parameter_declaration ::=
            parameter [ signed ] [ range] list_of_param_assignments ;
            | parameter integer list_of_param_assignments ;
            | parameter real list_of_param_assignments ;
            | parameter realtime list_of_param_assignments ;
            | parameter time list_of_param_assignments ;
specparam_declaration ::= specparam [ range ] list_of_specparam_assignments ;
```

C.2.1.2 Port declarations

```
inout_declaration ::= inout [ net_type ] [ signed ] [ range ]
            list_of_port_identifiers
input_declaration ::= input [ net_type ] [ signed ] [ range ]
            list_of_port_identifiers
output_declaration ::=
            output [ net_type ] [ signed ] [ range ] list_of_port_identifiers
            | output [ reg ] [ signed ] [ range ] list_of_port_identifiers
            | output reg [ signed ] [ range ] list_of_variable_port_identifiers
            | output [ output_variable_type ] list_of_port_identifiers
            | output output_variable_type list_of_variable_port_identifiers
```

From IEEE Std. 1364–2001. Copyright 2001 IEEE. All rights reserved.

C.2.1.3 Type declarations

event_declaration ::= **event** list_of_event_identifiers ;
genvar_declaration ::= **genvar** list_of_genvar_identifiers ;
integer_declaration ::= **integer** list_of_variable_identifiers ;
net_declaration ::=
        net_type [**signed**]
           [delay3] list_of_net_identifiers ;
     | net_type [drive_strength] [**signed**]
           [delay3] list_of_net_decl_assignments ;
     | net_type [**vectored** I **scalared**] [**signed**]
          range [delay3] list_of_net_identifiers ;
     | net_type [drive_strength] [**vectored** I **scalared**] [**signed**]
          range [delay3] list_of_net_decl_assignments ;
     | **trireg** [charge_strength] [**signed**]
          [delay3] list_of_net_identifiers ;
     | **trireg** [drive_strength] [**signed**]
          [delay3] list_of_net_decl_assignments ;
     | **trireg** [charge_strength] [**vectored** I **scalared**] [**signed**]
          range [delay3] list_of_net_identifiers ;
     | **trireg** [drive_strength] [**vectored** I **scalared**] [**signed**]
          range [delay3] list_of_net_decl_assignments ;
real_declaration ::= **real** list_of_real_identifiers ;
realtime_declaration ::= **realtime** list_of_real_identifiers ;
reg_declaration ::= **reg** [signed] [range]
    list_of_variable_identifiers ;
time_declaration ::= time list_of_variable_identifiers ;

C.2.2   Declaration data types

C.2.2.1 Net and variable types

net_type ::=
      supply0 I **supply1**
      | **tri**   I **triand** I **trior** I **tri0** I **tri1**
      | **wire**   I **wand** I **wor**
output_variable_type ::= **integer** I **time**
real_type ::=
      real_identifier [= constant_expression]
      | real_identifier dimension { dimension }
variable_type ::=
      variable_identifier [= constant_expression]
      | variable_identifier dimension { dimension }

C.2.2.2 Strengths

drive_strength ::=
      (strength0 , strengthl)
      | (strength1 , strength0)

```
              | ( strength0 ,highz1 )
              | (strength1 , highz0 )
              | ( highz0 , strength1 )
              | ( highz1 , strength0 )
strength0 ::= supply0 | strong0 | pull0 | weak0
strength1 ::= supply1 | strong1 | pull1 | weak1
charge_strength ::= ( small ) | ( medium ) | ( large )
```

C.2.2.3 Delays

```
delay3 ::= # delay_value | # (delay_value [, delay_value [, delay_value] ] )
delay2 ::= # delay_value | # (delay_value [, delay_value] )
delay_value ::=
        unsigned_number
        | parameter_identifier
        | specparam_identifier
        | mintypmax_expression
```

C.2.3   Declaration lists

```
list_of_event_identifiers ::= event_identifier [ dimension { dimension } ]
        { , event_identifier [ dimension { dimension } ] }
list_of_genvar_identifiers ::= genvar_identifier { , genvar_identifier }
list_of_net_decl_assignments ::= net_decl_assignment { , net_decl_assignment }
list_of_net_identifiers ::= net_identifier [ dimension { dimension } ]
        { , net_identifier [ dimension { dimension } ] }
list_of_param_assignments ::= param_assignment { , param_assignment }
list_of_port_identifiers ::= port_identifier { , port_identifier }

list_of_real_identifiers ::= real_type { , real_type }
list_of_specparam_assignments ::= specparam_assignment { , specparam_assignment }
list_of_variable_identifiers ::= variable_type { , variable_type }
list_of_variable_port_identifiers ::= port_identifier [ = constant_expression ]
{ , port_identifier [ = constant_expression ] }
```

C.2.4   Declaration assignments

```
net_decl_assignment ::= net_identifier = expression
param_assignment ::= parameter_identifier = constant_expression
specparam_assignment ::=
        specparam_identifier = constant_mintypmax_expression
        | pulse_control_specparam
pulse_control_specparam ::=
        PATHPULSE$ = (reject_limit_value [ , error_limit_value ] ) ;
        | PATHPULSE$specify_input_terminal_descriptor$specify output_terminal_
        descriptor
```

```
                        = (reject_limit_value [ , error_limit_value ] ) ;
     error_limit_value ::= limit_value
     reject_limit_value ::= limit_value
     limit_value ::= constant_mintypmax_expression
```

C.2.5 Declaration ranges

```
     dimension ::= [ dimension_constant_expression : dimension_constant_expression ]
     range ::= [ msb_constant_expression : lsb_constant_expression ]
```

C.2.6 Function declarations

```
     function_declaration ::=
             function [ automatic] [ signed] [ range_of_type ] function_identifier;
             function_item_declaration { function_item_declaration }
             function_statement
             endfunction
           | function [ automatic] [ signed] [ range_of_type ]
             function_identifier ( function_port_list) ;
             block_item_declaration { block_item_declaration }
             function_statement
             endfunction
     function_item_declaration ::=
             block_item_declaration
           | tf_input_declaration ;
     function_port_list ::= { attribute_instance } tf_input_declaration { , { attribute_instance }
             tf_input_declaration }
     range_or_type ::= range | integer | real | realtime | time
```

C.2.7 Task declarations

```
     task_declaration ::=
             task [ automatic] task_identifier;
             { task_item_declaration }
             statement
             endtask
           | task [ automatic] task_identifier ( task_port_list ) ;
             { block_item_declaration }
             statement
             endtask
     task_item_declaration ::=
             block_item_declaration
           | { attribute_instance } tf_input_declaration ;
           | { attribute_instance } tf_output_declaration ;
           | { attribute_instance } tf_inout_declaration ;
```

```
task_port_list ::= task_port_item { ,task_port_item }
task_port_item ::=
         { attribute_instance } tf_input_declaration
       | { attribute_instance } tf_output_declaration
       | { attribute_instance } tf_inout_declaration
tf_input_declaration ::=
            input [ reg] [ signed ] [ range ] list_of_port_identifiers
          | input [ task_port_type ] list_of_port_identifiers
tf_output_declaration ::=
            output [ reg] [ signed ] [ range ] list_of_port_identifiers
          | output [ task_port_type ] list_of_port_identifiers
tf_inout_declaration ::=
            inout [ reg] [ signed ] [ range ] list_of_port_identifiers
          | inout [ task_port_type ] list_of_port_identifiers
task_port_type ::=
            time | real | realtime | integer
```

C.2.8 Block item declarations

```
block_item_declaration ::=
         { attribute_instance } block_reg_Ldeclaration
       | { attribute_instance } event_declaration
       | { attribute_instance } integer_declaration
       | { attribute_instance } local_parameter_declaration
       | { attribute_instance } parameter_declaration
       | { attribute_instance } real_declaration
       | { attribute_instance } realtime_declaration
       | { attribute_instance } time_declaration
block_reg_declaration ::= reg [signed] [ range ]
         list_of_block_variable_identifiers ;
list_of_block_variable_identifiers ::=
         block_variable_type { , block_variable_type }
block_variable_type ::=
         variable_identifier
       | variable_identifier dimension { dimension }
```

C.3 Primitive instances

C.3.1 Primitive instantiation and instances

```
gate_instantiation ::=
         cmos_switchtype [delay3]
             cmos_switch_instance { " cmos_switch_instance } ;
       | enablegatetype [ drive_strength ] [ delay3 ]
             enable  gate_instance { , enablegate_instance } ;
       | mos_switchtype [delay3]
             mos_switch_instance { , mos_switch_instance } ;
```

```
            | n_input_gatetype [ drive_strength ] [ delay2 ]
                    n_inputgate_instance { , n_input_gate_instance } ;
            | n_output_gatetype [ drive_strength ] [ delay2 ]
                    n_output_gate_instance { , n_output_gate_instance } ;
            | pass_en_switchtype [ delay2 ]
                    pass_enable_switch_instance { , pass_enable_switch_instance } ;
            | pass_switchtype
              pass_switch_instance { , pass_switch_instance } ;
            | pulldown [ pulldown_strength ]
              pull_gate_instance { , pull_gate_instance } ;
            | pullup [ pullup_strength ]
              pull_gate_instance { , pull_gtate_instance } ;
cmos_switch_instance ::= [ name_of_gate_instance ] ( output_terminal , input_terminal ,
            ncontrol_terminal , pcontrol_terminal )
enable_gate_instance ::= [ name_of_gate_instance ] ( output_terminal , input_terminal ,
            enable_terminal )
mos_switch_instance ::= [ name_of_gate_instance ]
                ( output_terminal, input_terminal , enable_terminal)
n_input_gate_instance ::= [ name_of_gate_instance ]
                ( output_terminal , input_terminal { , input_terminal } )
n_output_gate_instance ::= [ name_of_gate_instance ]
                ( output_terminal { , output_terminal } , input_terminal )
pass_switch_instance ::= [ name_of_gate_instance ] ( inout_terminal , inout_terminal )
pass_enable_switch_instance ::= [ name_of_gate_instance ]
                ( inout_terminal , inout_terminal , enable_terminal )
pull_gate_instance ::= [ name_of_gate_instance ] ( output_terminal )
name_of_gate_instance ::= gate_instance_identifier [ range ]
```

C.3.2   Primitive strengths

```
pulldown_strength ::=
            ( strength0 , strength1 )
            | ( strength1 , strength0 )
            | ( strength0 )
pullup_strength ::=
            ( strength0 , strength1 )
            | ( strengthl , strength0 )
            | ( strength1 )
```

C.3.3   Primitive terminals

```
enable_terminal ::= expression
inout_terminal ::= net_lvalue
input_terminal ::= expression
ncontrol_terminal ::= expression
output_terminal ::= net_lvalue
pcontrol_terminal ::= expression
```

C.3.4   Primitive gate and switch types

cmos_switch type ::= **cmos** I **rcmos**
enable_gatetype ::= **bufif0** I **bufif1** | **notif0** | **notif1**
mos_switchtype ::= **nmos** I **pmos** I **rnmos** I **rpmos**
n_input_gatetype ::= **and** I **nand** I **or** I **nor** I **xor** I **xnor**
n_output_gatetype ::= **buf** I **not**
pass_en_switchtype ::= **tranif0** I **tranif1** **rtranif1** | **rtranif0**
pass_switchtype ::= **tran** | **rtran**

C.4   Module and generated instantiation

C.4.1   Module instantiation

module_instantiation ::=
        module_identifier [parameter_value_assignment]
                module_instance { , module_instance } ;
parameter _value_assignment ::= # (list_of_parameter_assignments)
list_of_parameter_assignments ::=
        ordered_parameter_assignment { , ordered_parameter_assignment } |
        named_parameter_assignment { , named_parameter_assignment }
ordered_parameter_assignment ::= expression
named_parameter_assignment ::= . parameter_identifier ([expression])
module_instance ::= name_of_instance ([list_of_port_connections])
name_of_instance ::= module_instance_identifier [range]
list_of_port_connections ::=
        ordered_port_connection { , ordered_port_connection }
        I named_port_connection { , named_port_connection })
ordered_port_connection ::= (attribute_instance) [expression]
named_port_connection ::= (attribute_instance) .port_identifier ([expression])

C.4.2   Generated instantiation

generated_instantiation ::= **generate** { generate_item } **endgenerate**
generate_item_or_null ::= generate_item | ;
generate_item ::=
        generate_conditional_statement
        | generate_case_statement
        | generate_loop_statement
        | generate_block
        | module_or_generate_item
generate_conditional_statement ::=
        if (constant_expression) generate_item_or_null [**else** generate_item_or_null]
generate_case_statement ::= **case** (constant_expression)
                genvar_case_item { genvar_case_item } **endcase**
genvar_case_item ::= constant_expression { , constant_expression } :

generate_item_or_null | **default** [:] generate_item_or_null
generate_loop_statement ::= **for** (genvar_assignment ; constant_expression ;
genvar_assignment)
         begin: generate_block_identifier { generate_item } **end**
genvar_assignment ::= genvar_identifier = constant_expression
generate_block ::= **begin** [: generate_block_identifier] { generate_item } **end**

C.5   UDP declaration and instantiation

C.5.1 UDP declaration

udp_declaration ::=
         { attribute_instance } **primitive** udp_identifier (udp_port_list) ;
         udp_port_declaration { udp_port_declaration }
         udp_body
         endprimitive
         | { attribute_instance } **primitive** udp_identifier (udp_declaration_port_list) ;
         udp_body
         endprimitive

C.5.2 UDP ports

udp_port_list ::= output_identifier , input_identifier { , input_identifier }
udp_declaration_port_list ::=
         udp_output_declaration , udp_input_declaration { , udp_input_ddeclaration }
udp_port_declaration ::=
         udp_output_declaration ;
         | udp_input_declaration ;
         | udp_reg_declaration ;
udp_output_declaration ::=
         { attribute_instance } **output** port_identifier
         | { attribute_instance } **output reg** port_identifier [= constant_expression]
udp_input_declaration ::= { attribute_instance } **input** list_of_port_identifiers
udp_reg_declaration ::= { attribute_instance } **reg** variable_identifier

C.5.3 UDP body

udp_body ::= combinational_body | sequential_body
combinational_body ::= **table** combinational_entry { combinational_entry} **endtable**
combinational_entry ::= level_input_list : output_symbol ;
sequential_body ::= [udp_initial_statement] **table** sequential_entry { sequential_entry}
endtable
udp_initial_statement ::= **initial** output_port_identifier = init_val;
init_val::= **1'b0 | 1'b1 | 1'bx | 1'bX | 1'B0 | 1'B1 | 1'Bx | 1'BX | 1 | 0**
sequential_entry ::= seq_input_list: current_state: next_state;

seq_input_list ::= level_input_list I edge_input_list
level_input_list ::= level_symbol { level_symbol }
edge_input_list ::= { level_symbol } edge_indicator { level_symbol }
edge_indicator ::= (level_symbol | level_symbol) I edge_symbol
current_state ::= level_symbol
next_state ::= output_symbol | -
output_symbol ::= **0** | **1** | **x** | **X**
level_symbol ::= **0** | **1** | **x** | **X** | **?** | **b** | **B**
edge_symbol ::= **r** | **R** | **f** | **F** | **p** | **P** | **n** | **N** | *****

C.5.4   UDP instantiation

udp_instantiation ::= udp_identifier [drive_strength] [delay2]
                          udp_instance { , udp_instance } ;
udp_instance ::= [name_of_udp_instance] (output_terminal , input_terminal
                          { , input_terminal })
name_of_udp_instance ::= udp_instance_identifier [range]

C.6   Behavioral statements

C.6.1   Continuous assignment statements

continuous_assign ::= **assign** [drive_strength] [delay3] list_of_net_assignments ;
list_of_net_assignments ::= net_assignment { , net_assignment }
net_assignment ::= net_lvalue = expression

C.6.2   Procedural blocks and assignments

initial_construct ::= **initial** statement
always_construct ::= **always** statement
blocking_assignment ::= variable_lvalue = [delay_or_event_control] expression
nonblocking_assignment ::= variable_lvalue **<=** [delay_or_event_control] expression
procedural_continuous_assignments ::=
          assign variable_assignment
          | **deassign** variable_lvalue
          | **force** variable_assignment
          | **force** net_assignment
          | **release** variable_lvalue
          | **release** net_lvalue
function_blocking_assignment ::= variable_lvalue = expression
function_statement_or_null ::= function_statement I { attribute_instance } ;

C.6.3   Parallel and sequential blocks

function_seq_block ::= **begin** [: block_identifier
          { block_item_declaration }] { function_statement } **end**

From IEEE Std. 1364–2001. Copyright 2001 IEEE. All rights reserved.

```
variable_assignment ::= variable_lvalue = expression
par_block ::= fork [ : block_identifier { block_item_declaration } ] { statement } join
seq_block ::= begin [ : block_identifier { block_item_declaration } ] { statement } end
```

C.6.4 Statements

```
statement ::=
          { attribute_instance } blocking_assignment ;
        | { attribute_instance } case_statement
        | { attribute_instance } conditional_statement
        | { attribute_instance } disable_statement
        | { attribute_instance } event_trigger
        | { attribute_instance } loop_statement
        | { attribute_instance } nonblocking_assignment ;
        | { attribute_instance } par_block
        | { attribute_instance } procedural_continuous_assignments ;
        | { attribute_instance } procedural_timing_control_statement
        | { attribute_instance } seq_block
        | { attribute_instance } system_task_enable
        | { attribute_instance } task_enable
        | { attribute_instance } wait_statement
statement_or_null ::=
          statement
        | { attribute_instance } ;
function_statement ::=
          { attribute_instance } function_blocking_assignment ;
        | { attribute_instance } function_case_statement
        | { attribute_instance } function_conditional_statement
        | { attribute_instance } function_loop_statement
        | { attribute_instance } function_seq_block
        | { attribute_instance } disable_statement
        | { attribute_instance } system_task_enable
```

C.6.5 Timing control statements

```
delay_control ::=
          # delay_value
        | # ( mintypmax_expression )
delay_or_event_control ::=
          delay_control
        | event_control
        | repeat ( expression ) event_control
disable_statement ::=
          disable hierarchical_task_identifier ;
        | disable hierarchical_block_identifier;
event_control ::=
          @ event_identifier
```

```
            | @ ( event_expression )
            | @*
            | @ ( * )
event_trigger ::=
            -> hierarchical_event_identifier ;
event_expression ::=
                expression
            | hierarchical_identifier
            | posedge expression
            | negedge expression
            | event_expression or event_expression
            | event_expression , event_expression
procedural_timing_control_statement ::=
            delay_or_event_control statement_or_null
wait_statement ::=
            wait ( expression ) statement_or_null
```

C.6.6 Conditional statements

```
conditional_statement ::=
            if ( expression )
                    statement_or_null [ else statement_or_null ]
            | if_else_if_statement
if_else_if_statement ::=
            if ( expression ) statement_or_null
            { else if ( expression ) statement_or_null }
                    [ else statement_or_null ]
function_conditional_statement ::=
            if ( expression ) function_statement_or_null
            [ else function_statement_or_null ]
            | function_if_else_if_statement
function_if_else_if_statement ::=
            if ( expression ) function_statement_or_null
            { else if ( expression ) function_statement_or_null }
            [ else function_statement_or_null ]
```

C.6.7 Case statements

```
case_statement ::=
            case ( expression )
                    case_item { case_item } endcase
            | casez ( expression )
                    case_item { case_item } endcase
            | casex ( expression )
                    case_item { case_item } endcase

case_item ::=
```

```
                expression { , expression } : statement_or_null
              | default [ : ] statement_or_null
    function_case_statement ::=
              case ( expression )
              function_case_item ( function_case_item } endcase
            | casez ( expression )
              function_case_item { function_case_item } endcase
            | casex ( expression )
              function_case_item { function_case_item } endcase
    function_case_item ::=
              expression {, expression } : function_statement_or_null
            | default [ : ] function_statement_or_null
```

C.6.8   Looping statements

```
    function_loop_statement ::=
              forever function_statement
            | repeat ( expression ) function_statement
            | while ( expression ) function_statement
            | for ( variable_assignment; expression; variable_assignment)
                    function_statement
    loop_statement ::=
              forever statement
            | repeat ( expression ) statement
            | while ( expression ) statement
            | for ( variable_assignment; expression; variable_assignment ) statement
```

C.6.9   Task enable statements

```
    system_task_enable ::= system_task_identifier [ ( expression { , expression } ) ] ;
    task_enable ::= hierarchical_task_identifier [ ( expression { , expression } ) ] ;
```

C.7   Specify section

C.7.1   Specify block declaration

```
    specify_block ::= specify { specify_item } endspecify
    specify_item ::=
              specparam_declaration
            | pulsestyle_declaration
            | showcancelled_declaration
            | path_declaration
            | system_timing_check
    pulsestyle_declaration ::=
              pulsestyle_onevent list_of_path_outputs ;
```

              I **pulsestyle_ondetect** list_of_path_outputs ;
showcancelled_declaration ::=
         showcancelled list_of_path_outputs ;
         I **noshowcancelled** list_of_path_outputs ;

C.7.2   Specify path declarations

path_declaration ::=
        simple_path_declaration ;
        I edge_sensitive_path_declaration ;
        I state_dependent_path_declaration ;
simple_path_declaration ::=
        parallel_path_description = path_delay _value
        I full_path_description = path_delay_value
parallel_path_description ::=
        (specify _input_terminal_descriptor [polarity_operator] => specify
        _output_terminal_descriptor)
full_path_description ::=
        (list_of_path_inputs [polarity_operator] *> list_of_path_outputs)
list_of_path_inputs ::=
        specify_input_terminal_descriptor { , specify_input_terminal_descriptor }
list_of_path_outputs ::=
        specify_output_terminal_descriptor { , specify_output_terminal_descriptor }

C.7.3   Specify block terminals

specify_input_terminaldescriptor ::=
        input_identifier
        I input_identifier [constant_expression]
        I input_identifier [range_expression]
specify_output_terminal_descriptor ::=
        output_identifier
        I output_identifier [constant_expression]
        I output_identifier [range_expression]
input_identifier ::= input_port_identifier I inout_port_identifier
output_identifier ::= output_port_identifier I inout_port_identifier

C.7.4   Specify path delays

path_delay_value ::=
        list_of_path_delay _expressions
        I (list_of_path_delay_expressions)
list_of_path_delay _expressions ::=
        t_path_delay _expression

```
                    | trise_path_delay_expression , tfall_path_delay _expression
                    | trise_path_delay_expression , tfall_path_delay_expression ,
                    tz_path_delay_expression
                    | t01_path_delay_expression , t10_path_delay_expression ,
                    t0z_path_delay_expression,
                    tz1_path_delay_expression , t1z_path_delay_expression , tz0_path_delay_
                    expression
                    | t01_path_delay_expression , t10_path_delay_expression ,
                     t0z_path_delay_expression,
                     tz1_path_delay_expression , t1z_path_delay_expression ,
                     tz0_path_delay_expression
                     t0x_path_delay_expression , tx1_path_delay_expression ,
                     t1x_path_delay_expression,
                     tx0_path_delay_expression , txz_path_delay_expression ,
                     tzx_path_delay_expression
    t_path_delay_expression ::= path_delay_expression
    trise_path_delay_expression ::= path_delay_expression
    tfall_path_delay_expression ::= path_delay_expression
    tz_path_delay_expression ::= path_delay_expression
    t01_path_delay_expression ::= path_delay_expression
    t10_path_delay_expression ::= path_delay_expression
    t0z_path_delay _expression ::= path_delay_expression
    tz1_path_delay_expression ::= path_delay_expression
    t1z_path_delay_expression ::= path_delay_expression
    tz0_path_delay_expression ::= path_delay_expression
    t0x_path_delay_expression ::= path_delay_expression
    tx1_path_delay_expression ::= path_delay_expression
    t1x_path_delay_expression ::= path_delay_expression
    tx0_path_delay_expression ::= path_delay_expression
    txz_path_delay_expression ::= path_delay_expression
    tzx_path_delay_expression ::= path_delay_expression
    path_delay_expression ::= constant_mintypmax_expression
    edge_sensitive_path_declaration ::=
            parallel_edge_sensitive_path_description = path_delay_value
            | full_edge_sensitive_path_description = path_delay _value
    parallel_edge_sensitive_path_description ::=
            ( [ edge_identifier ] specify_input_terminal_descriptor =>
            specify_output_terminal_descriptor [ polarity_operator ] : data_source_expres-
            sion )
    full_edge_sensitive_path_description ::=
            ( [ edge_identifier ] list_of_path_inputs *>
            list_of_path_outputs [ polarity_operator ] : data_source_expression )
    data_source_expression ::= expression
    edge_identifier ::= posedge | negedge
    state_dependent_path_declaration ::=
            if ( module_path_expression ) simple_path_declaration
            | if ( module_path_expression ) edge_sensitive_path_declaration
            | ifnone simple_path_declaration
    polarity_operator ::= + | -
```

C.7.5   System timing checks

C.7.5.1 System timing check commands

```
system_timing_check ::=
        $setup_timing_check
      | $hold _timing_check
      | $setuphold_timing_check
      | $recovery_timing_check
      | $removal_timing_check
      | $recrem_timing_check
      | $skew timing_check
      | $timeskew_timing_check
      | $fullskew_timing_check
      | $period_timing_check
      | $width_timing_check
      | $nochange_timing_check
$setup_timing_check ::=
        $setup (data_event , reference_event , timing_check_limit [ , [ notify_reg ] ] ) ;
$hold _timing_check ::=
        $hold ( reference_event , data_event , timing_check_limit [ , [ notify_reg] ] ) ;
$setuphold_timing_check ::=
        $setuphold ( reference_event , data_event, timing_check_limit ,
        timing_check_limit
              [ , [ notify_reg ] [ , [ stamptime_condition] [, [ checktime_condition]
              [ , [ delayed_reference] [ , [ delayed_data ] ] ] ] ] ) ;
$recovery_timing_check ::=
        $recovery ( reference_event , data_event, timing_check_limit [ , [ notify_reg ] ] ) ;
$removal_timing_check ::=
        $removal ( reference_event , data_event , timing_check_limit [ , [ notify_reg ] ] ) ;
$recrem_timing_check ::=
        $recrem ( reference_event , data_event , timing_check_limit , timing_check_limit
              [ , [ notify_reg] [ , [ stamptime_condition ] [ , [ checktime_condition ]
              [ , [ delayed_reference ] [ , [ delayed_data] ] ] ] ] ) ;
$skew_timing_check ::=
        $skew ( reference_event , data_event , timing_check_limit [ , [ notify_reg ] ] ) ;
$timeskew_timing_check ::=
        $timeskew ( reference_event , data_event , timing_check_limit
              [ , [ notify_reg ] [ , [ event_based_flag ] [ , [ remain_active_flag ] ] ] ] ) ;
$fullskew_timing_check ::=
        $fullskew ( reference_event, data_event , timing_check_limit , timing_check_limit
              [ , [ notify_reg ] [ , [ event_based_flag ] [ , [ remain_active_flag ] ] ] ] ) ;
$period_timing_check ::=
        $period (controlled_reference_event , timing_check_limit [ , [ notify_reg ] ] ) ;
$width_timing_check ::=
        $width ( controlled_reference_event , timing_check_limit , threshold [ , [ noti-
        fy_reg ] ] ) ;
$nochange_timing_check ::=
```

$nochange (reference_event , data_event , start_edge_offset ,
end_edge_offset [, [notify_reg]]) ;

C.7.5.2 System timing check command arguments

checktime_condition ::= mintypmax_expression
controlled_reference_event ::= controlled_timing_check_event
data_event ::= timing_check_event
delayed_data ::=
        terminal_identifier
        I terminal_identifier [constant_mintypmax_expression]
delayed_reference ::=
        terminal_identifier
        I terminal_identifier [constant_mintypmax_expression]
end_edge_offset ::= mintypmax_expression
event_based_flag ::= constant_expression
notify_reg ::= variable_identifier
reference_event ::= timing_check_event
remain_active_flag ::= constant_mintypmax_expression
stamptime_condition ::= mintypmax_expression
start_edge_offset ::= mintypmax_expression
threshold ::=constant_expression
timing_check_limit ::= expression

System timing check event definitions

timing_check_event ::=
        [timing_check_event_control] specify_terminal_descriptor [**&&&**
        timing_check_condition]
controlled_timing_check_event ::=
        [timing_check_event_control specify_terminal_descriptor [**&&&**
        timing_check_condition]
timing_check_event_control ::=
        posedge
        I **negedge**
        I edge_control_specifier
specify_terminal_descriptor ::=
        specify_input_terminal_descriptor
        I specify _output_terminal_descriptor
edge_control_specifier ::= **edge** [edge_descriptor [, edge_descriptor]]
edge_descriptor ::=
        01
        | **10**
        | z_or_x zero_or_one
        | zero_or_one z_or_x
zero_or_one ::= **0** | **1**
z_or_x ::= **x** I **X** I **z** I **Z**

```
timing_check_condition ::=
        scalar_timing_check_condition
        | ( scalar_timing_check_condition )
scalar_timing_check_condition ::=
        expression
        | ~expression
        | expression == scalar_constant
        | expression === scalar_constant
        | expression != scalar_constant
        | expression !== scalar_constant
scalar_constant ::=
        1'b0 | 1'b1 | 1'B0 | 1'B1 | 'b0 | 'b1 | 'B0 | 'B1 | 1 | 0
```

C.8   Expressions

C.8.1 Concatenations

```
concatenation ::= { expression { , expression } }
constant_concatenation ::= { constant_expression { , constant_expression } }
constant_multiple_concatenation ::= { constant_expression constant_concatenation }
module_path_concatenation ::= { module_path_expression { , module_path_expression } }
module_path_multiple_concatenation::={ constant_expression module_path_concatenation }
multiple_concatenation ::= { constant_expression concatenation }
net_concatenation ::= { net_concatenation_value { , net_concatenation_value } }
net_concatenation_value ::=
        hierarchical_net_identifier
        | hierarchical_net_identifier [ expression ] { [ expression ] }
        | hierarchical_net_identifier [ expression ] { [ expression] } [ range_expression ]
        | hierarchical_net_identifier [ range_expression ]
        | net_concatenation
variable_concatenation ::= { variable_concatenation_value { ,
variable_concatenation_value } }
variable_concatenation- value ::=
        hierarchical_variable_identifier
        | hierarchical_variable_identifier [ expression ] { [ expression ] }
        | hierarchical_variable_identifier [ expression ] { [ expression ] } [ range_
        expression ]
        | hierarchical_variable_identifier [ range_expression ]
        | variable_concatenation
```

C.8.2   Function calls

```
constant_function_call ::= function_identifier { attribute_instance }
                ( constant_expression { , constant_expression } )
function_call ::= hierarchical_function_identifier { attribute_instance }
                ( expression { , expression } )
```

genvar_function_call ::= genvar_function_identifier { attribute_instance }
           (constant_expression { , constant_expression })
system_function_call ::= system_function_identifier
     [(expression { , expression })]

C.8.3   Expressions

base_expression ::= expression
conditional_expression ::= expression1 **?** { attribute_instance } expression2 : expression3
constant_base_expression ::= constant_expression
constant_expression ::=
     constant_primary
     | unary_operator { attribute_instance } constant_primary
     | constant_expression binary_operator (attribute_instance } constant_expression
     | constant_expression **?** (attribute_instance } constant_expression :
     constant_expression I string
constant_mintypmax_expression ::=
     constant_expression
     | constant_expression : constant_expression : constant_expression
constant_range_expression ::=
     constant_expression
     | msb_constant_expression : lsb_constant_expression
     | constant_base_expression **+:** width_constant_expression
     | constant_base_expression **-:** width_constant_expression
dimension_constant_expression ::= constant_expression
expression1 ::= expression
expression2 ::= expression
expression3 ::= expression
expression ::=
     primary
     | unary_operator { attribute_instance } primary
     | expression binary_operator { attribute_instance } expression
     | conditional_expression
     | string
lsb_constant_expression ::= constant_expression
mintypmax...expression ::=
     expression
     | expression: expression: expression
     module_path_conditional_expression ::= module_path_expression **?**
     { attribute_instance }
          module_path_expression : module_path_expression
module_path_expression ::=
     module_path_primary
     | unary_module_path_operator { attribute_instance } module_path_primary
     | module_path_expression binary_module_path_operator { attribute_instance }
     module_path_expression
     | module_path_conditional_expression
module_path_mintypmax_expression ::=

```
                module_path_expression
                | module_path_expression : module_path_expression :
        module_path_expression
        msb_constant_expression ::= constant_expression
        range_expression ::=
                expression
                | msb_constant_expression : lsb_constant_expression
                | base_expression +: width_constant_expression
                | base_expression -: width_constant_expression
        width_constant_expression ::= constant_expression
```

C.8.4   Primaries

```
        constant_primary ::=
                constant_concatenation
                | constant_function_call
                | ( constant_mintypmax_expression )
                | constant_multiple_concatenation
                | genvar_identifier
                | number
                | parameter_identifier
                | specparam_identifier
        module_path_primary ::=
                number
                | identifier
                | module_path_concatenation
                | module_path_multiple_concatenation
                | function_call
                | system_function_call
                | constant_function_call
                | ( module_path_mintypmax_expression )
        primary ::=
                number
                | hierarchical_identifier
                | hierarchical_identifier [ expression ] { [ expression ] }
                | hierarchical_identifier [ expression ] { [expression ] } [ range_expression ]
                | concatenation
                | multiple_concatenation
                | function_call
                | system_function_call
                | constant function_call
                | ( mintypmax_expression )
```

C.8.5   Expression left-side values

```
        net_lvalue ::=
                hierarchical_net_identifier
```

From IEEE Std. 1364–2001. Copyright 2001 IEEE. All rights reserved.

```
              | hierarchical_net_identifier [ constant_expression ] { [constant_expression ] }
              | hierarchical_net_identifier [ constant_expression ] { [ constant_expression ] } [
                      constant_range_expression ]
              | hierarchical_net_identifier [ constant_range_expression ]
              | net_concatenation
variable_lvalue ::=
              hierarchical_variable_identifier
              | hierarchical_variable_identifier [ expression ] { [ expression ] }
              | hierarchical_variable_identifier [ expression ] { [expression ] } [range_expres-
              sion ]
              | hierarchical_variable_identifier [ range_expression ]
              | variable_concatenation
```

C.8.6   Operators

```
unary_operator ::=
         + | - | ! | ~ | & | ~& | | | ~| | ^ | ~^ | ^~
binary_operator ::=
         + | - | * | / | % | == | != | === | !== | && | || | **
         | < | <= | > | >= | & | || | ^ | ^~ | ~^ | > | << | <<< | >>>
unary _module_path_operator ::=
         ! | ~ | & | ~& | | | ~| | ^ | ~^ | ^~
binary _module_path_operator ::=
         == | != | && | || | & | || | ^ | ^~| ~^
```

C.8.7   Numbers

```
number ::=
          decimal_number
        | octal_number
        | binary_number
        | hex_number
        | real_number
real_number ::= unsigned_number . unsigned_number
        | unsigned_number [ . unsigned_number] exp [ sign]
unsigned_number exp ::= e | E
decimal_number: :=
          unsigned_number
        | [ size ] decimal_base unsigned_number
        | [ size ] decimal_base x_digit { _ }
        | [ size ] decimal_base z_digit { _ }
binary_number ::= [ size ] binary_base binary_value
octal_number ::= [ size ] octal_base octal_value
hex_number ::= [ size ] hex_base hex_value
sign ::= + | -
size ::= non_zero_unsigned_number
non_zero_unsigned_number ::= non_zero_decimaLdigit { -| decimal_digit }
```

```
unsigned_number ::= decimal_digit { _ I decimal_digit }
binary_value ::= binary_digit { _ I binary_digit }
octal_value ::= octaldigit { _ I octal_digit }
hex_value ::= hex_digit { _ I hex_digit }
decimal_base ::= '[slS]d 1'[slS]D
binary_base ::= '[slS]b 1'[slS]B
octal_base ::= '[slS]o 1'[slS]O
hex_base ::= '[slS]h 1'[slS]H
non_zero_decimal_digit ::= 1 | 2 | 3 | 4 | 5 | 6| 7| 8 | 9
decimal_digit::= 0 | 1 | 2 | 3 | 4 | 5 | 6 | 7 | 8 | 9
binary_digit ::= x_digit I z_digit I 0 | 1
octal_digit ::= x_digit I z_digit | 0 | 1 | 2 | 3 | 4 | 5 | 6 | 7
hex_digit ::=
        x_digit | z_digit I 0 | 1 | 2 | 3 | 4 | 5 | 6 | 7 | 8 | 9
        | a | b | c | d | e | f | A | B | C | D | E | F
x_digit ::= x | X
z_digit ::= z | Z | ?
```

C.8.8 Strings

```
string ::= " { Any_ASCII_Characters_except_new_line } "
```

C.9   General

C.9.1 Attributes

```
attribute_instance ::= ( * attr_spec { , attr_spec} * )

attr_spec ::=
        attr_name = constant_expression
      I attr_name
attr_name ::= identifier
```

C.9.2 Comments

```
comment ::=
        one_line_comment
      I block_comment
one_line_comment ::= // comment_text \n
block_comment ::= /* comment_text */
comment_text ::= { Any_ASCII_character }
```

C.9.3 Identifiers

```
arrayed_identifier ::=
```

```
                    simple _arrayed _identifier
                  I escaped_arrayed_identifier
block_identifier ::= identifier
cell_identifier ::= identifier
config_identifier ::= identifier
escaped_arrayed_identifier ::= escaped_identifier [ range ]
escaped_hierarchical_identifier ::=
        escaped_hierarchical_branch
              { . simple_hierarchical_branch I . escaped_hierarchical_branch }
escaped_identifier ::= \ {Any_ASCII_character_except_white_space} white_space
event_identifier ::= identifier
function_identifier ::= identifier
gate_instance_identifier ::= arrayed_identifier
generate_block_identifier ::= identifier
genvar_function_identifier ::= identifier /* Hierarchy disallowed */
genvar_identifier ::= identifier
hierarchical_block_identifier ::= hierarchical_identifier
hierarchical_event_identifier ::= hierarchical_identifier
hierarchical_function_identifier ::= hierarchical_identifier
hierarchical_identifier ::=
        simple hierarchical_identifier
      I escaped_hierarchical_identifier
hierarchical_net_identifier ::= hierarchical_identifier
hierarchical_variable_identifier ::= hierarchical_identifier
hierarchical_task_identifier ::= hierarchical_identifier
identifier ::=
        simple_identifier
      I escaped_identifier
inout_port_identifier ::= identifier
input_port_identifier ::= identifier
instance_identifier ::= identifier
library_identifier ::= identifier
memory_identifier ::= identifier
module_identifier ::= identifier
module_instance_identifier ::= arrayed_identifier
net_identifier ::= identifier
output_port_identifier ::= identifier
parameter_identifier ::= identifier
port_identifier ::= identifier
real_identifier ::= identifier
simple_arrayed_identifier ::= simple_identifier [ range ]
simple_hierarchical_identifier ::=
    simple_hierarchical_branch [ .escaped_identifier ]
simple_identifier ::= [ a-zA-Z_ ] { [ a-zA-Z0-9_$ ] }
specparam_identifier ::= identifier
system_function_identifier ::= $[ a-zA-Z0-9_$]{ [a-zA-Z0-9_$] }
system_task_identifier ::= $[ a-zA-Z0-9_$]{ [a-zA-Z0-9_$] }
task_identifier ::= identifier
terminal_identifier ::= identifier
```

```
text_macro_identifier ::= simple_identifier
topmodule_identifier ::= identifier
udp_identifier ::= identifier
udp_instance_identifier ::= arrayed_identifier
variable_identifier ::= identifier
```

C.9.4 Identifier branches

```
simple_hierarchical_branch ::=
        simple_identifier [ [ unsigned_number ] ]
                [ { .simple_identifier [ [ unsigned_number ] ] } ]
escaped_hierarchical_branch ::=
        escaped_identifier [ [ unsigned_number ] ]
                [ { .escaped_identifier [ [ unsigned_number ] ] } ]
```

C.9.5 White space

```
white_space ::= space I tab I newline I eof
```

Notes:

1. Embedded spaces are illegal.
2. A simple_identifier and arrayed_reference shall start with an alpha or under-score (_) character, shall have at least one character, and shall not have any spaces.
3. The period (.) in simple_hierarchical_identifier and simple_hierarchical- branch shall not be preceded or followed by white_space.
4. The period in escaped_hierarchical_identifier and escaped_hierarchical- branch shall be preceded by white_space, but shall not be followed by white_space.
5. The $ character in a system_function_identifier or system_task_identifier shall not be followed by white_space. A system_function_identifier or system_task_identifier shall not be escaped.
6. End of file.

APPENDIX D   System Tasks and Functions

This brief appendix summarizes the role and syntax of Verilog's predefined system tasks and functions for (1) displaying the results of simulation, (2) controlling file I/O, (3) specifying the timescale for simulation, (4) accessing the timebase of simulation, and (5) converting the format of data. (See [1–4] for timing checks and other tasks and functions for modeling programmable logic arrays (PLAs), conducting stochastic analysis, specifying probability distributions, and directing the output of simulation to a value-change dump file.)

D.1 Display Tasks

D.1.1 $display

$display displays information to standard output and adds a newline character to the end of its output. (See *$write*).

> Syntax: display_tasks ::= display_task_name (list_of_arguments)
>
>   display_task_name ::= **$display** | **$displayb** | **$displayo** |
>
>   **$displayh** | **$write** | **$writeb** | **$writeo** | **$writeh**
>
> Example: **$display** ("This is an example");
>
> Example: **$display** ("opcode = %b", opcode);

The default format of an expression argument, that has no format specification, is decimal. The *$fdisplayb*, *$fdisplayo*, and *$fdisplayh* tasks specify binary, octal, and hex default formats, respectively. The only difference between the *$display* and *$write* tasks is that the *$display* tasks automatically add a newline character to the end of their output, and the *$write* tasks do not.

The arguments (parameters) of the task are displayed in the order of their appearance in the parameter list, and can be a quoted string, an expression that returns a value, or a null parameter. Strings are output literally, subject to any included escape sequences. Escape sequences may be inserted in a quoted string to display special characters or to specify the display format for a subsequent expression. Escape sequences are interpreted according to the following table:

\	The next character is a literal or nonprintable character.
%	The next character specifies the display format for a subsequent expression parameter. An expression parameter (following the string) must be supplied for each % character that appears in a string.
%%	Displays the % character.

A null parameter (i.e. ,,) produces a single space character in the display.

Note: The *$display* task executes immediately when encountered in a behavior, and not necessarily after all simulation activity is complete. The *$strobe* task executes after all simulation activity is complete.

Note: If the host operating system buffers the text generated by *$write* instead of flushing it directly to the output, it is necessary to include an explicit newline character (\n) in the *$write* task, to immediately send the text to the output. Otherwise, use the *$display* system task.

Special Characters

\n	Newline character
\t	Tab character
\\	The \ character
\"	The " character (double quote)
\o	A character specified in one to three octal digits

Format Specifications The following escape sequences specify the display format for a subsequent expression in a string parameter:

%h or %H	Display in hexadecimal format
%d or %D	Display in decimal format
%o or %O	Display in octal format
%b or %B	Display in binary format
%c or %C	Display in ASCII character format
%v or %V	Display net signal value and strength
%m or %M	Display hierarchical name
%s or %S	Display as a string
%t or %T	Display in current time format
%e or %E	Display 'real' value in exponential format
%f or %F	Display 'real' value in decimal format
%g or %G	Display 'real' value in exponential or decimal format, using the format that has the shorter printed output.

Except for *%m*, a newline character requires that a corresponding expression follow the string in the parameter list. The value of the expression replaces the format specification when the string is displayed. The decimal format is the default format.

The *%e*, *%f*, and *%g* format specifications for real numbers have a minimum field width of 10, with three fractional digits (as in the C language). The *%t* format is used with the **$timeformat** system task.

Size of displayed data   The values of expression arguments of the *$display* and *$write* tasks are sized automatically when written to a file or to a terminal output, (i.e. the value stored as a bit pattern is converted to an appropriate number of characters in decimal, octal, or hex value). For example, an 8-bit word, having a maximum decimal value of 511, would require three decimal characters, and two hex characters. Leading zero's are printed, except for decimal output. Insertion of a zero between the % character and the letter of the format specifier suppresses the automatic sizing of displayed data.

Display of High Impedance and Unknown Values

Decimal Format.   When an expression containing unknown or high impedance values is displayed in decimal format, a lowercase *x* (*z*) indicates that all bits are unknown (high impedance), and uppercase *X* (*Z*) indicates that some bits are known. Decimal numbers are right justified in a fixed-width field to conform to the output of the *$monitor* system task, which requires a fixed-columnar format.

Hexadecimal and Octal Formats.   When an expression containing unknown or high impedance values is displayed in hexadecimal (*%h*) (octal (*%o*)) format, each group of 4 (3) bits represents a single hexadecimal (octal) character. The convention for *x*, *X*, *z*, and *Z* is the same as for the decimal format.

Binary Format.   Each bit of a binary (*%b*) value is displayed separately using the *0, 1*, *x*, and *z* characters.

Signal Strength Format.   A *%v* format specification displays the strength of a scalar net in a three-character format. The first two characters are either a two-letter mnemonic or a pair of decimal digits indicating the signal's strength, as shown in the following table:

Mnemonic Level	Strength Name	Strength
Su	Supply drive	7
St	Strong drive	6
Pu	Pull Drive	5
La	Large capacitor	4
We	Weak drive	3
Me	Medium capacitor	2
Sm	Small capacitor	1
Hi	High impedance	0

Driving strengths (Su, St, Pu, We) are associated with primitive gate outputs and with continuous assignment outputs. Charge storage strengths (La, Me, Sm) are associated with nets of type **trireg**. A mnemonic is used when a signal having a logic value of *0* or *1* has no range of strengths. If the signal has a range of strengths, the logic value is preceded by two decimal digits from the preceding table to indicate the maximum and minimum strength levels.

If a signal has an unknown logic value, a mnemonic is used when the *0* and *1* value of the signal have the same strength level. Otherwise, the signal value is displayed as *X*, preceded by two decimal digits. The high impedance strength cannot have a known logic value; the only logic value allowed for this level is *Z*. A mnemonic is always used with the values *L* and *H* to indicate the strength level. The third character indicates the signal's current logic value, and may be any one of the following:

0	Denotes a logic 0 value
1	Denotes a logic 1 value
X	Denotes an unknown value
Z	Denotes a high impedance value
L	Denotes a logic 0 or a high impedance value
H	Denotes a logic 1 or a high impedance value

Hierarchical Name Format. The *%m* format prints the hierarchical name of the module, task, function, or named block that invokes the system task containing the specifier. It can be used in conjunction with other system tasks to locate and report simulation activity, such as timing violations.

String Format. The *%s* format specifier prints ASCII codes as characters. The associated parameter is interpreted as a sequence of 8-bit hexadecimal ASCII code, with each 8 bits representing a single character.

D.1.2 $monitor

$monitor continuously monitors and displays the values of any variables or expressions specified as parameters to the task. Parameters are specified in the same format as for *$display*. When a variable or expression changes, the simulator automatically displays the entire argument list at the end of the time step. If two or more variables change simultaneously, only one output is generated. Only one *$monitor* task display list may be active at a time, but new *$monitor* tasks can be invoked any number of times during a simulation. (See *$monitoron* and *$monitoroff*, for a discussion of interactive use of *$monitor* see [1].)

Syntax: monitor_tasks ::= monitor_task_name [(list_of_arguments)]; |
            $monitoron | $monitoroff
            monitor_task_name ::= **$monitor | $monitorb | $monitoro | $monitorh**

D.1.3 $monitoron

$monitoron controls a flag to reenable a previously disabled *$monitor*. A reenabled *$monitor* immediately prints a display, regardless of whether a value change has taken place.

> Syntax: **$monitoron;**

D.1.4 $monitoroff

$monitoroff controls a flag to disable monitoring.

> Syntax: **$monitoroff;**

D.1.5 $fmonitor

$fmonitor is the counterpart of *$monitor*; it is used to direct simulation results to a file.

> Syntax: **$fmonitor** ([multi_channel_descriptor], P1, P2, ..., Pn);

The default format of an expression argument that has no format specification is decimal. The *$fmonitorb*, *$fmonitoro*, and *$fmonitorh* tasks specify binary, octal, and hex default formats, respectively.

D.1.6 $strobe

$strobe displays simulation data at a selected time, after all simulation activity at that time is complete and immediately before time is advanced. Parameters are specified in the same format as for *$display*. (See *$fstrobe*.)

> Syntax: **$strobe** (P1, P2, ..., Pn);

D.1.7 $write

$write displays information to standard output without adding a newline character to the end of its output. (See *$display* for additional details.)

> Syntax: **$write** (list_of_arguments);

The default format of an expression argument, that has no format specification, is decimal. The companion *$writeb*, *$writeo*, and *$writeh* tasks specify binary, octal, and hex default formats, respectively.

D.2 File I/O Tasks

Note: Additional file I/O tasks are introduced in Verilog 2001 to address the limited capabilities of Verilog 1995. (For a comprehensive treatment, see [2].)

D.2.1 $fclose

$fclose closes the channels specified in the MCD and prevents further writing to the closed channels.

> Syntax: file_closed_task ::= **$fclose** (MCD);

D.2.2 $fdisplay

$fdisplay is the counterpart of **$display**; use *$fdisplay* to direct simulation data to a file.

> Syntax: **$fdisplay** ([multi_channel_descriptor], list_of_arguments);

D.2.3 $fopen

$fopen opens the file specified by a parameter and returns a 32-bit unsigned MCD (integer multi-channel-descriptor) uniquely associated to the file. It returns 0 if the file could not be opened. (See *$fclose*.)

> Syntax: file_open_function ::= **integer**
>   multi_channel_descriptor = **$fopen** ("[name_of_file]");

Each bit of an MCD corresponds to a single output channel. The least significant bit (i.e., channel 0) refers to the standard output (i.e., log file and screen), unless redirected to a file. If a file cannot be opened, the MCD is returned as the value 0. The bits of the MCD are assigned in sequence, bits 1 through 31, as different files are referenced.

Note: The MCD feature of Verilog allows the same data to be written to multiple files by forming the bitwise-or of the MCD of the file. The file(s) receiving information can be altered dynamically and interactively during simulation.

D.2.4 $readmemb

$readmemb reads binary numbers from a text file and loads them into a Verilog memory, or subblocks of a memory, specified by an identifier.

> Syntax: **$readmemb** ("filename", memory_name [, start_addr [, finish_addr]]);

In this syntax, *memory_name* is the identifier of the memory that will be loaded with data from the file specified by *filename*, and *start_addr* is the address at which the first number is to be written. The default is the left-hand address given in the declaration of the memory. The numbers read from the file are assigned to successive locations in memory. Loading of numbers continues to *finish_addr* or until the memory is full. The file may contain addresses, which are denoted by the @ symbol, followed by the number. When an address is encountered, the subsequent data are loaded into the memory, beginning at the address. The text file may contain only white space, comments (either type), and binary numbers (also see *$readmemh*). The length and base of the numbers may not be specified.

D.2.5 $readmemh

$readmemh reads hexadecimal numbers from a text file, and loads them into a Verilog memory, or subblocks of a memory, specified by an identifier.

Syntax: **$readmemh** ("filename", memname[. start_adddr [, finish_addr]]);););
Example:

```
parameter ram_file_1 = "ram_data_file";
reg [15:0] RAM_1 [0:'hff];
initial $readmemh (ram_file_1, RAM_1);
```

In this syntax, *memory_name* is the identifier of the memory that will be loaded with data from the file specified by *filename*, and *start_addr* is the address at which the first number is to be written. The default is the left-hand address given in the declaration of the memory. The numbers read from the file are assigned to successive locations in memory. Loading of numbers continues to *finish_addr* or until the memory is full. The file may contain addresses, which are denoted by the @ symbol, followed by the number. When an address is encountered, the subsequent data are loaded into the memory, beginning at the address. The text file may contain only white space, comments (either type), and hexadecimal numbers (also see *$readmemb*). The length and base of the numbers may not be specified.

D.2.6 $fstrobe

$fstrobe writes simulation data to a file at a selected time, after all simulation activity at that time is complete and immediately before time is advanced. Parameters are specified in the same format as for **$display**. (See **$strobe**.)

Syntax: **$fstrobe** ([multi_channel_descriptor], list_of_arguments);

The default format of an expression argument that has no format specification is decimal. The *$fstrobeb*, *$fstrobeo*, and *$fstrobeh* tasks specify binary, octal, and hex default formats, respectively.

Note: The *$fdisplay* task executes immediately when encountered in a behavior, and not necessarily after all simulation activity is complete. The *$fstrobe* task executes after all simulation activity is complete, (i.e. at the end of a simulation time step).

D.2.7 $fwrite

$fwrite is the counterpart of *$write*; it writes information to designated file output, without adding a newline character to the end of its output. (See *$write* for additional details.)

Syntax: **$write** ([multi_channel_descriptor], P1, P2, ..., Pn);

The default format of an expression argument that has no format specification is decimal. The companion *$fwriteb*, *$fwriteo*, and *$fwriteh* tasks specify binary, octal, and hex default formats, respectively.

D.3   Time Scale Tasks

D.3.1 $printtimescale

The *$printtimescale* task displays the time unit and precision for a referenced module. If an optional argument is not given, the task displays the time unit and precision of the module that is the current scope.

Syntax: **$printtimescale** [(hierarchical_name)]

D.3.2 $timeformat

$timeformat determines how the *%t* format specifier, in system output tasks, reports time information, and specifies the time unit for delays entered interactively.

Syntax: **$timeformat** [(units_number, precision_number, suffix_string, minimum_field_width)];

The integer-valued *units_number* represents the time unit as follows:

Units_number	Time Unit	Units_number	Time Unit
0	1s	−8	10 ns
−1	100 ms	−9	1 ns
−2	10 ms	−10	100 ps
−3	1 ms	−11	10 ps
−4	100 us	−12	1 ps
−5	10 us	−13	100 fs
−6	1 us	−14	10 s
−7	100 ns	−15	1 fs

This system task sets the time unit for subsequent delays entered interactively, and sets the time unit, precision number (i.e., number of decimal digits to display), suffix string to be displayed after the time value, and a minimum field width for all *%t* formats specified in all modules that follow in the source description until another *$timeformat* system task is invoked. The default arguments of *$timeformat* are given in the table below:

Argument	Default
units_number	The smallest *time_precision* argument of all the timescale compiler directives in the source description
precision_number	0
suffix_string	A null character string
minimum field width	20

Example: *$timeformat* $(-10, 1, $"x100 ps", 10) specifies that the output produced by a *%t* format specifier will be displayed in units of 100's of picoseconds.

D.4 Simulation Control Tasks

D.4.1 $finish

$finish terminates simulation and returns control to the host operating system.

Syntax: **$finish;**

D.4.2 $finish(n)

$finish(n) terminates simulation and takes the following action, depending on the diagnostic control parameter, n:

n = 0   Prints nothing
n = 1   Prints the simulation time and location
n = 2   Prints simulation time and location, and run statistics

Syntax: **$finish(n);**

D.4.3 $stop

$stop suspends simulation, issues an interactive prompt, and passes control to the user.

D.4.4 $stop(n)

$stop(n) suspends simulation, issues an interactive prompt, and takes the following action, depending on the diagnostic control parameter, n:

n = 0   Prints nothing
n = 1   Prints the simulation time and location
n = 2   Prints simulation time and location, and CPU utilization and run statistics

REFERENCES

[1] *IEEE Standard Hardware Description Language Based on the Verilog Hardware Description Language,* Language Reference Manual (LRM), IEEE Std.1364-1995. Piscataway, NJ: Institute of Electrical and Electronic Engineers, 1996.
[2] *IEEE Standard Hardware Description Language Based on the Verilog Hardware Description Language,* Language Reference Manual (LRM), IEEE Std.1364-2001. Piscataway, NJ: Institute of Electrical and Electronic Engineers, 2001.
[3] Ciletti, M.D. *Modeling, Synthesis, and Rapid Prototyping with the Verilog HDL.* Upper Saddle River, NJ: Prentice Hall, 1999.
[4] Ciletti, M.D. *Advanced Digital Design with the Verilog HDL.* Upper Saddle River, NJ: Prentice Hall, 2003.

APPENDIX E ⎯ Compiler Directives

A compiler directive may be used to control the compilation of a Verilog description. The grave accent mark, `, denotes a compiler directive. A directive is effective from the point at which it is declared to the point at which another directive overrides it, even across file boundaries. Compiler directives may appear anywhere in the source description, but it is recommended that they appear outside a module declaration. This appendix presents those directives that are part of IEEE-1364, and the new directives introduced in Verilog 2001. Other nonstandard directives may also be used with certain tools, depending on the vendor.

E.1 `celldefine and `endcelldefine

The `celldefine and `endcelldefine directives mark a module as a cell for use with PLI in other applications.

E.2 `defaultnettype

The `defaultnettype directive allows the user to override the ordinary default type (**wire**) of implicitly declared nets. It must be used outside a module. It specifies the default type of all nets declared in modules that are declared after the directive.

Syntax: default_nettype_compiler_directive ::= `default_nettype net_type
net_type ::= **wire | tri | tri0 | wand | triand | tri1 | wor | trior | trireg**

E.3   `define and `undef

The `**define** directive defines a text macro for substitution in the source code. For example, a state code of 3`b010 can be replaced by the following directive:

> `**define** *wait_state 3'b010*

Notice that the directive and the text macro are separated by only white space, and the line declaring the text macro is not terminated by a semicolon. The `**undef** directive undefines a previously defined text macro.

> Syntax: text_macro_definition ::= `**define** text_macro_name macro_text
> text_macro_name ::= *text_macro*_identifier [(list_of_formal_arguments)]
> list_of_formal_arguments ::= formal_argument_identifier { ,
> formal_argument_identifier }

The syntax for using a text macro is as follows:

> Syntax: text_macro_usage ::= '*text_macro*_identifer [(list_of_actual_arguments)]
> list_of_actual_arguments ::= actual_argument { ,actual_argument }
> actual_argument ::= expression

The following is syntax for the `**undef** compiler directive:

> Syntax: undefined_compiler_directive ::= '**undef** text_macro_name

E.4   `ifdef, `else, `endif

These compiler directives conditionally include lines of a Verilog source description in a compilation. The `**ifdef** directive is used with a variable name. The compiler checks whether the named variable is defined (by a previous `**define** directive). If so, the lines of code that follow the directive are included in the compilation. If the variable is not defined, and if the `**else** directive exists, the lines of code that follow the `**else** directive are compiled. The `**endif** directive establishes the boundary of the code that is conditionally compiled. This group of directives affords versatility to a description. For example, the compilation may select between different implementations of the same functionality, select between different delay information, and select different stimulus for a simulation.

> Example: The following directives check whether the DISABLE_TIMESCALES variable is defined:

> '**ifdef** DISABLE_TIMESCALES
> '**else** 'timescale 1 ns / 10 ps

If DISABLE_TIMESCALES is not defined, the '**timescale** directive is compiled.

Example: **module** or_gates (y_out, x1_in, x2_in);
              output   y_out;
              input   x1_in, x2_in;

              `ifdef BEHAVIORAL
                y_out = x1_in | x2_in;
              `else
                or G1 (y_out, x1_in, x2_in);
              endmodule

Syntax: conditional_compilation_directive ::=
              `ifdef text_macro_name
              first_group_of_lines
              [**`else**
              second_group_of_lines
              `endif]

E.5   `ifndef, `elsif

Verilog 2001 introduced two more compiler directives for conditional compilation. The **`ifndef** directive tests whether a text macro has not been defined; the directive **`elsif** helps clarify conditional compilation, as shown in the following example:

Example:

       `ifdef behavioral
         wire a = b | c | d | e;
       `elsif gate
         or G1 (a, b, c, d, e);
       `else
         initial $display ("ERROR: Missing model");

The same compilation in Verilog 1995 would require the following statements:

     `ifdef behavioral
       wire a = b | c | d | e;
     `else
     `ifdef gate
       or G1 (a, b, c, d, e);
     `else
       initial $display ("ERROR: Missing model");
     `endif
     `endif

E.6 `include

The `include directive inserts the contents of a file into another file during compilation.

Syntax: include_compiler_directive ::= **'include** "filename"

E.7 `resetall

The `resetall directive sets all compiler directives to their default values.

E.8 `timescale

The `timescale directive specifies the **time_unit** and **time_precision** for measurement of delay, and time values in all modules that follow the directive until another `timescale directive is read.

Syntax: timescale_directive ::= **'timescale** time_unit / time_precision

The units and precision associated with the directive are as follows:

Character String	Physical Unit
s	seconds
ms	milliseconds
us	microseconds
ns	nanoseconds
ps	picoseconds
fs	femtoseconds

Example: The directive **'timescale** 10 ns/10 ps specifies that numerical values of time information are to be interpreted in units of 10s of ns, to the accuracy of 10 ps. In the code below, the minimum rising delay value (3.213) for the instantiation of the nand primitive will be interpreted as 32.13 ns. If the timescale directive is changed to **'timescale** 10 ns/1 ps, the maximum falling delay value (4.237) will be interpreted as 42.370 ns by a simulator.

nand #(3.213: 3.225:3.643, 4.112:4.237:4.413) (y, x1, x2);

(See also the **$timeformat** system task.)

E.9 `nounconnected_drive and `unconnected_drive

The `unconnected_drive and `nounconnected_drive directives cause all unconnected input ports of modules between the directives to be pulled up or pulled down, depending on the argument of the `unconnected_drive directive. The allowed arguments are **pull0** and **pull1**.

APPENDIX F   **Websites**

Additional resources can be obtained at the following websites (other sites will be posted on our companion website):

Industry Organization

www.accellera.org	Accellera
www.vsia.com	Virtual Socket Interface Alliance
www.opencores.org	Opencores
www.systemc.org	System C

FPGA and Semiconductor Manufacturers

www.actel.com	Actel Corp.
www.altera.com	Altera, Inc.
www.atmel.com	Atmel Corp.
www.latticesemconductor.com	Lattice Semiconductor Corporation
www.mcu.motsps.com/hc11/	Motorola
www.mcu.motsps.com/hc05/	Motorola

Media and Archives

www.ednmag.com	EDN magazine
(Annual PAL, PLD, and FPGA directory)	
www.eetimes.com	EE Times
www.isdmag.com	Integrated System Design Magazine

http://xup.msu.edu   Xilinx University Resource Center[1]
http://www.mrc.uidaho.edu/vlsi/   See this site for additional links

EDA Tools and Resources

www.cadence.com   Cadence Design Systems, Inc.
www.co-design.com   Co-Design Automation, Inc.
www.mentorg.com   Mentor Graphics Corp.
www.model.com/verilog   Model Technology
www.montereydesign.com   Monterey Design Systems
www.qualis.com   Qualis, Inc.
www.simucad.com   Simucad, Inc.
www.synopsys.com   Synopsys, Inc.
www.synplicity.com   Synplicity, Inc.
www.xilinx.com   Xilinx, Inc.

Consultants

www.sunburst-design.com   Sunburst Design, Inc.
www.sutherland.com   Sutherland HDL, Inc.
www.whdl.com   Willamette HDL, Inc.

---

[1]The Xilinx University Resource Center website, maintained and hosted by the Department of Electrical and Computer Engineering at Michigan State University, provides a collection of resources already located on the web, as well as original content. A robust on-line support system consisting of a mailing list, discussion board, and e-mail is in place and monitored to answers any questions that you may have.

Index